The Common Core Coaching Book

Teaching Practices That Work
Diane Lapp and Douglas Fisher, Series Editors
www.guilford.com/TPTW

Designed specifically for busy teachers who value evidence-based instructional practices, books in this series offer ready-to-implement strategies and tools to promote student engagement, improve teaching and learning across the curriculum, and support the academic growth of all students in our increasingly diverse schools. Written by expert authors with extensive experience in "real-time" classrooms, each concise and accessible volume provides useful explanations and examples to guide instruction, as well as step-by-step methods and reproducible materials, all in a convenient large-size format for ease of photocopying. Recent titles have Web pages where purchasers can download and print the reproducible materials.

The Common Core Coaching Book

Strategies to Help Teachers Address the K–5 ELA Standards

Laurie Elish-Piper
Susan K. L'Allier

*Series Editors' Note by
Diane Lapp and Douglas Fisher*

THE GUILFORD PRESS
New York   London

© 2014 The Guilford Press
A Division of Guilford Publications, Inc.
72 Spring Street, New York, NY 10012
www.guilford.com

Printed in the United States of America

This book is printed on acid-free paper.

Last digit is print number: 9   8   7   6   5   4   3   2   1

Library of Congress Cataloging-in-Publication Data

Elish-Piper, Laurie.
    The common core coaching book : strategies to help teachers address the
K-5 ELA standards / Laurie Elish-Piper and Susan K. L'Allier.
        pages cm — (Teaching practices that work)
    Includes bibliographical references and index.
    ISBN 978-1-4625-1557-8 (paperback)
    1. Language arts (Elementary)—Standards—United States.
    2. Language arts (Elementary)—Activity programs—United States.
    I. L'Allier, Susan K. II. Title.
    LB1576.E4225 2014
    372.6—dc23
                                                    2014000608

◆•◆

About the Authors

Laurie Elish-Piper, PhD, is Distinguished Teaching Professor, Presidential Engagement Professor, and Director of the Jerry L. Johns Literacy Clinic in the Department of Literacy Education at Northern Illinois University, where she also serves as Deputy Provost. Dr. Elish-Piper's research and teaching focus on literacy leadership and coaching. She has published and presented widely with Susan K. L'Allier on literacy coaching at the elementary level, including articles in *The Reading Teacher* and *Elementary School Journal*. She has worked extensively with school districts to develop and implement literacy coaching programs at the elementary and middle school levels, and she teaches graduate courses related to literacy coaching and leadership. Dr. Elish-Piper has coauthored seven books, including *Literacy Strategies for Teacher Candidates*, *A Declaration of Readers' Rights: Renewing Our Commitment to Students*, and *Teaching Reading Pre-K–Grade 3*. Prior to joining the faculty at Northern Illinois University, she worked as an elementary teacher, a middle school reading teacher, and an educational therapist in a clinical setting.

Susan K. L'Allier, EdD, is Associate Professor and Coordinator of the Reading Program in the Department of Literacy Education at Northern Illinois University. She and Laurie Elish-Piper have conducted multiple research studies to examine the relationship between literacy coaching and student literacy achievement. In addition to their journal articles, chapters, and presentations about literacy coaching, they also have published a video "workshop in a box" titled *The Literacy Coaching Series*, which enables viewers to see and analyze interactions between literacy coaches and teachers. Prior to joining the faculty at Northern Illinois University, Dr. L'Allier worked as an elementary teacher, a lead teacher, and a principal.

Series Editors' Note

As our schools continue to grow in linguistic, cultural, and socioeconomic diversity, educators are committed to implementing instruction that supports both individual and collective growth within their classrooms. In tandem with teacher commitment, schools recognize the need to support teacher collaboration on issues related to implementing, evaluating, and expanding instruction to ensure that all students will graduate from high school with the skills needed to succeed in the workforce. Through our work with teachers across the country, we've become aware of the need for books that can be used to support professional collaboration by grade level and subject area. With these teachers' questions in mind, we decided that a series of books was needed that modeled "real-time" teaching and learning within classroom instruction. Thus the series *Teaching Practices That Work* was born.

Books in this series are distinguished by offering instructional examples that have been studied and refined within authentic classroom settings. Each book is written by one or more educators who are well connected to everyday classroom instruction. Because the series editors are themselves classroom teachers as well as professors, each instructional suggestion has been closely scrutinized for its validity.

Recently educators have been tasked to consider how they can use all that they know about teaching and learning to accomplish the major challenge of the Common Core State Standards, which is to prepare all students to be college and career ready. To accomplish this goal, administrators and teachers are turning to their literacy coaches and instructional leaders to provide purposeful professional development that encourages teacher confidence in the instruction they already know and do well, and also expands their insights about teaching, learning, and assessing.

Although greatly needed, there is currently nothing similar to *The Common Core Coaching Book* on the market. The practical, easy-to-implement ideas shared by Laurie Elish-Piper and Susan K. L'Allier are based on insights gained from their many years working with literacy coaches, intervention specialists, and others who support teachers in the planning, teaching, and assessing of student learning across the grades and content areas. Hitting a grand slam, these authors identify practices that enable both new and veteran literacy coaches to responsively facilitate, collaborate, and consult with elementary teachers as they address the Common Core standards through instruction. The model they propose invites coaches to use contrastive analysis when working with individual teachers, as well as small and large groups of teachers, to compare their current knowledge and practices with the new knowledge and tasks required of them. The authors provide coaches with ideas for listening closely to the needs of teachers and then co-planning and modeling instructional practice, while also promoting continuous learning through engaged collaboration. Coaches implementing the ideas shared in this book will find themselves creating school environments where mutual respect and collaboration define the collegial norm.

We invite you into the "real-time" teaching offered in this book and hope you'll find this series useful as you validate and expand your coaching repertoire. And if you have an idea for a book, please contact us!

DIANE LAPP
DOUGLAS FISHER

Acknowledgments

First, we want to thank Diane Lapp and Doug Fisher for their support, vision, and enthusiasm as we wrote this book. Their encouragement to maintain a practical and user-friendly approach helped us produce a book that we believe literacy leaders, coaches, and reading specialists will find informative, useful, and supportive.

For the past several years we have been working with school districts to develop, implement, and enhance literacy coaching programs and to conduct research about those programs. We have learned so much from these experiences, and we are forever indebted to the literacy leaders who invited us into their districts to do this work: Dr. Christie Aird, Dr. Maria McClurkin, Dr. Susan Kosmoski, Candy Kramer, and Judy Heller.

We also wish to thank the many reading specialist candidates with whom we've worked for almost two decades at Northern Illinois University. We have learned so much from their questions and insights, and we have been inspired by their commitment, professionalism, and collegiality. We are proud to have contributed to the preparation of so many exemplary literacy coaches, reading specialists, and literacy leaders who have such a positive impact on the professional development of teachers and the literacy learning of students.

We also want to thank our mentors, colleagues, and families for their support and encouragement, which sustained us as we wrote this book. Finally, we wish to extend our hearty thanks to our editor, Craig Thomas, and the fabulous professionals at The Guilford Press, including Mary Beth Anderson, Bianca Hunter, Katherine Lieber, Christopher Etsell, Paul Gordon, and Judith Grauman. We truly appreciate their guidance, efficiency, and attention to both the big ideas and the details.

Contents

PART THREE

Small-Group Coaching toward the Common Core

PART FOUR

Individual Coaching toward the Common Core

PART FIVE

Putting It All Together:
Profiles of Highly Effective Literacy Coaches

PART ONE

Coaching toward the Common Core

We have the opportunity to work with many literacy professionals—reading specialists, reading teachers, literacy coaches, reading interventionists, and so on. While their job titles may vary, there is one element of their current work that is the same—the focus on the Common Core State Standards (CCSS). To date, 45 states have adopted the CCSS, and the ramifications for teaching, learning, and assessment are enormous. The standards offer great promise toward making all students college and career ready at graduation; however, they present challenges in terms of helping teachers enact the Standards into their practice. With testing related to the Common Core to begin in 2014, there is a clear sense of urgency to ensure that teachers have the professional development and coaching needed to address the Standards in their teaching (Calkins, Ehrenworth, & Lehman, 2012).

The CCSS for the English language arts (ELA) are organized around college and career anchor standards for the strands of Reading, Writing, Speaking and Listening, and Language. These anchor standards describe what students need to know and be able to do by graduation. Within each strand, these anchor standards are clustered to represent the major components of the strand. An overview of the major components of the ELA standards is provided in Table 1.

The ELA standards promote five instructional shifts that will change the way K–5 teachers provide instruction (EngageNY, 2012; Fisher, Frey, & Uline, 2013). These shifts identify broad areas of emphasis to help teachers and literacy leaders review and revise curriculum and to determine professional development needed to address the Common Core (see Table 2). Thus, examination of these instructional shifts provides a manageable way to help teachers learn about and begin to implement instruction aligned to the Common Core.

TABLE 1. Overview of the ELA Common Core Standards

Standard strand	Anchor Standard components
Reading 10 Anchor Standards	Literature • Key Ideas and Details • Craft and Structure • Integration of Knowledge and Ideas • Range of Reading and Level of Text Complexity Informational Text • Key Ideas and Details • Craft and Structure • Integration of Knowledge and Ideas • Range of Reading and Level of Text Complexity Foundational Skills • Print Concepts (K–1) • Phonological Awareness (K–1) • Phonics and Word Recognition • Fluency
Writing 10 Anchor Standards	• Text Types and Purposes • Production and Distribution of Writing • Research to Build and Present Knowledge • Range of Writing
Language 6 Anchor Standards	• Conventions of Standard English • Knowledge of Language • Vocabulary Acquisition and Use
Speaking and Listening 6 Anchor Standards	• Comprehension and Collaboration • Presentation of Knowledge and Ideas

The Common Core is a major educational initiative that will affect teaching, learning, assessment, and professional development for many years to come. How can school districts gear up to teach toward the Common Core? Literacy coaching provides a viable, cost-effective, research-based approach to aligning teaching practice with the Common Core.

Overview of This Book

This book is designed for any professional charged with literacy coaching at the K–5 levels in this era of the Common Core. The primary focus of the book is on effective coaching strategies to support teachers. All of the coaching strategies in Part Two through Part Four highlight specific instructional shifts, strands, or individual standards from the Common Core. While these illustrative examples are offered to demonstrate both the coaching strategy and the CCSS content, it is important to

TABLE 2. Instructional Shifts Associated with the ELA Common Core Standards

What are the instructional shifts?	What do they mean for practice?
Balancing literary and informational texts	By third grade, 50% of texts read by students should be informational and 50% should be literary. This includes texts used across the curriculum, not just in language arts.

Increasing text complexity	To become college and career ready, students will read increasingly complex texts to build reading skills and strategies. Text complexity has three components:
	
	1. Quantitative
	  • Word length or frequency
	  • Sentence length
	  • Cohesion
	  • Often measured by Lexile level
	
	2. Qualitative
	  • Levels of meaning or purpose
	  • Structure
	  • Language conventionality and clarity
	  • Knowledge demands (on the reader)
	
	3. Reader and task considerations
	  • Reader knowledge, motivation, and experiences
	  • Task purpose and complexity
	  • Questions posed

Developing evidence-based responses	Students must be taught to think about texts carefully and find specific evidence to support responses. Close reading is an approach that will address this instructional shift.
Writing from sources	Students must be taught to write to inform and argue in response to ideas, events, and facts in texts they read. Students will write opinions (arguments), informative/explanatory pieces, and—to a lesser degree—narratives that incorporate evidence from multiple sources. They will also conduct research projects.
Building academic vocabulary	Teachers must help students build the vocabulary needed to read and comprehend grade-level complex texts and to learn across the disciplines.

note that you may wish to change the Common Core focus depending on the specific needs of your school and teachers. For example, for Strategy 3: Conducting an Article Study Group, we highlight the process using the instructional shift toward complex texts. That coaching strategy, however, could be just as effective with a different Common Core focus such as writing to sources or using digital media to present knowledge and ideas.

Part One of this book contains two chapters. Chapter 1 provides a brief overview of literacy coaching, adult learning, the change process, building a literacy leadership team, and guidelines for coaching toward the CCSS. Chapter 2 introduces the targeted coaching model, which is comprised of research-based coaching strategies aimed at improving student learning. Part Two provides specific coaching strategies for working with large groups of teachers about the CCSS. Part Three focuses on coaching strategies for small groups of teachers such as grade-level teams and professional learning communities (PLCs). Part Four presents coaching strategies for use with individual teachers who are working to enact the CCSS into their practice. Finally, Part Five shares profiles of highly effective coaches to illustrate ways to address six common obstacles of literacy coaching.

1

Getting Ready for Coaching

What Is Literacy Coaching?

Whether you are a reading specialist, reading teacher, reading interventionist, literacy specialist, or literacy coach, chances are you have seen your roles and responsibilities evolve to include more teacher support, specifically in the form of literacy coaching (Bean et al., 2013). Literacy coaching is an approach to professional development that is ongoing and job embedded. This means that teachers receive professional development support on site at their schools, in their classrooms, and in direct relation to the challenges and issues they face in their teaching (Toll, 2005).

Literacy coaching can take many forms, but there are typical literacy coaching activities that are often used in schools. These include providing large- and small-group professional development such as conducting workshops; facilitating teacher study groups and professional learning communities; conferencing with teachers to discuss curriculum, instruction, assessments, and student learning; modeling lessons; co-planning lessons; co-teaching lessons; and observing lessons. Each of these coaching activities, as well as others, are described in more detail in Chapter 2. Unlike traditional models of professional development where teachers attend a single workshop and are expected to figure out on their own how to "make it work" in their classrooms, literacy coaching offers ongoing support that is directly tied to teachers' daily work in their classrooms with their own students.

A Note on the Use of the Term *Literacy Coach* in This Book

For the purposes of this book, we will use the term *literacy coach* to refer to any professional who delivers job-embedded professional development for teachers, regardless of that professional's official job title or the amount of time he or she spends coaching. For example, literacy coaching might be offered by a reading specialist, reading teacher, teacher leader, assistant principal, district literacy coordinator, or literacy coach; however, for clarity and consistency in language, we will use the term *literacy coach* throughout the book.

Coaching Adults

Many individuals with literacy coaching responsibilities have not had specific training in how to work with adults. Typically, literacy coaches were trained as teachers and reading specialists, and they may find that they are uncomfortable and unprepared to work with adults—especially their own colleagues! Working with adults is clearly different than teaching children, but what are those differences? And, how can a literacy coach prepare to work effectively with adults? You are probably familiar with the term *pedagogy,* which refers to the art and science of teaching children, but you may not have heard of *andragogy,* the art and science of helping adults learn. This concept was developed and popularized by Malcolm Knowles (1970), who set forth six principles to clarify how adults learn.

1 Adults want to know why they need to learn something.

2 Adults are most interested in learning when it has immediate relevance to their job or personal life.

3 Adult learning tends to be problem centered rather than content oriented.

4 Adults need to be involved in the planning, evaluation, and implementation of their instruction.

5 Experience, including mistakes, provides the basis for learning activities.

6 Adults respond best to internal rather than external motivators.

Literacy Coaching and Adult Learning Theory in Action

You might wonder, "What do these principles look like when they are implemented?" A visit to Bethune Elementary School provides a quick snapshot of andragogy in action. Gracie Walters is a reading specialist who spends about half of her time supporting teachers through literacy coaching. Gracie attends grade-level meetings, co-plans lessons and units, and co-teaches lessons on a regular basis. She also facilitates study groups and helps teachers use assessment data to plan their groups and instruction. Gracie has been coaching for 3 years, and she recently shared some key insights with us about what makes her coaching effective.

> "I love teaching children so when I found out that I was going to be doing literacy coaching as part of my job, I freaked out! I got so nervous thinking about working with adults that I didn't even know where to start. Fortunately, I was able to attend a couple of workshops on coaching and read some great resources [see Figure 1].

Knight, J. (2007). *Instructional coaching: A partnership approach to improving instruction.* Thousand Oaks, CA: Corwin.

L'Allier, S. K., Elish-Piper, L., & Bean, R. M. (2010). What matters for elementary literacy coaching? Guiding principles for instructional improvement and student achievement. *The Reading Teacher, 63*(7), 544–554.

Toll, C. A. (2005). *The literacy coach's survival guide: Essential questions and practical answers.* Newark, DE: International Reading Association.

FIGURE 1. Literacy coaching resources.

"Once I started working with teachers, I realized that they are people just like me. I thought back to when I attended professional development sessions or had questions about my practice. I considered what I wanted and what frustrated me too. I remembered the workshops I'd attended where I left wondering, 'Why did I have to go to that? How is that relevant to anything I do in my job?' I also recalled being overwhelmed with too much information, too many new ideas, and too many things to do—all at once! I needed someone to help me decide what ideas might be helpful for my students and which one I should try first. In addition to thinking about my own experiences, I talked with some of the teachers in my school and asked them what they wanted from coaching. They offered valuable insights such as 'I want to solve the problems and challenges I have in my teaching' and 'I want to learn what I can do to improve teaching and learning in my classroom—tomorrow!'

"I realized that many of these ideas align directly with principles of adult learning (Knowles, 1970), and when I embraced these principles and kept in mind the teachers I was working with, my coaching really took off! Of course, I'm always learning and improving as a literacy coach, but the first key step was making sure I focused on the adults I was coaching and how they learn."

Literacy Coaching and Change

Literacy coaches tend to be on the forefront of change, and the implementation of the Common Core is certainly an apt example. Because new initiatives, programs, curriculum, and standards all require professional development support, literacy coaches are often charged with leading the change process. While some educators embrace change with open arms, others find change to be scary, overwhelming, or frustrating. Therefore, it is essential that literacy coaches keep two key ideas in mind as they lead the charge for change. First, they must understand and consider the change process itself; second, they must situate themselves as part of a literacy leadership team so that change is supported by a cadre of professionals at the school level, not just by a single literacy coach!

Understanding the Change Process

A quote attributed to Mark Twain proclaims, "Nobody likes change except a wet baby." While that statement may ring true for some teachers, the reality is that change is a consistent part of education. As new initiatives and standards are adopted, educators find themselves faced with expectations to change their instructional practices. As literacy coaches faced with helping teachers navigate the many challenges associated with teaching toward the Common Core, it is important to understand that the change process follows a fairly predictable pattern, and there are specific things you can do to help teachers move ahead in the process.

In our work in schools, we have found the concerns-based adoption model (CBAM) is a useful tool to guide literacy coaching (Hall & Hord, 1987). This developmental model outlines the stages that teachers typically go through as they learn about, grapple with, and implement a new initiative, curriculum, or instructional approach. While individual teachers may not progress in a clear, linear manner through the stages of CBAM, most teachers do move through the stages in a fairly predictable manner that starts with a focus on "self," moves to a focus on "task," and ends with a focus on "results." The model is framed by the notion that the concerns educators experience at different stages of adopting an innovation provide insights regarding the type of coaching support they need at that specific point in time. Let's look at the CBAM (Figure 2) to learn what these stages are and how literacy coaches can use them to guide their work.

The change process is developmental in nature and typically starts with a focus on self. Teachers generally begin at the bottom rung with the Awareness phase when they simply wonder, "What is this new innovation?" For example, teachers at this stage of the change process may be asking questions such as "What are the Com-

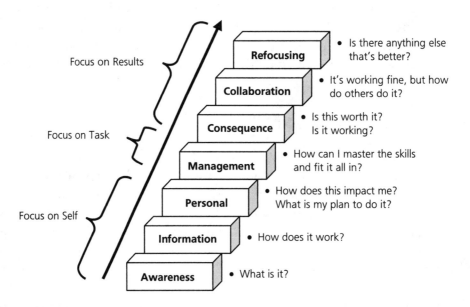

FIGURE 2. The concerns-based adoption model (CBAM). From Elish-Piper, L'Allier, and Zwart (2009). Copyright 2009 by the Illinois Reading Council. Reprinted by permission.

mon Core State Standards?" Next, teachers generally move to the Information stage wherein they seek details about the innovation and how it works. Teachers at the Information stage for the CCSS may ask questions such as "How are the Standards organized?" "How do the Standards change from one grade level to the next?" or "What are the specific Common Core expectations for students at my grade level?" Teachers who are at the Personal stage are focused on issues such as "How am I going to teach toward the Common Core Standards in my classroom?" "What is my plan for addressing text complexity with my students?" or "What will I do to teach my students to do opinion writing in response to the texts they read?"

When teachers begin to focus on task considerations, they have reached the Management stage, where they must address the logistics of implementing the innovation. They are most concerned with challenges such as "How can I identify texts and plan instruction to include a balance of literary and informational texts?" "How do I schedule the day to address the Common Core for ELA and Math as well as the other areas of the curriculum?" or "It's taking me forever to plan close reading lessons for a single day. How am I ever going to have time to plan and implement everything?"

As teachers begin to focus on results, they enter the Consequence stage of the process where they are grappling with the impact and effectiveness of the innovation. They may ask questions such as "How effective is my instruction related to the Common Core Reading Standards?" "How well are my students doing with developing their Speaking and Listening skills?" or "What can I do to enhance my writing instruction to align with the CCSS expectations for my students?" At the Collaboration stage, teachers begin considering how others are implementing the innovation and whether they can enhance their own use of it. They may ask questions such as "Who is further along with addressing the research-related standards, and what can I learn from them?" or "How can I work with others to enhance what I'm already doing regarding building students' academic vocabulary?" The final stage of the change process is Refocusing wherein teachers begin to ask questions such as "What else can we do to enhance teaching and learning beyond just implementing the Common Core?"

A clear understanding of the CBAM enables literacy coaches to align professional development efforts with the stages of the model to ensure that teachers receive the specific type of coaching support they need (Hall & Hord, 2006). Using the metaphor of a bridge, Sweeny (2002) offered specific types of coaching activities to support teachers as they traversed the span from where they were to where the innovation required them to be. We have adapted that model to focus on the Common Core (see Table 1). While the list of sample coaching activities is not comprehensive, it shows how coaching can move from information, to implementation, to results—depending on where the teachers in your school are in their enactment of the Common Core.

Building a Literacy Leadership Team to Support Change

While the literacy coach may be at the forefront of change in implementing the Common Core, he or she should not be leading the charge alone! It is essential to build a

TABLE 1. Using CBAM to Coach toward the Common Core

CBAM stage	Focus of concern	Sample coaching activities to support teachers
Awareness	Self	• Introduce the CCSS with a focus on the problem the Standards are designed to address—preparing students to be college and career ready. • Clarify state and district requirements associated with the CCSS such as dates for implementation and assessment.
Information	Self	• Explain and show organization of the CCSS. • Implement the unpacking process for the Standards. • Facilitate an article study to provide key information on the CCSS. A good article for this purpose is: McLaughlin, M., & Overturf, B. J. (2012). The Common Core: Insights into the K–5 standards. *The Reading Teacher, 66*(2), 153–164.
Personal	Self	• Conference with individual teachers to discuss "what gets in the way of helping students meet the CCSS" and how the literacy coach can help. • Work with teachers to set realistic goals; provide coaching support to reach those goals.
Management	Task	• Share inventory of resources available in the school. • Share sample schedules and organizational structures. • Model lessons in classrooms. • Co-plan lessons and units of study. • Co-teach lessons and units of study. • Develop implementation guides with grade-level teams.
Consequence	Results	• Review assessment data and student work to determine impact. • Provide targeted professional development to address areas where student performance does not meet the Standards.
Collaboration	Results	• Provide time and space to share lessons and resources. • Provide time to visit classrooms to observe others' practice. • Provide opportunities for lesson study as described in Strategy 12.
Refocusing	Results	• Engage teachers in self-assessment. • Encourage teachers to research ways to enhance practice or build on the innovation.

literacy leadership team so that the professional development efforts and changes are sustainable and not dependent on a single person. To that end, we embrace a model of literacy leadership that involves teacher leaders who represent each grade level so that there is shared ownership, buy in, and support for an innovation (Allen, 2006), in this case, the Common Core.

We recently viewed a great video on Ted Talks (*www.ted.com*) about starting a movement. In this 3-minute video, Derek Sivers (2010) explains how leaders need others to join the movement in order for it to have any impact. He uses video footage of a "silly dancer" on a hill at a concert to illustrate this point. It is only when a second dancer joins the first one that the movement begins to take shape and others join in as well. The big lesson from this video applies directly to building a literacy leadership team to support the CCSS. Namely, to establish momentum for implementation of the Common Core, it is essential to build a team of equals so that the focus is on the innovation—not on you, the literacy coach. Until you have a team of equals to collaborate with on the process, it is unlikely that you will be able to make significant progress toward implementing the change.

While there are a number of ways to build this type of literacy leadership team, the most common is identifying one teacher from each grade level to serve as a leader. In essence, these teacher leaders become "instructional leaders among their peers" (Sweeney, 2003, p. 88). For example, the first-grade teacher on the literacy leadership team will take the responsibility for facilitating first-grade team meetings as well as working with the literacy coach to develop and implement professional development and coaching support. Generally, the literacy coach recruits and asks for volunteers to serve in this important role. Experienced teachers who are well respected by their colleagues are ideal candidates to serve as teacher leaders. Good communication skills, an open mind, and a commitment to professional learning are also essential attributes for teacher leaders. In some schools, additional compensation or release time may be available for teacher leaders.

When recruiting potential teacher leaders, it is helpful to share expectations for the position as well as plans for providing training so that teachers can determine if being a teacher leader is appropriate and "doable" for him or her at that point in time. Expectations may include a full-day training/planning session each semester, weekly attendance at literacy leadership team meetings, and facilitating grade-level or PLC meetings on a regular basis. In addition to knowing the expectations, Sweeney (2003, p. 90) offers a series of questions that may be helpful to share with potential teacher leaders so they can determine whether they wish to sign on for the role or not. These questions include:

"Am I ready to do this?"

"Will I be alienated if I take a leadership role?"

"What kinds of expertise do I need?"

"Do I have enough time to take on this new role?"

By working as part of a literacy leadership team, the literacy coach is able to affect greater changes than he or she could produce alone (Fullan & Knight, 2011). Additionally, since the mandate to implement the Common Core is so far-reaching and complex, it only makes sense to build the strongest, most skilled leadership team. Throughout this book, we will offer suggestions on how to enlist the support of teacher leaders. In addition, many of the coaching strategies can be implemented by teacher leaders with their own grade-level colleagues.

Guidelines for Coaching toward the Common Core

While coaching toward the Common Core may strike you as an enormous, unwieldy task, we offer several important guidelines to help you focus and prioritize your coaching efforts. These guidelines reflect the current state of knowledge regarding effective literacy coaching and provide direction regarding top priorities for literacy coaching.

1 **Build capacity.** By building the capacity of teacher leaders, you can create a strong team to support implementation of the CCSS. The ultimate focus of all literacy coaching must be on building the instructional capacity of each teacher in the school to ensure that all students are taught by highly effective teachers.

2 **Create sustainability.** By building a strong leadership team, you can ensure that progress will continue even if individual teachers, teacher leaders, literacy coaches, or administrators leave the school. Using consistent, predictable structures and protocols for team meetings, PLCs, and teacher leader meetings will allow these processes to become part of the fabric of your school so the focus is on the CCSS rather than on figuring out how to run a meeting, discuss an article, or examine student work.

3 **Spend as much time as possible working directly with teachers and teacher leaders.** While literacy coaches are often asked to do managerial or administrative tasks such as organizing books rooms, inputting assessment data, or ordering instructional resources, those tasks do not directly improve the quality of teaching or learning in the school. If the tasks you are being asked to complete as a literacy coach do not support building capacity or sustainability, work with your administrator to assign those tasks to others such as paraprofessionals, secretarial staff, or school volunteers so you can devote your coaching time to activities that directly support teachers and teacher leaders.

4 **Focus on student learning.** By focusing on student learning and student work, you and your colleagues can concentrate on what is actually happening in classrooms in your school rather than wandering through all of the options of what could be or what should be. For example, by examining student writing samples and identifying areas that are consistently weak at a specific grade level, you, the teacher leader, and teachers can engage in professional development directly related to that area. In addition, even the most hesitant teachers tend to sit up and take notice when they compare their student work with standards, with other grade levels, or even with the work of students in other classrooms at the same grade level.

By keeping these four broad guidelines in mind, you can ensure that your literacy coaching work will be focused, productive, and effective.

Tools for Effective Coaching

Literacy coaching is a relatively new approach to professional development in many schools. Therefore, the roles, responsibilities, and best practices for literacy coaching are still evolving. In this chapter, we address a number of "nuts-and-bolts" issues that can make or break your literacy coaching work, and we offer useful tools to help you enhance the quality and effectiveness of coaching. First, we discuss how to determine a focus for your literacy coaching by establishing a coaching purpose statement. We then share the targeted coaching model (L'Allier & Elish-Piper, 2011, 2012) to provide guidance on which research-based literacy coaching activities contribute to student achievement gains, and we offer simple suggestions for making these activities part of your daily schedule. We also provide information about how to draw on and link three layers of coaching so you can use your literacy coaching time efficiently and effectively. Finally, we share information about how you can adjust your coaching stances and language to be responsive and supportive to teachers by providing just the type of coaching they need.

Prioritizing Coaching Time

Most of the literacy coaches we know find that there are more things on their "to-do" lists than there are hours in the day! One coach we have worked with for several years, Kim Dauber, lamented how she often found herself at the end of a busy day wondering, "What did I accomplish today?" More often than not, she told us, she could recount a long list of "random acts of coaching" that had kept her busy but didn't have any significant impact on building capacity, enhancing teacher practice, or improving student learning. When we shared this concern with other coaches, they generally nodded in agreement, sharing stories of typical days when they ran from one meeting to the next and spent countless hours managing assessment data and organizing book rooms. In light of this common quandary faced by literacy coaches, we began to consider findings from research and the wisdom of practice shared by successful, veteran coaches. Using these valuable sources, we have identified two useful tools to help coaches determine how to spend their time in the most effective ways possible.

What Is Your Purpose as a Literacy Coach?

Hopefully you have a clear job description that outlines your literacy coaching responsibilities. However, many of the literacy coaches we know do not have job descriptions, which can make their work nebulous and frustrating (Elish-Piper, L'Allier, & Zwart, 2009). If you don't have a job description, we urge you to sit down with your administrator or supervisor and begin developing one. Doing so is the first step in determining the focus of your coaching work. Next, we recommend that you write down and share widely your purpose statement for literacy coaching so that all of the teachers and specialized professionals in the building clearly understand the focus of your work. Two sample purpose statements are provided in Figure 1.

Sharing your purpose statement with the administrators and teachers at your school is important to make sure you are all in agreement regarding the type of work you should be doing (and not doing) as a literacy coach. However, we have found that this purpose statement serves another important function—being a personal "sounding board" for how you spend your time. For example, Mike Thomas, the literacy coach who wrote the first statement in Figure 1, reported that he uses this statement to determine whether a task is something he should be spending his precious, limited coaching time doing, or whether the task could be done by others such as secretarial or paraprofessional staff members or school volunteers. As Mike explained:

"I loved the idea that we were going to organize the book room by level and genre to support our work with the Common Core. I knew that this reorganized

---

Sample Purpose Statement 1: Mike Thomas

The purpose of my literacy coaching work is to build teacher instructional capacity related to the Common Core; to improve student literacy learning; and to build a supportive, collaborative professional learning community for teachers at my school.

Sample Purpose Statement 2: Ariel Washington

My literacy coaching has three purposes:

1. To help teachers enhance their practice.
2. To help students improve their literacy achievement.
3. To build a strong literacy leadership team to support purposes 1 and 2.

FIGURE 1. Literacy coaching purpose statements.

book room would be a great resource for teachers, but I didn't like the idea that I would be the one spending many, many hours sorting, cataloging, and organizing the books. A little thinking led me to realize that Margie, the paraprofessional who reshelves books in the book room and also in the school library, could complete this task with just a little time and support from me. By having Margie do this work, I would be able to spend most of my coaching time working with groups of teachers to review assessment data and model, co-plan, and co-teach lessons aligned to the Common Core. I felt like that was a much better use of my coaching time and more aligned to my coaching purpose statement. When I explained this to my principal, she supported my plan and thanked me for being so careful and deliberate about how I spend my coaching time."

We recommend that you review your coaching purpose statement frequently to ensure that it aligns with district and school priorities as well as your job description. We also encourage you to share your coaching purpose statement frequently, post it on your planning book or in your electronic calendar, and refer to it often to make sure that you are not getting caught up in the "random acts of coaching" that can fill a coach's day but result in few meaningful outcomes.

The Targeted Coaching Model

In addition to the coaching purpose statement, we offer the targeted coaching model (L'Allier & Elish-Piper, 2011, 2012) as a tool to help coaches determine how to spend their time in the most effective ways possible. The model is based on research we conducted in several large school districts over a 6-year period, involving 30 literacy coaches, 280 teachers, and over 7,000 students. The targeted coaching model (Figure 2) is depicted as a three-ring target with the bull's eye representing student reading and writing gains because that is the goal of all literacy coaching—to improve learning outcomes for students.

Literacy coach certification is positioned in the outer ring of the model because it is essential that coaches possess strong specialized knowledge about literacy instruction, assessment, and curriculum. In our research (Elish-Piper & L'Allier, 2010), coaches who had certification in reading/literacy produced greater gains in the classrooms where they coached than literacy coaches who did not have reading/literacy certification. This component of the model aligns with the International Reading Association's recommendation that literacy coaches possess "in-depth knowledge of reading processes, acquisition, assessment, and instruction" (2004, p. 3).

The second ring of the model shows that the amount of time literacy coaches spend working directly with classroom teachers is important. In our research, we found that the highest average student reading and writing gains were produced in classrooms served by literacy coaches who spent the most time working directly with teachers. Likewise, the lowest average student literacy gains were produced in classrooms served by literacy coaches who spent the smallest percentage of time with teachers (Elish-Piper & L'Allier, 2010). Therefore, the targeted coaching model

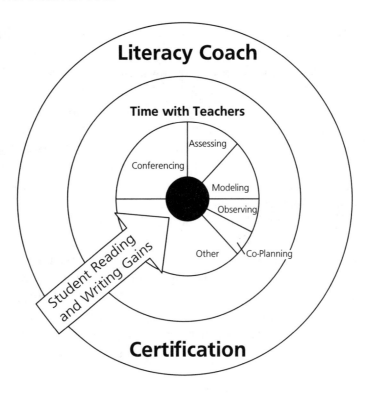

FIGURE 2. The targeted coaching model.

advocates that coaches spend as much of their time working directly with teachers as possible.

The inner ring of the model shows the specific literacy coaching activities that predicted student literacy gains. In our research, five literacy coaching activities were found to be significant predictors of student literacy gains: conferencing with teachers, working with assessments, modeling, observing, and co-planning (Elish-Piper & L'Allier, 2011). Each of the coaching activities in the targeted coaching model is described in Table 1. One section of the inner ring of the model is labeled "Other," because the five specified activities do not account for all of the important literacy coaching activities that may influence students' reading and writing gains. Therefore, depending on the specific goals and needs in a school, the literacy coach may also want to devote coaching time to large- and small-group coaching activities such as providing professional development workshops and facilitating grade-level meetings, study groups, PLCs, and lesson study groups.

Putting the Targeted Literacy Coaching Model into Action

Having a literacy coaching purpose statement and considering the targeted coaching model are two important steps that coaches can take to ensure that they are spending their coaching time wisely and effectively. However, just being aware of your coaching priorities does not mean they will be easy to implement in your work. Rachel Graham is a full-time literacy coach who is in her fourth year of coaching.

TABLE 1. Research-Based Literacy Coaching Strategies in the Targeted Coaching Model

Coaching activity	Description
Conferencing	Individual and small-group professional conversations with teachers to address specific problems, questions, or issues related to teaching practice, curriculum, or students. Conferencing refers primarily to scheduled meetings with teachers, but it also includes "on the fly" professional discussions that occur in the teachers' lounge, hallway, and parking lot.
Working with Assessments	Individual and small-group sessions to score and interpret assessment results. Sessions may also focus on reviewing assessment results to determine goals, to select appropriate instructional materials, and to plan instruction. The examination or evaluation of student work samples is also included within this coaching activity.
Modeling	Demonstration lessons delivered in a classroom setting for one or more teachers to observe. When the literacy coach models, he or she generally demonstrates a new instructional approach, such as close reading, so that teachers can see it in action with real students.
Observing	The literacy coach observes in a classroom, at the request of the individual teacher, to offer insights, feedback, suggestions, and support regarding some aspect of instruction, classroom management, or differentiation.
Co-planning	Individual and small-group sessions to plan lessons and units collaboratively, with the literacy coach or teacher leader facilitating the process.

She told us that she initially struggled with applying both her purpose statement and the targeted coaching model in her work, but eventually she developed an approach that worked well in her school. Let's see what Rachel learned and how it might help you as you work to focus and prioritize your coaching work.

"The first thing I did was to meet with my principal to share the targeted coaching model and my literacy coaching purpose statement. We then worked to reduce some of the time-consuming activities in my daily schedule that didn't align with the purpose statement and model. For example, we changed my morning bus duty so I'd be free to work with teachers before school started. We also assigned some tasks such as inputting assessment data and ordering reading resource materials to one of the school secretaries. We developed a plan to 'roll out' the targeted coaching model and to share my literacy coaching purpose statement with the teachers so they would all understand my role and our school's coaching priorities. We then discussed how I could create an initial focus for my coaching by working on one of the instructional shifts from the Common Core. We decided that this would give our school staff a unified professional development focus. We agreed that I would also work with our teacher leaders so they could facilitate some grade-level and PLC meetings which would allow me to spend the majority of my coaching time on the important activities from the targeted coaching model. Finally, I developed a log to record my coaching activities on a daily basis so I could monitor how I was spending my coaching time and make sure that I wasn't getting caught up in time-consuming activities that didn't match my purpose or the model."

Three Layers of Coaching

As we've been discussing in Chapter 1 and this chapter, literacy coaching is not a single activity but rather it is a range of job-embedded professional development opportunities and supports for teachers. Because of the complexity of teaching and learning, as well as the many changes needed in instructional practice to teach toward the Common Core, no single literacy coaching activity is sufficient to enhance teacher practice. We like the layered literacy coaching metaphor that Jennifer Allen (2007) uses. We envision this metaphor as three layers of literacy coaching support that is implemented with (1) large groups of teachers, (2) small groups such as grade-level teams or PLCs, and (3) individual teachers (see Figure 3).

To lay the groundwork for coaching toward the Common Core, we recommend starting with large groups of teachers such as the whole school or all primary- or all intermediate-grade teachers. Large-group coaching activities focus on building and establishing the "big picture" related to the CCSS. There are three main benefits to large-group coaching activities. First, they use coaching time efficiently; second, they build a common focus, purpose, or goal across many teachers in the school; and third, they help to create a collaborative climate and shared knowledge base that can serve as the foundation for coaching that goes more deeply into enhancing teacher practice and improving student literacy learning. Part Two of this book offers seven specific literacy coaching strategies designed for use with large groups of teachers. While large-group coaching activities are valuable and an essential part of any literacy coaching program, they are not sufficient to support teachers in their work to teach toward the Common Core.

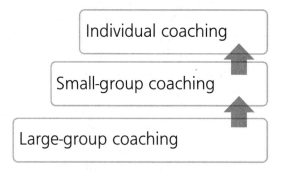

FIGURE 3. Layers of literacy coaching.

Small-group coaching activities are an essential layer of coaching toward the Common Core because these types of coaching activities are tailored specifically to the needs of small groups of teachers such as grade-level teams or PLCs. Small-group coaching activities may be facilitated by the literacy coach, but they may also be facilitated by teacher leaders who work closely with the literacy coach. When teacher leaders are able to facilitate grade-level meetings, PLCs, and article study groups, the responsibility for literacy coaching (and leadership) is shared across professionals in the school. This is an important move toward creating a sustainable coaching model that is not solely dependent on a single person. In Part Three we describe five specific small-group literacy coaching activities. These small-group coaching activities focus on supporting teachers to work collaboratively to dig down into the Common Core by engaging in processes such as developing implementation guides, reviewing assessments, examining student work, reviewing units of instruction, and conducting lesson studies. Generally, there is a direct link from large-group coaching activities to small-group coaching. For example, Kelly Maxwell, a literacy specialist who spends about half of her time on literacy coaching, implemented several large-group coaching activities at her school to lay the foundation so all teachers would be familiar with the Common Core and understand the instructional shifts. Once teachers started to ask questions that indicated they were entering the Management phase of the CBAM (Hall & Hord, 1987), she knew it was time to turn her attention to adding a layer of small-group coaching activities so that teachers at each grade level could work collaboratively to determine how they would modify their teaching to address specific aspects of the Common Core.

In some situations, two layers of coaching may be sufficient. This is especially true in schools with strong teacher leaders and a collaborative climate that supports professional development. However, there are often situations when teachers require or request individual coaching support to address specific aspects of their teaching. Newer teachers, those who have recently changed grade levels, and those who either lack confidence or struggle with the logistics of implementing new instructional practices, are prime candidates for individual coaching. Generally, individual coaching flows directly from small-group coaching activities. For example, a teacher may approach the coach and explain that he or she understands the implementation guide the team created as part of a small-group coaching activity, but is having difficulty moving his or her instruction and students' learning forward. Or, a teacher may participate fully in a small-group lesson study but still request that the coach work with him or her to co-plan and co-teach several lessons to ensure that he or she gains control and confidence over this new instructional approach. Individual coaching activities include goal setting, modeling, co-planning, co-teaching, and observing. When all of these coaching activities are linked together, they constitute a coaching cycle. These individual coaching strategies and the coaching cycle are described in great detail in Part Four. While individual coaching can be very time-consuming, it can produce powerful results.

Coaching Stances and Coaching Language

Regardless of the type of literacy coaching activity in which the coach is engaged, there are two important factors that contribute to the coach's effectiveness: coaching stance and coaching language. By listening carefully to what teachers say, literacy coaches are able to adjust the coaching stance they use to support teachers and the language they use to communicate effectively with them (Lipton & Wellman, 2007). A coaching stance refers to the way that the literacy coach positions him- or herself in terms of the type of support he or she provides and whether the coach or the teacher takes the lead in providing information and problem solving. The three literacy coaching stances are facilitating, collaborating, and consulting (L'Allier & Elish-Piper, 2012; Lipton & Wellman, 2007). The coaching stances are described in Table 2.

We have presented the three coaching stances separately, but literacy coaches often shift from one stance to another within a single coaching conversation. As teachers share their ideas, ask questions, and pose concerns, the literacy coach listens carefully to determine the appropriate stance. Teachers generally provide clear cues with the language they use when talking with literacy coaches. By listening carefully and considering what teachers say, the literacy coach can determine the appropriate stance to take and language to use. Table 3 illustrates how teacher cues can be used to determine the appropriate coaching stance and coaching language for that situation.

TABLE 2. Literacy Coaching Stances

Coaching stance	Description of support	Who provides information and leads problem solving
Facilitating	The literacy coach serves as someone for teachers to "think and problem solve with." The coach asks open-ended questions and paraphrases what teachers say. This stance is most appropriate when teachers have a good deal of knowledge about the issue and just want to have someone with whom to share ideas and discuss options.	The teacher
Collaborating	The literacy coach serves as a partner for teachers in this stance. Both the teacher and the literacy coach bring knowledge to the coaching conversation and share in the problem-solving process. In this stance, the coach often uses inclusive language such as "we," "us," and "our" to show that he or she is working as a partner with the teacher.	The teacher and the literacy coach
Consulting	The literacy coach takes the lead in this stance when teachers are frustrated, overwhelmed, or extremely unfamiliar with the topic or issue. In this stance, the literacy coach brings most of the information to the coaching activity and takes the responsibility for leading the problem-solving process.	The literacy coach

TABLE 3. Coaching Stances, Teacher Cues, and Coaching Language

Coaching stance	Teacher cues	Coaching language
Facilitating	[The coach knows that the teacher has knowledge and experience with the topic.] [The teacher appears to be seeking confirmation or a chance to talk through what he or she is already doing or thinking.] "I have been working on this, and I'd like to talk through with you how it has been going."	"What did you notice [about the data, the lesson, the students' reading behaviors]?" "What do you think helped the students make progress?" "In light of what you know about your students and have already done in the area of _____, what are you planning to do next?"
Collaborating	"I was thinking that I'd do [insert name of strategy]. What do you think?" "Can I bounce some ideas around with you for a lesson I'm planning?" "I just got the data from my students' assessments. Can I talk through some of the data with you?"	"Let's think about this together." "Let's brainstorm some ideas." "That's a great idea. I was also thinking of. . . ." "How about if we work through this together?"
Consulting	"I just don't know what else to try [to help my students . . .]." "What did you do about this when you were teaching?" "I've heard about this strategy, but I don't really know how to implement it [or if it is appropriate for my students or situation]. Can you give me some advice?" "Don't give me lots of choices. Please just tell me which one you think is the best option for my students."	"What has worked for me with students was. . . ." "Some of our colleagues have found this worked well with their students. . . ." "Here is a research-based practice that I think might work well with your students."

Note. Adapted from L'Allier and Elish-Piper (2011). Copyright 2011 by LearnSure, Inc. Adapted by permission.

Coaching Stances and Language in Action

Elena Castillo is in her second year of literacy coaching. She spends about a third of her time coaching and the remaining two-thirds working with small groups of struggling readers. Elena learned in her first year of coaching that she needed to listen carefully to what teachers said so that she could adjust her coaching stance to provide the support they wanted and needed at that time. She explained:

"I used to always jump to the consulting stance, trying to solve the teachers' problems by being the expert. I quickly learned that this approach didn't work lots of the time because many teachers wanted to exchange information and insights about their teaching challenges and others had already devised possible solutions to their instructional problems that they just wanted to talk through with me. I also wasn't always an expert on the topics or issues that the teachers were struggling with in their practice. Once I learned to listen closely and carefully, I realized when teachers just wanted someone to listen to them talk through their thinking as compared to when they wanted to collaborate to solve a problem. I also learned that there are times when teachers do want the coach to assume a consulting stance and offer specific suggestions. Once I learned to adjust my coaching stance, I was able to do a better job of responding to and supporting the teachers in my school."

Using "The Question" to Initiate a Coaching Conversation

Literacy coaches may find some teachers are hesitant to participate in coaching or to engage in conversations about their teaching or their students' learning. Even when coaches employ appropriate literacy coaching stances and language, these teachers avoid participating in literacy coaching activities. We have found that "The Question," offered by Cathy Toll (2005), is a surefire way to get even the most hesitant teacher to open up and talk about his or her teaching practice. Toll's question asks, "When you think about the reading and writing you want your students to do and the kind of teaching you want to do, what gets in the way?" (p. 121). This question invites teachers to identify the obstacles or challenges they experience in their teaching and can offer an opportunity to open up a meaningful coaching conversation.

Hugo Martinez, a literacy specialist who has been coaching for 4 years, recently recounted a story to us about how he used "The Question" with a group of teachers who seemed very hesitant to participate in coaching. He explained:

"I have this team of veteran teachers in fourth grade. They have many years of teaching experience and they are well respected in our school, but they never want to talk about their students' assessment results or to look at how they might need to update their teaching approaches to address the Common Core instructional shifts. I thought I had tried everything—offering to help, sharing new resources, facilitating grade-level meetings to review assessment data and student work, but nothing seemed to work. They just seemed to dismiss coaching by saying things like, 'We are doing just fine. We don't need any coaching support. You should spend your time helping the new teachers.' When I finally came across 'The Question,' I figured it was worth a try. At a grade-level meeting I asked, 'When you think about the kind of reading and writing your students are expected to do for the Common Core, what gets in the way?' The teachers just opened up and started listing all of the challenges they faced—identifying complex texts, knowing how to select texts to teach specific standards related to the integration of knowledge and ideas, and determining which aspects of craft and structure to teach with which texts. We immediately began to work together to address these challenges. It's amazing how well 'The Question' worked with this group of teachers. I must admit that I have started to rely on it to get coaching conversations rolling."

Conclusion

The tools in this chapter will help new as well as experienced literacy coaches. First, developing your coaching purpose statement and using the targeted coaching model to prioritize the coaching activities on which you spend time can increase the effectiveness of your literacy coaching work. Second, using a three-layered approach to coaching wherein you work with large groups, small groups, and individual teachers will help you support teachers efficiently and effectively. Finally, using responsive coaching stances and language will enable you to support teachers by providing just the type of coaching they want and need at that point in time.

The next three parts of this book are focused on specific coaching strategies that move teaching toward the Common Core. Part Two focuses on coaching strategies that can be used with large groups of teachers; Part Three addresses small-group coaching strategies; and Part Four presents coaching strategies to use with individual teachers. As you read about these strategies and determine which ones are most appropriate for use in your coaching work, be sure to keep in mind the key ideas about coaching toward the Common Core that have been discussed here in Part One. Figure 4 provides a visual summary of these key ideas.

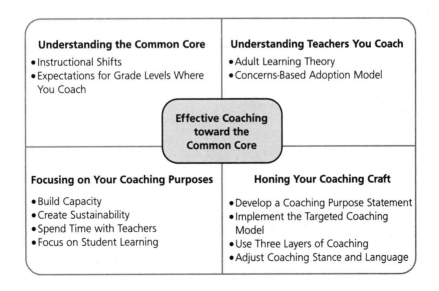

FIGURE 4. Key coaching considerations.

PART TWO

Large-Group Coaching toward the Common Core

If you are just getting started with coaching toward the Common Core, the whole process might seem so complicated or enormous that you don't even know where to begin. You may only have a small amount of time to devote to coaching, or the teachers in your school may not be familiar or comfortable with the Common Core. What can you do to get started? How can you use your coaching time most efficiently? How can you support the largest number of teachers in your school? Using the concept of layers of literacy coaching introduced in Chapter 2, we recommend getting started with large groups of teachers. Depending on the size of your school, large groups might include the whole staff, all of the primary teachers, or all of the intermediate-grade teachers.

Working with large groups of teachers is clearly the most time-efficient approach to coaching. However, there are additional benefits to coaching large groups of teachers. First, coaching large groups will allow you to make sure that all of the teachers in your school understand the basics of the Common Core. Because you will be working with lots of teachers on the same CCSS content, you can help to build a common focus, purpose, or goal across your whole school. For example, if you target instructional shifts such as close reading, writing to sources, or building academic vocabulary, all of the teachers in your school will be learning about, thinking about, and exploring that instructional shift at the same time. This means that it is likely that you'll start hearing teachers initiate conversations with one another related to the shift, and they may even begin sharing ideas, resources, and pins of CCSS things they love on Pinterest! Because you and the teachers will all be working toward the same goal, you will begin to build a collaborative climate and shared knowledge base that are necessary foundations for helping teachers to update and enhance their instructional practices.

Part Two contains seven specific literacy coaching strategies designed for use with large groups of teachers. The first two strategies focus on getting your school ready for coaching. Strategy 1 shares ideas about establishing a climate in your school that will be conducive to coaching. Strategy 2 offers suggestions for building shared knowledge and language related to the Common Core so you, your principal, and your teachers are using the same terms to represent the same ideas. For example, you will be able to make sure that everyone understands what close reading refers to—examining text closely and strategically as compared with holding a book closer to one's eyes!

Strategies 3 and 4 provide ideas about using familiar structures as the framework for coaching. More specifically, in Strategy 3 you'll learn how to conduct article study groups so that teachers can read, respond to, and reflect on professional articles related to the Common Core. With so many great articles written on various aspects of the Common Core, article study groups are easy to implement, and they offer many benefits in terms of building teacher knowledge and promoting applications to classroom practice. In Strategy 4, we'll share ways to use your limited coaching time effectively by embedding coaching activities and support into already-scheduled faculty meetings.

The focus of Strategies 5 and 6 is on helping teachers unpack and understand the alignment of the Common Core standards. In Strategy 5 we provide step-by-step procedures to guide teachers through the purpose, organization, and key ideas in the CCSS. In Strategy 6 you'll learn about how you can coach teachers to examine and understand the vertical alignment of the Standards from one grade level to the next. Finally, Strategy 7 offers useful information about how you can plan, deliver, and evaluate powerful professional development sessions with large groups of teachers in your school.

By implementing many or all of the strategies in Part Two, you will be able to work with the teacher leaders, teachers, and principal in your school to establish a strong foundation for teaching toward the Common Core. Then, by layering on appropriate small-group and individual coaching activities as described in Parts Three and Four, you and your colleagues can continue to move the instructional practices in your school toward the expectations of the Common Core.

Establishing a Climate
for Literacy Coaching

What Is It?

Literacy coaching is most effective when a school has already established a climate of mutual respect and collaboration (Bryk, Sebring, Allensworth, Luppescu, & Easton, 2010; Stiegler & Hiebert, 1999). This climate usually evolves as administrators, teachers, and other specialized professionals work together to develop a common vision and mission that includes high expectations for student learning and a sense of collective responsibility for helping students meet those expectations (Desimone, 2002; Learning Forward, 2010). The climate for literacy coaching is strengthened further when there is a literacy curriculum and assessment system in place. In addition, the principal plays a key role in fostering a school climate that embraces collaboration and change by providing opportunities for ongoing professional development (Leithwood, Seashore-Louis, Anderson, & Wahlstrom, 2004).

The success of literacy coaching is also dependent on the coach. Coaches must be knowledgeable not only about literacy acquisition, development, instruction, and assessment (Frost & Bean, 2006) but also about how adults learn and how to support the change process (Hall & Hord, 1987, 2006; Knowles, Holton, & Swanson, 2005; Terehoff, 2002). They must have good communication and interpersonal skills in order to facilitate their work with large groups, small groups, and individuals (International Reading Association, 2004). Coaches may not possess all of the necessary knowledge and skills when they begin their work, but they should be cognizant of their strengths and areas of need in order to develop a plan to enhance their coaching effectiveness.

The two questionnaires in this strategy (see Forms 1.1 and 1.2 at the end of this chapter) will help you determine how prepared your school and you are for literacy coaching. In addition, you will be able to increase that preparedness by developing and implementing action plans to strengthen any aspects that warrant further attention. Implementing those action plans will increase schoolwide readiness and result in your feeling more confident about your ability to engage in a wide variety of literacy coaching activities.

The School Climate and Literacy Coaching

The questionnaire in Form 1.1 will help you examine how ready your school is for literacy coaching.

How Do I Do It?

1 Read the questions listed under "Aspects to Consider" and the list of "Indicators of Readiness" on Form 1.1.

2 If possible, write down one or more examples for each indicator.

3 Place an "X" in the box that best describes your school's readiness in relation to each question.

- ◆ *We are ready!* Being able to list one or more examples for each indicator will provide specific evidence that, for this aspect of school climate, your school is ready for literacy coaching.
- ◆ *We are almost ready.* Providing an example for almost every indicator suggests that your school is making progress in this area.
- ◆ *We have a long way to go.* An inability to provide examples for most of the indicators suggests that this aspect of school climate needs considerable attention.

4 Analyze the results and develop an action plan for enhancing the school's readiness for literacy coaching. Outline your action plan in the box at the bottom of Form 1.1.

- ◆ Under "Short-Term Goals," you may want to focus on those aspects you marked as "We are almost ready." Consider ways that you could work with others to address the missing indicators. Giving just a little attention to these aspects may be very beneficial in strengthening a climate of shared vision, professional development, and collaboration.
- ◆ Aspects that you marked as "We have a long way to go" probably need a more long-term action plan. You may want to begin the process by meeting with your principal to discuss your observations about these aspects, determine

which aspect(s) might be addressed first, brainstorm possible approaches, and decide who might be involved in the next steps of the planning.

The Strategy in Action

Jamie Langdon is a reading specialist whose job description specifies that she spend 25% of her time engaged in literacy coaching. When she completed the questionnaire, Jamie noted that the district's literacy curriculum was not very explicit and had not been mapped to the CCSS that had recently been adopted by the state. After receiving approval from their principals and the assistant superintendent of instruction, she and other literacy leaders across the district met weekly throughout an entire year to review and revise the curriculum so that it was clear, complete, and aligned with the CCSS. Then, she and her colleagues developed a districtwide professional development initiative for sharing, refining, and implementing the curriculum. As Jamie facilitated this professional development initiative within her school, she not only focused on the curriculum (Item 4 on the questionnaire) but also on building good communication (Item 3) and shared language (Item 5). Furthermore, Jamie set the stage for future professional development (Item 1) as she and the teachers discussed what additional knowledge and skills they might need in order to implement the curriculum even more effectively.

Establishing a Personal Coaching Foundation

The questionnaire in Form 1.2 will help you examine how ready you are for literacy coaching.

How Do I Do It?

1 Read and thoughtfully consider each question listed on Form 1.2.

2 For each question, place an "X" in the box that best describes your readiness for coaching: "Yes," "Somewhat," "Not really."

3 For questions to which you responded "Somewhat" or "Not really," read the suggestions for enhancing your readiness.

4 Develop an action plan by circling the suggestions you feel would be most helpful. You may think of additional activities that would be helpful. Write those ideas in the space provided beneath the item "Additional action(s) you might take."

5 Prioritize the circled items and develop a timeline for completing the activities.

The Strategy in Action

If you are not sure what your action plan might look like, Maria Lopez's experience might provide some guidance. As a reading specialist for the past 3 years, Maria has primarily provided additional reading instruction to struggling readers. She has learned that, in the upcoming year, she will be taking on some coaching responsibilities. After responding to Form 1.2, she developed an action plan based on her need to understand the alignment of the district's curriculum with the CCSS (Item 1). First, she examined the district's literacy curriculum. Then, she located and read materials that helped her gain a clear understanding of the CCSS. Maria found the following materials to be particularly helpful:

◆ Calkins, L., Ehrenworth, M., & Lehman, C. (2012). *Pathways to the Common Core: Accelerating achievement.* Portsmouth, NH: Heinemann.

◆ McLaughlin, M., & Overturf, B. J. (2013). *The Common Core: Teaching K–5 students to meet the reading standards.* Newark, DE: International Reading Association.

◆ Appendix A (Research Supporting Key Elements of the Standards) and Appendix B (Text Exemplars and Sample Performance Tasks) from the CCSS (National Governors Association Center for Best Practices [NGA] & Council Chief State School Officers [CCSSO], 2010).

Next, Maria asked Cecil Foster, a second-grade teacher in the building, to meet with her. Maria viewed Cecil as an expert on the Common Core since he had attended two workshops focused on the Common Core and had served on the districtwide committee that had recently completed an initial mapping of the curriculum to the CCSS. Maria's discussion with Cecil strengthened her understanding of how the district's curriculum was aligned to the CCSS. Finally, as she observed in the classrooms, Maria looked for specific evidence of how teachers were integrating the CCSS into their instruction. The careful examination of the curriculum, professional reading, discussions with Cecil, and classroom observations all helped her feel better prepared to consider how coaching at the school, grade, and individual teacher levels might strengthen instruction that incorporated the Common Core.

FORM 1.1

How Ready Is My School for Literacy Coaching?

Aspects to Consider	Indicators of Readiness	Examples from My School
1. Is there a climate of professional development? ☐ We are ready! ☐ We are almost ready. ☐ We have a long way to go.	a. Professional development efforts focus on enhancing teacher knowledge and practice. b. Professional development efforts focus on improving student achievement. c. Professional development efforts include teacher participation at the planning, implementation, and evaluation stages.	a. b. c.
2. Is the principal a curricular leader? ☐ We are ready! ☐ We are almost ready. ☐ We have a long way to go.	a. The principal is knowledgeable about the school's curriculum, including the literacy curriculum. b. The principal provides the time and resources necessary for professional development related to literacy and other curricular areas. c. The principal attends and, when possible, actively participates in meetings and workshops related to curricular issues.	a. b. c.
3. Is there good communication among the teachers, including a respect for differing views? ☐ We are ready! ☐ We are almost ready. ☐ We have a long way to go.	a. There are multiple opportunities for teachers to converse (e.g., whole-school professional development sessions, grade-level meetings, professional learning communities). b. In informal settings, teachers talk to one another about strategies and resources. c. Good lines of communication have been established among teachers and other professional staff such as speech and language therapists, psychologists, and social workers.	a. b. c.

(continued)

Aspects to Consider	Indicators of Readiness	Examples from My School
4. Is there a defined literacy curriculum that is implemented across the grades? ☐ We are ready! ☐ We are almost ready. ☐ We have a long way to go.	a. The literacy curriculum includes goals, learning standards, instructional strategies, assessments, and resources. b. The curriculum is aligned with district, Common Core, and state and federal standards, as appropriate. c. Classroom observations provide evidence that the curriculum is being implemented as delineated.	a. b. c.
5. Is there shared understanding of language related to literacy acquisition, development, instruction, and assessment? ☐ We are ready! ☐ We are almost ready. ☐ We have a long way to go.	a. Discussions about topics such as emergent literacy, developmentally appropriate activities, and age-appropriate content show a common understanding of terms related to literacy acquisition and development. b. Clear, concise definitions/descriptions of terms related to literacy instruction (e.g., shared reading, guided reading, phonemic awareness, phonics) have been established. c. There is a common understanding of the terminology related to literacy assessment (e.g., universal screening, diagnostic assessment, progress monitoring) and of the assessments that are given in the school (e.g., *Measures of Academic Progress, Fountas and Pinnell Benchmark Assessment System*, curriculum-based assessments).	a. b. c.
6. Is there a schoolwide assessment system in place?	a. The school's assessment plan includes universal screening, diagnostic assessment, and progress monitoring.	a.

(continued)

Aspects to Consider	Indicators of Readiness	Examples from My School
☐ We are ready! ☐ We are almost ready. ☐ We have a long way to go.	b. There are clear procedures for aggregating and sharing the assessment data. c. The assessment data are being used to develop goals at the school level, grade level, classroom level, and individual student level.	b. c.
7. Are there schoolwide goals for improving students' literacy development? ☐ We are ready! ☐ We are almost ready. ☐ We have a long way to go.	a. Schoolwide goals have been developed and shared. b. An implementation plan for each goal has been developed and shared. c. The implementation plan for each goal is being executed.	a. b. c.
8. Are teachers open to having others in their classrooms? ☐ We are ready! ☐ We are almost ready. ☐ We have a long way to go.	a. Novice teachers observe more experienced teachers. b. Teachers engage in co-teaching and parallel teaching on a regular basis. c. The push-in model of providing support for students who struggle is being used when appropriate.	a. b. c.
9. Is the schedule conducive for literacy coaching? ☐ We are ready! ☐ We are almost ready. ☐ We have a long way to go.	a. There is common planning time for grade levels so that the coach and all members of a particular grade level can meet on a regular basis. b. The schedule provides time for coaching when many teachers are implementing literacy instruction (e. g., during literacy blocks). c. The schedule enables the coach to be free of additional duties right before or after school as those are optimal times for the coach to meet with teachers.	a. b. c.

(continued)

Action Plan for Enhancing the School's Readiness for Coaching			
Short-Term Goals	**Tasks**	**People Who Can Help**	**Date for Task Completion**
Long-Term Goals	**Tasks**	**People Who Can Help**	**Date for Task Completion**

How Ready Am I for Literacy Coaching?

Questions to Consider	What Can You Do to Enhance Your Readiness for Coaching?
1. Do I understand the scope and sequence of the literacy curriculum and how it is aligned with the district, Common Core, and other standards? ☐ Yes ☐ Somewhat ☐ Not really	a. Carefully read the literacy curriculum. Note unclear aspects that you want to discuss with others. b. Read the standards that are expected to be met by the students in your district. Write down any questions you have about the standards. Think about who would be able to answer your questions. c. Determine whether the curriculum includes explicit alignment with the required standards. If it does not, think about the steps that might be necessary to ensure that there is alignment between the curriculum and the required standards. How might you, as the literacy coach, be involved in that process? d. Additional action(s) you might take:

2. Do I understand what literacy instruction looks like in my school (in regular education classrooms, in bilingual classrooms for English learners, in self-contained classrooms for students with special needs, in pull-out or push-in instructional settings)?
 	
☐ Yes
 	
☐ Somewhat
 	
☐ Not really
	a. Determine the grade levels or specific settings where your understanding of literacy instruction could be enhanced.
	b. To learn about the literacy instruction at those grade levels or within those specific settings, make multiple observations.
	c. Reflect on your observations.
	  ◆ Is the instruction aligned with the literacy curriculum?
	  ◆ What differences are there across settings? Which differences seem appropriate and why? Which differences may warrant discussion with teachers?
	d. Additional action(s) you might take:

3. Am I familiar with all of the literacy-related resources in my school and where those resources are located? ☐ Yes ☐ Somewhat ☐ Not really	a. Complete a survey of the resources in each classroom. b. Complete a similar survey with each specialized professional who implements literacy instruction (e.g., Title I teachers, reading specialists, teachers of students with learning disabilities or other special needs). They often have materials that they are not currently using but that might be useful to other teachers. c. Determine where all of the leveled books are housed. You may find them in classrooms, a designated book room, or the library/learning center. Note how many different titles are available at each guided reading level. d. Additional action(s) you might take:

(continued)

Questions to Consider	What Can You Do to Enhance Your Readiness for Coaching?
4. Do I understand the demographics of my school? ☐ Yes ☐ Somewhat ☐ Not really	a. If your state or district provides a school report card for each school, carefully examine the report card for your school. These report cards usually provide information about the distribution of students across the grades and the diversity of students in terms of gender, race/ethnicity, language, and socioeconomic status. Student performance on state assessments is also generally included. If your state or district does not provide a school report card, work with your principal to obtain the information listed previously. b. In addition to the classroom teachers and their grade levels, make a list of the other professionals and paraprofessionals in your building. What role does each person play and with which students do they interact? c. Make a list of the ways that parents are involved with the school (e.g., volunteering in classrooms or the library/learning center, working in after-school programs, participating in the parent–teacher organization or association, attending parent conferences and other parent events). d. Additional action(s) you might take:
5. Have I worked with the principal to lay the foundation for literacy coaching? ☐ Yes ☐ Somewhat ☐ Not really	a. Work with your principal to develop a job description and purpose statement for the literacy coaching aspect of your position. b. At a faculty meeting, the principal can share the job description and you can share your purpose statement. You also can share a list of ways that you could provide support to the teachers as they work to improve student learning. c. After the faculty meeting, send out the list discussed at the meeting and invite teachers to contact you if they would be interested in collaborating with you. d. Additional action(s) you might take:
6. Do I know who the other literacy leaders are in the school and what they have done to be recognized as literacy leaders? ☐ Yes ☐ Somewhat ☐ Not really	a. If there is a school leadership team, list the members and grade level(s)/area each represents. b. If there is a literacy or language arts committee in the school, list the members and grade level(s) each represents. c. If there are teacher leaders, list their names and the grade levels they represent. d. Make a list of the informal literacy leaders in the school and why they are considered leaders. e. Additional action(s) you might take:

(continued)

Questions to Consider	What Can You Do to Enhance Your Readiness for Coaching?
7. Do I know who the "experts" are in my school? ☐ Yes ☐ Somewhat ☐ Not really	a. Make a list of the teachers who you know from personal observation have expertise in certain areas (e.g., guided reading, writing workshop, conferencing with individual students). b. Add to that list as you make classroom observations and as you listen to teachers' discussions at faculty meetings, grade-level meetings, and professional development workshops. c. Additional action(s) you might take:
8. Am I knowledgeable about all aspects of literacy development, instruction, and assessment? ☐ Yes ☐ Somewhat ☐ Not really	a. When you think about the pillars of reading instruction (phonemic awareness, word identification including phonics, fluency, vocabulary, and comprehension), list specific aspects where your knowledge could be enhanced. As you look at the current "hot" topics in literacy such as the Common Core and progress monitoring, list those about which you would like more information. b. Start with two or three topics about which you want to know more. Locate articles and other materials related to those topics. c. As you read, think about how your new learning is related to your school's literacy curriculum and to the literacy instruction you are seeing in the classrooms. d. Additional action(s) you might take:
9. Do I understand the key ideas related to adult learning, change theory, and coaching? ☐ Yes ☐ Somewhat ☐ Not really	a. For more information about adult learning, consider reading: ◆ Terehoff, I. I. (2002). Elements of adult learning in teacher professional development. *NASSP Bulletin, 86*(232), 65–77. ◆ Trotter, Y. D. (2006). Adult learning theories: Impacting professional development programs. *Delta Kappa Gama Bulletin, 72*(2), 8–13. b. For more information about change theory, consider reading: ◆ Reeves, D. B. (2009). *Leading change in your school.* Alexandria, VA: ASCD. ◆ Hall, G. E., & Hord, S. M. (2006). *Implementing change: Patterns, principles, and potholes* (2nd ed., Chap. 1). Boston: Allyn & Bacon. c. There are many recently published professional books about literacy coaching. Go to *www.amazon.com* and type "literacy coaching" in the search box. Browse through the tables of contents from several of these books and purchase one or two that include chapters related to your specific interests. d. Attend workshops related to literacy coaching. e. Meet regularly with other coaches to discuss literacy coaching. This group might want to participate in a book study that focuses on a professional book about literacy coaching. f. Additional action(s) you might take:

(continued)

Questions to Consider	What Can You Do to Enhance Your Readiness for Coaching?
10. Have I established my credibility as a teacher? ☐ Yes ☐ Somewhat ☐ Not really	a. If you have been a teacher in the building where you coach, you probably have established a certain level of credibility. If, for example, you taught second grade, your credibility may extend to all primary teachers. b. To establish credibility with teachers at levels where you have not taught or if you are coaching in a building where you have not taught, consider one or more of the following: ◆ Offer to conduct read-alouds in each classroom. ◆ Offer to teach a guided reading group in a few classrooms for a week or two. ◆ Offer to do some demonstration teaching around one of the key Common Core standards with which the teachers are grappling. c. Additional action(s) you might take:
11. Am I a good listener? ☐ Yes ☐ Somewhat ☐ Not really	a. Monitor yourself as you engage in conversations with teachers. Are you listening at least as much as you are talking? b. Demonstrate active listening by restating what you've heard and asking questions. The following examples are responses that might be made by a coach who is an active listener: ◆ You note that your students have been successful with supporting their answers by referring to specific parts of the text (or some other aspect of a Common Core standard). What activities have contributed to your students' success? ◆ You're telling me that your students are having trouble determining the supporting details for a main idea (or some other aspect of a Common Core standard). What do you think is getting in the way of their success? ◆ You said you are working on helping your students compare and contrast themes across texts. What could I do to support you? c. Additional action(s) you might take:
12. Have I reflected on previous curricular initiatives in my school? ☐ Yes ☐ Somewhat ☐ Not really	a. Make a list of factors that contributed to the success of those initiatives. b. Make a list of factors that inhibited the success of those initiatives. c. Consider how you can incorporate the successful factors and avoid the inhibiting factors as you support teachers with current and future literacy initiatives. d. Additional action(s) you might take:

Building Shared Understanding and Language

What Is It?

Schools that value and promote teacher learning often implement professional development models such as professional learning communities (PLCs; DuFour, DuFour, & Eaker, 2008), lesson study (Hurd & Licciardo-Musso, 2005), and literacy coaching (Toll, 2005). In many schools, multiple models of professional development are used in tandem to reap the benefits of each approach. While the models differ in some ways, they do have several important similarities. First, each seeks to establish a common vision focused on improved student learning. To that end, these professional development approaches build teacher knowledge about how to support all students' learning. By establishing this shared knowledge base, teachers also develop a common language about teaching, learning, and instructional practices to facilitate productive discussions and collaboration across groups, teams, and the school. In order to promote this type of shared understanding, a collegial climate is essential wherein teachers feel comfortable to share their practice, discuss their challenges, and collaborate with their peers (Hord & Tobia, 2012).

An effective way to build shared understanding and language around the CCSS is to identify key concepts and strategies addressed in the Standards and to use these consistently in the school setting. Using the five major instructional shifts associated with the CCSS for grades K–5 (EngageNY, 2012; Fisher et al., 2013) is a viable way to organize this process (see Figure 2.1). Through this process, literacy coaches will be able to identify shared knowledge and language and to determine areas where professional development support and greater cohesion are needed.

◆ 39 ◆

> **1.** Balancing informational and literary texts.
> **2.** Increasing text complexity.
> **3.** Developing text-based responses.
> **4.** Writing from sources.
> **5.** Building academic vocabulary.

FIGURE 2.1. Instructional shifts associated with the CCSS in grades K–5.

How Do I Do It?

Before you can build shared knowledge and language across the teachers you coach, it is important for you to determine the status of the group regarding the Common Core. By following the process outlined below, you can gather that information, identify areas for improvement, and develop a plan for building shared knowledge and language.

Identifying Shared Knowledge and Language and Areas of Need

1 Administer a needs assessment related to the Common Core to the teachers in your school. The needs assessment in Form 2.1 focuses on the five instructional shifts associated with the CCSS.

2 Form 2.2 provides a template you can use to tally and analyze the information from the needs assessment. You may want to organize your tallies by grade level when you analyze responses.

3 Write your conclusions in the "Key Findings from Needs Assessment" box found at the bottom of Form 2.2.

   a Identify areas where most teachers report having sufficient knowledge and feel prepared to address the shift.
   b Identify areas where many of the teachers report not having sufficient knowledge and do not feel prepared to address that shift in their instruction.
   c Record relevant information in the "Notes" column to help you with your planning.

Developing Shared Knowledge and Language

1 Using the results of the needs assessment, determine an initial instructional shift to focus on with the teachers.

2 Introduce the shift by doing a collective brainstorming activity with the teachers. Use the prompts below to structure the brainstorming. Record the teachers' responses so you can use them to guide this professional development process.

- What do you know about this instructional shift?
- What key concepts and terms come to mind related to this instructional shift?
- What examples of this instructional shift can you think of?
- What non-examples of this instructional shift can you think of?
- What questions do you have about this instructional shift?

3 Using information from the collective brainstorming, develop a short resource guide (see Figure 2.2) that clarifies the instructional shift, including key concepts and related language. Have teachers read and discuss it with a partner. Ask each group of partners to write down a question they have related to the shift. Provide time to discuss the questions.

4 If the teachers still need additional information about the instructional shift, you may wish to implement an article study group as described in Strategy 3.

5 To remind the teachers about their new learning and shared language related to the instructional shift, post key ideas and language in group areas such as the teacher work room, team planning area, and teacher lunchroom. Provide teachers with a bookmark that lists the same key ideas and language related to the instructional shift.

6 Be sure to use the language related to the instructional shift consistently, and encourage teachers to do so too. By providing multiple exposures to the knowledge and language related to the instructional shift and offering various opportunities for the teachers to discuss, question, and share responses, they will be able to build and deepen their shared understanding of the instructional shift.

7 This strategy can be adapted easily to focus on any aspect of teaching, curriculum, or assessment.

Opinion Writing Resource Guide

Students in grades 4 and 5 are expected to produce written opinions in response to texts they read. This type of writing addresses each of these characteristics:

- Introduce a topic or text clearly.
- State an opinion (make an argument).
- Create an organizational structure with related ideas grouped to support the writer's opinion.
- Provide reasons (claims) that are supported by facts and details (evidence) from the text.
- Link opinion and reasons using words and phrases (e.g., *for instance, in order to, in addition*).
- Provide a concluding statement or section related to the opinion presented.

FIGURE 2.2. Instructional shift: Writing from sources. Check out Appendix C of the CCSS (NGA & CCSSO, 2010) for an example of opinion (argument) writing in grade 4.

The Strategy in Action

Brittney Wilkerson is a full-time literacy coach at Washington Elementary School. By administering the needs assessment to the teachers at her school, she learned that the fourth- and fifth-grade teachers did not have sufficient knowledge or confidence related to writing from sources. After doing the collective brainstorming, Brittney learned that the teachers were already having their students use sources for informational/explanatory writing, but they did not seem comfortable teaching students how to use sources to write opinions. She used that information to prepare a short resource guide with key ideas related to opinion writing (see Figure 2.2). She shared the resource guide with the teachers and engaged them in a spirited discussion about what they learned, how they might apply the ideas to their teaching, and the questions they still had about opinion writing. Their next step will be to review the relevant writing samples in Appendix C of the Common Core (NGA & CCSSO, 2010). More specifically, Brittney plans to have them read the grade 4 sample of opinion writing, paying attention to whether the sample addresses all of the key ideas on the resource guide. She then plans to initiate a conversation about which aspects of opinion writing they are already addressing in their instruction and which will need to be added. After that process is complete, Brittney anticipates that they will then be ready to focus more specifically on effective methods for teaching opinion writing.

Needs Assessment for Instructional Shifts in the ELA Common Core

Directions: Please respond to each of the prompts as honestly as possible. This information will help us determine professional development and coaching opportunities in our school. Your input is very important!

> SA = Strongly Agree
> A = Agree
> D = Disagree
> SD = Strongly Disagree

1. **Balancing Informational and Literary Texts**

    a. Please explain the term *informational texts* as you understand it in relation to the Common Core.

    b. Please explain the term *literary texts* as you understand it in relation to the Common Core.

(continued)

   c. I have sufficient knowledge of ways to balance informational and literary   SA   A   D   SD
      texts in my classroom.

   d. I feel prepared to balance informational and literary texts in my teaching.   SA   A   D   SD

   e. Please describe your understanding of what it means to "balance
      informational and literary texts" at your grade level.

2. Increasing Text Complexity

   a. I have sufficient knowledge about the quantitative factors associated   SA   A   D   SD
      with text complexity.

   b. I have sufficient knowledge about the qualitative factors associated with   SA   A   D   SD
      text complexity.

   c. I have sufficient knowledge about the reader and task factors associated   SA   A   D   SD
      with text complexity.

   d. I feel prepared to address increasing text complexity in my teaching.   SA   A   D   SD

   e. Please explain the concept of "text complexity" as you understand it in
      relation to your grade level.

3. Developing Text-Based Responses

   a. I have sufficient knowledge about text-based discussions.   SA   A   D   SD

   b. I have sufficient knowledge about close reading.   SA   A   D   SD

   c. I have sufficient knowledge about ways to teach students to develop   SA   A   D   SD
      text-based responses.

(continued)

    d. I feel prepared to teach students to develop text-based responses.   SA   A   D   SD

    e. Please explain the concept of "close reading" as you understand it in relation to your grade level.

4. Writing from Sources

    a. I have sufficient knowledge about writing from sources.   SA   A   D   SD

    b. I feel prepared to teach students to write from sources.   SA   A   D   SD

    c. Please explain the concept of "writing from sources" as you understand it in relation to your grade level.

5. Building Academic Vocabulary

    a. I have sufficient knowledge about building students' academic vocabulary.   SA   A   D   SD

    b. I feel prepared to teach students to build their academic vocabulary.   SA   A   D   SD

    c. Please explain the concept of "building academic vocabulary" as you understand it in relation to your grade level.

FORM 2.2

Summary of Teacher Needs Assessment

Needs Assessment Section	Knowledge of Instructional Shifts and Terminology + = Most teachers ✓ = Some teachers – = Few teachers	Preparedness for Application + = Most teachers ✓ = Some teachers – = Few teachers	Notes
Balancing informational and literary texts			
Increasing text complexity			
Developing text-based responses			
Writing from sources			
Building academic vocabulary			

Key Findings from Needs Assessment:

Conducting an Article Study Group

What Is It?

Article study groups bring together teachers to read and discuss professional journal articles related to some aspect of their teaching practice. Article study groups are similar to literature circles and book clubs in that they invite participants to share their reactions, insights, questions, and concerns through small-group discussion (Burbank, Kauchak, & Bates, 2010). Such groups allow teachers to be part of a community of learners who support the enhancement of their own professional development and practice (Commeyras, Bisplinghoff, & Olson, 2003). In addition, article study groups are flexible, easy to implement, cost- and time-effective, and applicable to any and all aspects of the Common Core.

To ensure that the articles selected for study groups are relevant, applicable, and accessible in terms of length, complexity, and amount of background knowledge needed, the literacy coach or a teacher leader generally selects them. For article study groups that operate over time, members may select their own articles to read and discuss. The literacy coach or a teacher leader typically serves as a facilitator to get the discussion going, to ensure that all members participate, and to keep the group focused on key ideas and applications from the article.

Participation in article study groups can help educators establish a common language and understanding of key educational issues and instructional practices as they read, discuss, and apply ideas from the article. This process can be an important step in building a school climate that encourages and supports ongoing professional development and collaboration. In addition, article study groups can serve as a gateway to other coaching activities as teachers reach out to the literacy coach for support to implement new practices they've read about into their teaching.

How Do I Do It?

To implement article study groups, there are three processes you'll complete. First, you need to prepare. Then you need to facilitate the session. And finally, you need to follow up with the group members. The basic steps for preparing, facilitating, and following up with article study groups are provided below.

Preparing for an Article Study Group

1 Determine the members of the article study group. If you work in a smaller school, the group may include all of the teachers, or it may include teachers from the primary grades or from the intermediate grades. Article study groups also work well with smaller groups such as grade-level teams, members of a specific committee such as the literacy or assessment committee, or self-selected groups based on interest.

2 Confer with the group members regarding the purpose for the article study group.

3 Identify at least one article that addresses the specific purpose of the group. A list of suggested articles related to various aspects of the Common Core is provided in Figure 3.1. If two or more articles are available, do brief article talks or share abstracts with the teachers so they can select the specific article to read and discuss. If only one appropriate article can be located, share a brief article talk or abstract so teachers can anticipate what they'll be reading.

4 Select a format that the article study group members can use to record their reactions and refer to during the discussion. A standard article discussion group format is provided in Form 3.1, and three alternative formats are provided in Table 3.1.

5 Determine the time, place, and location for the article study group to meet. Depending on the length of the article and the complexity of the ideas presented, a group meeting may be as short as 20 minutes or as long as 1 hour.

6 Clarify the expectations for the article study group. A sample set of expectations is provided in Figure 3.2.

7 Prepare to facilitate the meeting by reading and rereading the article carefully, writing your own comments using the same discussion format as the teachers, and developing several questions that you can use to move the discussion to a deeper more meaningful level, if needed. Sample questions include:

- "How does this connect to our school or your classroom?"
- "What is confusing or frustrating to you from this article? Why?"
- "What takeaway do you have from this article that will stick with you long after this meeting is over?"

Article	Content/Focus on the CCSS
Roskos, K., & Neuman, S. B. (2013). Common Core, commonplaces, and community in teaching reading. *The Reading Teacher, 66*(6), 469–473.	Overview of Reading Standards
Smith, M. W., Wilhelm, J. D., & Fredricksen, J. (2013). The Common Core: New standards, new teaching. *Phi Delta Kappan, 94*(8), 45–48.	General Overview
Shanahan, T. (2012/2013). The Common Core ate my baby and other urban legends. *Educational Leadership, 70*(4), 10–16.	Common Myths
Hollenbeck, A. F., & Saternus, K. (2013). Mind the comprehension iceberg: Avoiding Titanic mistakes with the CCSS. *The Reading Teacher, 66*(7), 558–568.	Comprehension
Hiebert, E. H. (2013). Supporting students' movement up the staircase of text complexity. *The Reading Teacher, 66*(6), 459–468.	Text Complexity
Stahl, K. A. D. (2012). Complex text or frustration-level text: Using shared reading to bridge the difference. *The Reading Teacher, 66*(1), 47–51.	Text Complexity
Fisher, D., & Frey, N. (2012). Close reading in elementary schools. *The Reading Teacher, 66*(3), 179–188.	Close Reading
Dalton, B. (2013). Engaging children in close reading. *The Reading Teacher, 66*(8), 642–649.	Close Reading
Boyles, N. (2012/2013). Closing in on close reading. *Educational Leadership, 70*(4), 36–41.	Close Reading
Dalton, B. (2012). Multimodal composition and the Common Core State Standards. *The Reading Teacher, 66*(4), 333–339.	Writing
Hiebert, E. H., & Pearson, P. D. (2012/2013). What happens to the basics? *Educational Leadership, 70*(4), 48–53.	Basic Skills

FIGURE 3.1. Recommended professional articles for article study groups about various aspects of the CCSS.

Facilitating an Article Study Group

1 Start and end the meeting on time.

2 For the standard article group discussion format (see Form 3.1), begin by asking teachers to share their ratings for the article and the reasons for their rating. Save your rating for last so as not to sway the responses of the group members. If the group is larger than a dozen teachers, you may want to consider dividing into two groups and having a teacher leader facilitate one of the groups.

3 Proceed through the remaining discussion prompts, asking for teachers to volunteer their responses and to connect them to ideas shared by other group members.

4 Use open-ended prompts to move the discussion along as needed. Some possible prompts are: "Tell us more." "Can you share an example?" "What are the rest of

TABLE 3.1. Article Study Group Discussion Formats

Discussion format	Description	Implementation considerations
3–2–1	Teachers record three big ideas from the article, two questions for discussion, and one idea for application.	This is an easy-to-implement format that requires little preparation on the part of teachers. They can compare the three big ideas they noted and discuss how they are similar and different from their peers' ideas. They can also pose their questions for discussion to get input and ideas from the group. Finally, they can share their ideas for application.
Text coding	Teachers code the article using the following codes: Important (*) Interesting (I) Confusing (C) Agree (A) Disagree (D) Apply (!) They also prepare to discuss why they coded the article as they did.	Text coding puts the focus more specifically on the text. This approach works well when the purpose is to read and discuss the text closely and thoroughly. Teachers can share what they marked with each of the codes as a way to structure the discussion.
Double-entry journal	Teachers identify several quotes from the article that they find important, relevant, or provocative. They record each *quote* and then write a *note* about what they were thinking when they read and reflected on the quote.	The double-entry journal ensures that the discussion focuses on specific information from the text. During the discussion, teachers can take turns sharing a quote and note and then inviting others to offer input and insights.

- Read the article carefully prior to the meeting.
- Record reactions to the article using the discussion format provided by the facilitator.
- Come to the meeting on time with a copy of the article and your responses on the discussion format sheet.
- Stay for the entire meeting.
- Be prepared to share your responses to the article, listen carefully to other group members, and keep an open mind.
- Focus on building your knowledge base and identifying meaningful applications to your practice.

FIGURE 3.2. Article study group expectations.

you thinking?" To move the discussion to a deeper level, you may also want to ask one or more of your prepared questions.

5 Reserve time near the end of the meeting for teachers to discuss application ideas associated with the article.

6 Ask teachers how you or other group members can help them move ahead with their application ideas.

7 Discuss and determine the next steps for the article discussion group. These steps will include:

   a Is the group meeting again?
   b If so, when and where?
   c What topic or focus does the group want to address in the next meeting?
   d If the group is not meeting again, how will members share their experiences with applying ideas from the article?

Following Up after an Article Study Group

1 Send an e-mail or put a note in each teacher's mailbox thanking him or her for participating in the article study group. Provide a brief recap of one or two of the main ideas from the discussion. Include a reminder about whether the group is meeting again. If the group is not meeting again, specify how they will share their experiences with applying ideas from the article. Conclude with an offer to follow up to provide support or share resources with the teachers. A sample e-mail message is shown in Figure 3.3.

2 Follow up with the teachers to discuss application ideas and how you can help.

3 If the group is meeting again, begin preparing for the next article study group discussion.

The Strategy in Action

Jenny Taylor is a reading specialist who spends about 25% of her time on literacy coaching. The rest of her time is devoted to providing small-group interventions for struggling readers. She finds that article discussion groups are a great use of her coaching time, and she currently is meeting with the intermediate-grade teachers to examine the topic of text complexity. So far, the group has read one article and decided to apply ideas from the article to help them analyze some of the texts they use in terms of complexity. At their next meeting, they will read and discuss another article and spend time looking at examples of the complex texts referenced in the article. She also plans to share Figure 2 of Appendix A from the CCSS (NGA &

To: Rachel Barnes, James Carter, Yuki Kim, Carolyn Miller, Madelyn Nelson, Sandi Peterson, Heather Quinn, Celi Silva, and Tyler Vaughn

From: Jenny Taylor

Hi all!

Thanks for participating in the article study group on Monday. The group did a great job discussing specific aspects of text complexity, especially qualitative factors such as levels of meaning, structure, language, and knowledge demands. The group will be meeting again on October 1 from 10:15 to 11:00 in the team center. Our focus will continue to be on text complexity. Our first task will be to share experiences with applying ideas from the article. If I can help as you work on applying ideas from the article, please let me know. I'm happy to co-plan, co-teach, model, share resources, or just be a partner to "think and problem-solve with."

Our second task at the October 1 meeting will be to discuss the new article that I will share with you by the end of the week.

Have a great afternoon!

Jenny

FIGURE 3.3. Sample e-mail message.

CCSSO, 2010) to provide a more detailed discussion of text complexity. Between the article study group meetings, Jenny has scheduled time to talk with the teachers individually before or after school or during their lunchtime to see what questions, concerns, and application experiences they have related to the article. In addition, she will remind them, as she often does, "Let me know what I can do to help as you move forward toward application. I'm here to help!"

Article Study Group Note Sheet

Name: _____

Article Title: _____

AS YOU READ THE ARTICLE . . .

1. How you would rate the text on a scale of 1 (low) to 10 (high)? Explain.

2. Describe how the article relates to your teaching or other professional experiences. (Mark specific passages or pages to share with the group.)

3. What questions are you still considering related to the article?

DURING THE GROUP DISCUSSION . . .

4. Some new ideas and insights I gained from the group discussion are:

AFTER THE GROUP DISCUSSION . . .

5. What ideas from the article do you plan to apply to your teaching? Be as specific as you can.

6. What can the other teachers in the article study group and/or the literacy coach do to support your application of these ideas?

····················· **Strategy 4** ·····················

Providing Professional Development at Faculty Meetings

What Is It?

A literacy coach can deliver professional development in a variety of ways: to large groups (e.g., the whole school or all primary-level teachers), to small groups (e.g., grade-level teams or groups based on a common interest), and to individual teachers (Bean, Draper, Hall, Vandermolen, & Zigmond, 2010; Elish-Piper & L'Allier, 2011). While large-group professional development is typically thought of something that occurs after school or on specifically designated days, the literacy coach can also embed large-group professional development into the monthly or bimonthly faculty meetings.

Literacy coaches can work with their principals to schedule time during the faculty meetings for professional development. Various options are possible. Some principals allocate 10–15 minutes per faculty meeting while other principals, especially in schools where there are two faculty meetings each month, designate a longer period of time during one faculty meeting for professional development. These short, but regular professional development opportunities send the message that professional development is valued. They also strengthen the school's commitment to lifelong learning and often lead to more in-depth professional development efforts at the school, grade, or individual level.

How Do I Do It?

Embedding professional development within faculty meetings enables you to discuss school and district initiatives, research, and instructional strategies that are relevant to the entire staff. However, you may feel somewhat nervous about presenting to such a large group of colleagues. By using the following steps to prepare for the sessions, you will be ready to deliver powerful, engaging professional development.

1 Prepare for a meeting with your principal. You want to go into that meeting with a plan for incorporating professional development into the faculty meetings. Consider the following factors when determining the type of professional development that might work best in your school.

a Time for professional development. Once-a-month faculty meetings may lend themselves to short professional development presentations at each meeting. Twice-a-month faculty meetings may mean that you could introduce a strategy to address a Common Core standard at the first meeting, ask the teachers to try the strategy with their students, and then, at the second meeting of the month, have them share how the strategy worked. Bimonthly meetings also afford you the opportunity to have a longer period of time during one faculty meeting to address more complex topics.

b Topics to be covered. A variety of topics about the Common Core could be shared during these short professional development sessions. You may want to begin by selecting from the following list:

- If there is a district or school goal related to the Common Core, align the professional development to that goal.
- Update the teachers about recent literacy research related to some aspect of the Common Core.
- Share instructional strategies that address an aspect of the Common Core with which students across the grades have been struggling.
- Have a teacher share an instructional "success story" about how his or her students are focusing on a specific CCSS and discuss how that approach could be used or modified for students at other grade levels.
- Share a piece from the public press (newspaper, magazine, online source) that focuses on the Common Core.

2 Meet with the principal.

a Discuss your plan with the principal.
b Keep an open mind to alternatives your principal may suggest.
c Finalize the plan and establish when the plan will begin.

- Suggest that the principal introduce the plan to the faculty. Results of research indicate that principal support and presence at such professional development sessions contribute to teacher participation (Matsumura, 2009).
- Suggest that the professional development occur at the beginning of the faculty meeting. If it is the last item on the agenda, earlier items may take longer than expected, resulting in little or no time for your professional development segment.

3 Prepare for each professional development session.

   a Select the topic and be prepared to share with the teachers your rationale for selecting that topic.

   b Prepare an overview that can be shown or distributed to the teachers. Examples of overview formats can be found in Figures 4.1, 4.2, 4.3, and 4.4.

   - Figure 4.1 displays a format that you could use to discuss recent research and instructional applications related a specific aspect of the Common Core.
   - You could use the format in Figure 4.2 to share and discuss an article from the popular press.
   - You could work with a teacher who is going to share an instructional strategy or approach at a faculty meeting to create an overview using the format in Figure 4.3.
   - The format in Figure 4.4 might work well when the professional develop-

Gaining Information from Graphical Elements

What Are Graphical Elements?	◆ Tables, charts, and graphs ◆ Diagrams—surface and cross-sectional ◆ Timelines ◆ Maps and their legends ◆ Flowcharts

Research Findings	◆ Grade 2, 4, and middle school students reported looking at the graphical elements only sometimes or rarely. ◆ Many students were unaware that graphical elements provide information not found in the written text. ◆ Students had no strategies for making sense of graphical elements. ◆ Students had the most difficulty with arrows, believing they are primarily used to connect a label to an object or to show a proposed path on a map. ◆ Research findings from McTigue, E. M., & Flowers, A. C. (2011). Science visual literacy: Learners' perceptions and knowledge of diagrams. *The Reading Teacher, 64*(8), 578–589; and Roberts, K. L., Norman, R. R., Duke, N. K., Morsink, P., Martin, N. M., & Knight, J. A. (2013). Diagrams, timelines, and tables—Oh, my!: Fostering graphical literacy. *The Reading Teacher, 67*(1), 12–23.

Strategies to Help Students Meet CCSS: RIT.7	◆ During read-alouds, use think-alouds to model what can be learned from the graphical elements in the texts. ◆ Explicitly teach students how to make sense of different graphical elements. ◆ Have students read and discuss texts where the graphics provide information not found in the written text. ◆ Have students create graphical components in their informational writing and provide feedback about those components. ◆ What other strategies have you found to be successful?

FIGURE 4.1. Sharing literacy research and related strategies.

ment focuses on an aspect of the Common Core about which teachers have asked for clarification or for ideas on how that aspect is being addressed by colleagues.

C Determine how the teachers and principal can be active participants during the session. Having a few teachers respond to one of the following questions can stimulate others to consider how they might apply what they've heard to their teaching.

* "How might the results of this research be applied to your teaching?"
* "How might this article impact how you talk with parents or other members of our community?"
* "Is this a strategy that would work with your students? What modifications would you need to make?"
* "What else would you like to know about this topic?"

d Inform the principal about the topic of the professional development so that he or she can introduce the professional development session to the faculty.

It's in the News!

A Parent's Guide to the Common Core
Retrieved from *http://education.com*

Who?   **Parents** who want to know more about the Common Core can easily find this guide on the Internet when using the search term "Common Core" or "Common Core and Parents."

What?   This guide provides an **overview** of the Common Core and **seven key concepts** related to the Common Core. For each concept, a **Parent Tip** is provided.

Why?   The term "Common Core" has been in the news frequently. This guide is a good starting point **for parents who are seeking more information**.

When?   **Right now.** Written in friendly language, this guide provides basic information that parents can read in about 5 minutes.

How?   The guide provides practical ideas of how **what parents do at home** is linked to the Common Core. Including links to other websites lets parents know **how they can learn more** about the Common Core.

Why This Article Is Important to Us

1. How have we informed our parents about the Common Core? What, if any, additional steps are needed?
2. How are we addressing the standards in our students' homework and in the literacy activities that we are recommending that parents do with their children?

FIGURE 4.2. Sharing a literacy topic from the news.

What's Working in Our Classrooms

Connie Trask's Instruction Related to Reading Anchor Standard 9:
Using Literature and Informational Text to Compare and Contrast Similar Topics

Literature:	Informational Texts:
Stellaluna (Cannell, 2008)	*The Life Cycle of a Bat* (Kalman, 2006) and *The Life Cycle of a Bird* (Kalman, 2002)

Mini-Lesson	Model and Guided Practice	Guided Practice
◆ I provided explicit instruction on compare-and-contrast language: *both, like, similar, different, but, however.* ◆ I used the topic of home and school activities to model sentences using the language.	◆ I read aloud *Stellaluna*. ◆ I used a think-aloud to write one similarity and one difference between birds and bats. ◆ I guided students to make additional comparisons and contrasts.	◆ Student partners read specific sections of informational books. ◆ Partners created written comparisons and contrasts to add to the class chart.

This is just one success story! Let's share some other ways that you are focusing on comparing and contrasting with your students.

FIGURE 4.3: Literacy in our classrooms.

Thinking More Deeply about Primary Sources

Our shared definition of the term "primary sources": Original textual and nontextual documents that we use to learn about a person, event, or period of time.

Connections to the Common Core State Standards:
◆ Important component related to the increased focus on informational text.
◆ Standard 1—Encourages close reading of texts such as journals/diaries and speeches and nontextual documents such as photographs and drawings.
◆ Standard 6—Indicates that students should have opportunities to interpret words and phrases as written by the original authors of the texts.
◆ Standard 7—Involves practice with evaluating the content of original texts and visual documents.
◆ Standard 8—Requires students to determine the arguments presented by the original authors.
◆ Standard 9—Expects students to compare and contrast the way a topic or theme is presented in two or more primary sources.

Turn and talk with a grade-level partner:
◆ How are you currently using primary sources with your students? Where did you find these sources?
◆ What additional primary sources might fit well with your social studies or science curriculum? How might you find these sources?

Debrief: Let's hear some examples of how primary sources are being used across the grades.

FIGURE 4.4. Building shared understanding of Common Core language.

4 Deliver the professional development session. Adhere to the time allocated for the session.

5 Follow up after the professional development session.

   a Put a copy of the overview form on your webpage or on the school's shared computer drive. If your session focused on a professional article or a piece from a newspaper, magazine, or online source, you also may want to include an electronic version of the text.

   b Teacher comments at the meeting may indicate that specific teachers or grade-level teams would be interested in delving more deeply into the topic. Schedule a meeting with those teachers or attend the next grade-level meeting to explore ways you might work together to enhance knowledge and/or skills related to the topic.

Unpacking the Common Core Standards

What Is It?

The Common Core standards document contains a plethora of information, including anchor standards, grade-level standards, and appendices that include performance tasks, text exemplars, and writing samples. The CCSS website (*www.ccss. org*) provides easy access to all of these materials; however, reading and understanding the Standards is not an easy task! Many teachers skip right to the Standards for their grade level, and then wonder what the terms mean, how the Standards fit together, and what skills and strategies are expected in previous and latter grade levels. They may be frustrated and overwhelmed by the length of the Standards document (66 pages for the Standards themselves and another 333 pages for Appendices A, B, and C; NGA & CCSSO, 2010). Additionally, they may be confused about how the Standards are organized, the function of the anchor standards, and what is meant by vertical alignment and instructional shifts. In short, many teachers need support to unpack and understand the design, organization, and intent of the CCSS.

Most teachers are aware that the goal of the Common Core standards is for all children to be college and career ready by the time they graduate from high school. They may wonder, however, how the work they do as a kindergarten or third-grade teacher leads to college and career readiness. The CCSS are unique in that they focus first on the outcome, college and career readiness, and then work back through the grade levels and areas of literacy to determine the progression of skills and strategies that students must acquire to reach the end goal.

The CCSS for the ELA focus on four key areas: Reading (Literature and Informational Texts), Writing, Speaking and Listening, and Language. Each area is framed around a set of anchor standards that span the grade levels, followed by a breakdown of the Standards at each specific grade level. In addition, Foundational Skills are included for students in grades K–5. The CCSS also include three appendices that provide important information regarding the Standards. Appendix A provides key research supporting the Standards as well as a glossary of key terms. Appendix B contains text exemplars and sample performance tasks, and Appendix C provides samples of student writing that have been annotated to show how they meet the criteria delineated in the grade-level standards. Given the sheer number of pages, concepts, and standards involved, it is no wonder that many teachers don't know where to begin!

The literacy coach can provide support to help teachers unpack the CCSS. The unpacking process includes helping teachers understand the purpose of the Standards, how the Standards are organized, the role of the anchor standards, and how to use the appendices (Calkins et al., 2012; McLaughlin & Overturf, 2012). In addition, unpacking the Standards includes understanding what they really state as compared with myths that teachers may have heard (Shanahan, 2012/2013). Several useful resources are listed in Figure 5.1 to help literacy coaches understand the CCSS fully so they can then lead teachers to unpack the Standards.

How Do I Do It?

Chances are that the teachers you work with may be a bit confused, overwhelmed, or frustrated regarding the Common Core. Therefore, we recommend that you use a systematic approach to help them unpack the Standards. This approach has three phases: Getting Started, Narrowing the Focus, and Reaching Common Ground (see Figure 5.2).

Calkins, L., Ehrenworth, M., & Lehman, C. (2012). *Pathways to the Common Core: Accelerating achievement*. Portsmouth, NH: Heinemann.

International Reading Association. (2012). *Literacy implementation guidance for the ELA Common Core State Standards*. Newark, DE: Author.

McTighe, J., & Wiggins, G. (2012). From Common Core to curriculum: Five big ideas. Retrieved from *http://grantwiggins.files.wordpress.com/2012/09/mctighe_wiggins_final_common_core_standards.pdf*.

McLaughlin, M., & Overturf, B. J. (2012). The Common Core: Insights into the K–5 standards. *The Reading Teacher, 66*(2), 153–164.

FIGURE 5.1. Resources to support unpacking the CCSS.

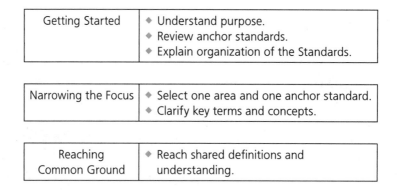

Getting Started	◆ Understand purpose.
	◆ Review anchor standards.
	◆ Explain organization of the Standards.

| Narrowing the Focus | ◆ Select one area and one anchor standard. |
| | ◆ Clarify key terms and concepts. |

| Reaching Common Ground | ◆ Reach shared definitions and understanding. |

FIGURE 5.2. Unpacking the CCSS.

Getting Started

1 Establish and clarify the purpose of the Common Core standards to ensure that the teachers understand how they are aimed at college and career readiness. You can do this by sharing this short video (6 minutes 25 seconds) about the ELA standards: "English Language Arts Standards: Key Changes and Evidence" (*www.youtube.com/watch?v=JDzTOyxRGLIPurpose*).

2 Either share or present information from page 8 in the Introduction of the CCSS. This section titled "How to Read This Document" provides a clear summary of how the information is organized in the Standards as well as the key features of the Standards.

3 Show the overall organization of the Standards by sharing Form 5.1. Discuss how the anchor standards in Reading, Writing, Speaking and Listening, and Language apply from kindergarten through grade 12. Note that the Foundational Skills standards apply only to grades K–5.

4 Discuss how the Standards are organized around broad concepts as shown by the bullet points in Form 5.1.

5 Provide time for the teachers to discuss the concepts and terms in Form 5.1. Invite the teachers to document their ideas, comments, and questions in the right column of Form 5.1.

6 Distribute copies of the anchor standards from the Common Core. These are available at *www.ccss.org* and can be found on these pages:

- ◆ Anchor Standards for Reading (p. 10)
- ◆ Anchor Standards for Writing (p. 18)
- ◆ Anchor Standards for Speaking and Listening (p. 22)
- ◆ Anchor Standards for Language (p. 26)

Narrowing the Focus

1 Based on district or school priorities or goals, narrow the focus for unpacking the Standards to a specific area such as reading or writing. For our example, we will focus on reading.

2 Ask the teachers to focus on just one anchor standard so they can unpack the standard fully. For example, you might direct the teachers to focus on Anchor Standard 1 in reading: "Read closely to determine what the text says explicitly and to make logical inferences from it; cite specific textual evidence when writing or speaking to support conclusions drawn from the text."

3 As a group, identify key terms from Anchor Standard 1. You and the teachers may identify terms such as *read closely, explicitly, logical inferences, cite, textual evidence,* and *support conclusions.*

Reaching Common Ground

1 To ensure that all of the teachers have a common understanding of the target standard—Anchor 1: Literature—ask them to work together in small groups to complete the following tasks (see Form 5.2).

   a Discuss what key terms in the standard mean: *read closely, explicitly, logical inferences, cite, textual evidence,* and *support conclusions.*
   b Take turns explaining the anchor standard in your own words.
   c Finally, ask each small group to prepare a 30-second summary of the most important things they learned about the target standard.
   d Collect Form 5.2 from each group to determine what terms might need further discussion in order to reach a shared understanding of those terms (as described in Strategy 2).

The time spent on this process will be well worth it, as the teachers will develop a framework of understanding that you can use to help them read and efficiently examine the remaining standards.

The Strategy in Action

Bernice Jackson is a veteran reading specialist who has over 20 years of experience, but this is only her second year of literacy coaching. She spends about a third of her time coaching teachers and the remaining two-thirds focused on assessing and providing small-group reading instruction for struggling readers in grades K–5. When Bernice first saw the CCSS, she reported being a bit confused, explaining:

"I didn't know if I should focus on the specific grade-level standards, anchor standards, instructional shifts, or something else! I was lucky that the district reading coordinator organized a summer book study on *Pathways to the Common Core* (Calkins et al., 2012). As a part of the book study, we developed a process to unpack the Standards [see Figure 5.2]. We were then ready to come back to our schools in the fall and use that process to help our teachers unpack the Standards too."

Bernice approached the unpacking of the Standards using the process the group developed. She began with a short informational presentation at the first staff meeting to complete the initial step in the process, "Getting Started." She then conducted short unpacking sessions related to one reading and one writing anchor standard at the next two staff meetings, spending between 15 and 20 minutes each time. Throughout the process she assured the teachers that they were making progress and reminded them that once they unpacked the Standards, they would be much more comfortable and prepared to begin addressing them in curriculum development and instruction. Bernice learned that several of her colleagues in other schools in the district implemented the unpacking process in the same manner but on a different schedule. For example, Sharon used part of a half-day institute to do the unpacking process in a single meeting. While their timelines differed, their processes were the same, and the results were consistently favorable.

Overview of the ELA Common Core Standards

Standards	My Notes, Comments, and Questions
Reading (Literature and Informational Text) (10 anchor standards K–12) ◆ Key Ideas and Details ◆ Craft and Structure ◆ Integration of Knowledge and Ideas ◆ Range of Reading and Level of Complexity	
Writing Standards (10 anchor standards K–12) ◆ Text Types and Purposes ◆ Production and Distribution of Writing ◆ Research to Build and Present Knowledge ◆ Range of Writing	
Speaking and Listening (6 anchor standards K–12) ◆ Comprehension and Collaboration ◆ Presentation of Knowledge and Ideas	
Language (6 anchor standards K–12) ◆ Conventions of Standard English ◆ Knowledge of Language ◆ Vocabulary Acquisition and Use	
Foundational Skills (no anchor standards; apply only to K–5) ◆ Print Concepts (K–1 only) ◆ Phonological Awareness (K–1 only) ◆ Phonics and Word Recognition ◆ Fluency	

Reaching Common Ground with the CCSS

Target Standard: _____

_____

Tasks	Responses
What are the key terms you need to know and understand related to the target standard? List the key terms discussed in the whole group and any additional terms proposed by members of your small group.	
What does each of those key terms mean? Try to write them in your own words or to provide examples to clarify what they mean.	
Write the anchor standard in your own words, adding clarifications and examples as appropriate.	
Write a short summary of the most important things you learned about the target standard.	

Strategy 6

Examining the Vertical Alignment of the Common Core Standards

What Is It?

The anchor standards for Reading, Writing, Speaking and Listening, and Language provide the foundation for the K–5 ELA standards. For each anchor standard, specific grade-level standards delineate the understandings and skills expected of students at each grade level. These understandings and skills are cumulative in nature; students at each grade are expected to maintain, deepen, and build on the understandings and skills from previous grades. The term *vertical alignment* is often used to describe this cumulative design (McLaughlin & Overturf, 2013).

As teachers learn about the CCSS, they often examine the standards for their specific grade level, thinking about how their current instruction is helping their students meet the grade-level expectations and what changes they might need to make. However, teachers may not be aware of the need to understand how their specific grade-level standards are related to the grade-level standards that come before and after the grade that they teach (Agamba & Jenkins, 2012). Knowledge about this vertical alignment will encourage teachers to confirm that students have mastered the expectations from previous grades and to reteach specific skills to students who have not achieved mastery. Understanding the vertical alignment will also help teachers target their instruction carefully to be sure they cover all elements described within each standard for their grade level.

An examination of the vertical alignment of standards seems to be most appropriate within large-group settings, such as the whole school or the primary and intermediate levels, because the process requires participation by representatives from multiple grade levels. Several standards can be examined during one session by dividing the teachers into small groups. After teachers have carefully looked at the vertical alignment of at least one standard from each of the four strands (i.e., Reading, Writing, Speaking and Listening, and Language), they may feel ready to preview the remaining standards and determine which ones need closer examination. That examination of additional standards could take place during future large-group sessions or during grade-level meetings facilitated by the teacher leaders.

How Do I Do It?

Examining the vertical alignment of standards may seem time-consuming and complex, but it is essential for building an in-depth knowledge about the Common Core, knowledge that will enable teachers to design instruction aligned with the Standards. While the teachers you work with may need more than one session to develop an understanding of how the CCSS are vertically aligned, you can use the following basic steps to prepare, facilitate, and follow up after each session.

Preparing for a Session Focused on the Vertical Alignment of the Standards

1 Talk with your principal to set the date and time for the first session. A session of about 30–45 minutes will be needed. If your school has two faculty meetings per month, the principal may designate one of those faculty meetings for the discussion of the vertical alignment of the CCSS. Other times set aside for professional development such as late-start or early-release days might also provide the necessary time for this activity.

2 Select the standards on which the faculty will focus. Here are some options:

- Select one strand to examine. For example, if you select the Writing standards strand, you could ask each small group to look carefully at a different standard from that strand (e.g., Text Type and Purposes—2; Production and Distribution of Writing—6; and Research to Build and Present Knowledge—7). Another option is to have each small group examine different clusters of standards within a specific strand (e.g., Text Type and Purposes—1, 2, and 3; Production and Distribution of Writing—4, 5, and 6; and Research to Build and Present Knowledge—7, 8, and 9).
- Select one standard or cluster of standards from each strand. For example, Group 1 might focus on a standard or cluster of standards from Reading Literature, Group 2 might look at a standard or cluster of standards from Writing, and so on.
- Select a set of standards that addresses aspects of literacy with which students at many grade levels are struggling or standards that teachers have noted on a needs assessment survey (see Form 2.1 in Strategy 2) as difficult to interpret and/or apply.

3 Determine how you will form the small groups. If your school has teacher leaders, they could facilitate the small-group activity. Each small group should include teachers from multiple grade levels and, if possible, the group members should represent a range of teaching experience and knowledge of the Common Core. Specialized professionals such at Title I teachers, teachers of the learning disabled, and speech and language pathologists can join groups.

4 Develop an examination sheet for each of the selected standards. Figure 6.1 shows an examination sheet for looking at the vertical alignment of Standard 6 of Reading Literature. The descriptors for all six grades are included as are the sample performance tasks for grades 1, 3, and 5 taken from Appendix B (NGA & CCSSO, 2010).

5 Develop a set of procedures that teachers can follow as they examine a specific standard. You may want to use the procedures outlined in Figure 6.2. A completed examination sheet for Standard 6 of Reading Literature is shown in Figure 6.3.

6 Carefully plan how you will introduce the task to the teachers, facilitate the small-group activity, and close the session. If your school has teacher leaders, you will want to meet with them prior to the session to preview the activity itself and discuss their role as facilitators.

Facilitating a Session Focused on the Vertical Alignment of the Standards

1 Introduce the task, clarify the purpose, explain the procedures, and set the time frame for the group work. In your introduction, it might be helpful to remind the teachers that the term *vertical alignment* refers to the ways that standards change as students progress vertically through the grades (i.e., from kindergarten to grade 1 to grade 2 and so on). However, when they look at the layout of the CCSS and the examination sheets for the small-group activity, they will see that the descriptions of each standard across grade levels are actually presented in a horizontal format.

2 Give the teachers a few minutes to get into their groups, select a record-keeper, and begin their work.

3 Circulate among the groups; try to spend time with each group more than once during the session. Sit down with each group, listen to the discussion, and provide guidance as necessary. To help the group clarify key points, you might ask, "Before you look at grade 5, can you summarize for the record keeper the difference between the standard expectations at grades 3 and 4?" To promote group input and participation, you might ask, "Have you had a chance to share the new performance tasks with everyone in the group?" If the small groups are facilitated by teacher leaders, they can provide the necessary guidance.

4 Allow 5 minutes for a whole-group debrief. The following two debriefing methods might work for you:

	Kindergarten	First Grade	Second Grade	Third Grade	Fourth Grade	Fifth Grade
Reading Literature: Standard 6 Language	With prompting and support, name the author and illustrator of a story and define the role of each in telling the story.	Identify who is telling the story at various points in a text.	Acknowledge differences in the points of view of characters, including by speaking in a different voice for each character when reading dialogue aloud.	Distinguish their own point of view from that of the narrator or those of the characters.	Compare and contrast the point of view from which different stories are narrated, including the difference between first- and third-person narrations.	Describe how a narrator's or speaker's point of view influences how events are described.
Academic Language (not including the verbs)						
Performance Tasks		Students identify the points at which different characters are telling the story in *Finn Family Moomintroll* (1990) by Tove Jansson.		When discussing E. B. White's book *Charlotte's Web* (1952), students distinguish their own point of view regarding Wilbur the Pig from that of Fern Arable, as well as from that of the narrator.		Students describe how the narrator's point of view in Walter Farley's *The Black Stallion* (1982) influences how events are described and how the reader perceives the character of Alexander Ramsay, Jr.

FIGURE 6.1. Examination sheet for the vertical alignment of reading literature: Standard 6.

1. Read all of the grade-specific standards for the anchor standard you are examining. Remember that students at one grade are expected to have mastered the skills and understandings at all of the previous grade levels as well. For example, third-grade students who are focusing on Standard 6 under Reading Literature should have already mastered the skills and understandings delineated under that standard for kindergarten, first grade, and second grade.

2. How are student expectations similar and different across grade levels? The following techniques might be helpful.
    - Circle the key words that are similar from grade to grade.
    - Put a box around the verbs. Discuss what action each verb requires and how the actions differ across grades.
    - You may wish to use different-colored highlighters instead of the circles and boxes.

3. What academic vocabulary do the students need to know to master the standard at each grade level? Write down the academic language in the second row of the examination sheet.

4. Look at the sample performance tasks. Discuss how each performance task addresses the elements of the related standard.

5. For grade levels that are missing performance tasks, create a performance task that could be used to determine student mastery at each of those grade levels.

FIGURE 6.2. Procedures for examining the vertical alignment of Standards.

- Ask the teacher leader from each group to share one big "aha" related to the vertical alignment of their standard or cluster of standards. If you do not have teacher leaders, each record keeper can share his or her group's "aha."
- You can share several insights about vertical alignment that you gained as you listened to the small-group discussions.

5 Take the last minute of the session to discuss future activities related to the vertical alignment of the standards. Discuss how the examination sheets and notes from each group will be distributed to grade-level teams so that, at the next grade-level meetings, teachers can review all of the charts and performance tasks for their grade level. Ask the participants to complete the feedback form (see Form 6.1) to help you to determine what standards still need to examined.

Following Up after the Session Focused on the Vertical Alignment of the Standards

1 Compile the examination sheets and record-keeper's notes from each group.

2 Collaborate with the teacher leaders or a representative from each grade level to determine how they can, during grade-level meetings, assist their colleagues in clarifying the language and developing appropriate performance tasks.

	Kindergarten	First Grade	Second Grade	Third Grade	Fourth Grade	Fifth Grade
Reading Literature: Standard 6 Language	With prompting and support, [name] the author and illustrator of a story and [define] the role of each in telling the story.	[Identify] who is telling the story at various points in a text.	[Acknowledge] differences in the [points of view] of characters, including by speaking in a different voice for each character when reading dialogue aloud.	[Distinguish] their own [point of view] from that of the narrator or those of the characters.	[Compare] and [contrast] the [point of view] from which different stories are narrated, including the difference between first-and third-person narrations.	[Describe] how a narrator's or speaker's [point of view] influences how events are described.
Academic Language (not including the verbs)	◆ author ◆ illustrator	◆ who is telling the story	◆ point of view ◆ character ◆ dialogue	◆ point of view ◆ narrator ◆ character	◆ point of view ◆ narrated ◆ first-person narration ◆ third-person narration	◆ narrator ◆ point of view
Performance Tasks	*Students name the author and illustrator of* Little Bear *(1957) and define what role Else Minarik (author) and Maurice Sendak (illustrator) had in telling (creating) the story.*	Students identify the points at which different characters are telling the story in *Finn Family Moomintroll* (1990) by Tove Jansson.	*Students acknowledge that the fire chief and the firemen in* The Fire Cat *(1960) by Esther Averill had different points of view about Pickles becoming a fire cat and show that difference when reading dialogue of the fire chief and the firemen.*	When discussing E. B. White's book *Charlotte's Web* (1952), students distinguish their own point of view regarding Wilbur the Pig from that of Fern Arable, as well as from that of the narrator.	*Students compare and contrast the points of view from which* A Taste of Blackberries *(1973) by Doris Buchanan Smith (first-person narration) and* Homer Price *(1943) by Robert McCloskey (third-person narration) are narrated.*	Students describe how the narrator's point of view in Walter Farley's *The Black Stallion* (1982) influences how events are described and how the reader perceives the character of Alexander Ramsay, Jr.

FIGURE 6.3. Completed examination sheet for the vertical alignment of reading literature: Standard 6.

3 Review the feedback forms to determine what aspects of the last session were helpful, what changes might enhance future sessions, and what standards should receive priority at the next session. Use this information as you plan the next session.

The Strategy in Action

Tyrell Washington is a full-time literacy coach at an elementary school that has two or three teachers at each grade level. For the past month, 1 hour of each of the 3 early release days has been spent examining the vertical alignment of reading standards. Weekly grade-level meetings have been used to share the information from the large-group sessions. Results from the feedback forms that Tyrell distributed indicated that the teachers felt they have examined all of the reading standards that were confusing or problematic for them and that they would like to move on to an examination of some of the writing standards. They knew that the writing standards might present a new challenge as there are writing samples, but not sample performance tasks, included in Appendix C of the CCSS.

For the next early release day, Tyrell selected three writing standards and developed an examination sheet for each standard (see Figure 6.4 for the examination sheet for Standard 8). During the professional development session, the teachers broke into three groups, with representatives from multiple grade levels in each group. Each group began by clarifying the differences in student expectations across grade levels and the academic language that the students would need to master, similar to the way they had worked with the reading standards. Then, each group brainstormed ways they were currently addressing the standard.

During the next week, the results of the three groups were shared during grade-level meetings. Grade-level teams then added examples of how they were addressing the standards and created a performance task for each standard for their grade level. At the beginning of the next early release session, the teachers met in their mixed grade-level groups to review the new examples and performance tasks. Discussion focused on whether each performance task clearly represented the grade-level standard and whether the tasks represented an increasing breadth and depth of understandings and skills as the students moved through the grades. This combination of cross-grade- and within-grade-level discussions enabled teachers to thoroughly understand the three writing standards, learning not only how each standard applied to their own grade level but to prior and subsequent grade levels as well.

	Kindergarten	First Grade	Second Grade	Third Grade	Fourth Grade	Fifth Grade
Writing: Standard 8 Language	With guidance and support from adults, recall information from experiences or gather information from provided sources to answer a question.	With guidance and support from adults, recall information from experiences or gather information from provided sources to answer a question.	Recall information from experiences or gather information from provided sources to answer a question.	Recall information from experiences or gather information from print and digital sources; take brief notes on sources and sort evidence into provided categories.	Recall relevant information from experiences or gather relevant information from print and digital sources; take notes and categorize information, and provide a list of sources.	Recall relevant information from experiences or gather relevant information from print and digital sources; summarize or paraphrase information in notes and finished work, and provide a list of sources.
What academic language do students need to know?						
Examples of how we are currently doing this.						
Examples of how we could do this in the future.						
What might the performance task look like?						

FIGURE 6.4. Examination sheet for the vertical alignment of writing: Standard 8.

Sample Feedback Form

Feedback about Our Work on the Vertical Alignment of Standards

How would you rate the following activities in helping you understand and prepare to apply the standard?	Very helpful	Helpful	Not helpful	What changes might increase the effectiveness of the activity?
1. Comparing and contrasting expectations across the grades.				
2. Listing the academic vocabulary for each grade level.				
3. Discussing the sample performance tasks.				
4. Creating sample performance tasks and/or revising the sample performance tasks.				

Which reading, writing, speaking and listening, or language standards would you like to examine during the next session? Is there a specific reason for your recommendation(s)?

Additional comments or suggestions related to the session:

Strategy 7

Presenting Powerful Professional Development

What Is It?

Large-group professional development sessions provide opportunities to build a sense of community within a school wherein teachers take collective responsibility for the learning of their students (Bryk et al., 2010). As members of the community, teachers work together to understand new curricular initiatives such as the Common Core and to address schoolwide needs such as increasing student motivation or supporting students to understand informational texts better (Bean, 2009; Vogt & Shearer, 2011).

Effective practices for professional development cover a wide range of topics (Bean, 2009; L'Allier & Elish-Piper, 2006–2007; Rosemary & Feldman, 2006). However, there is general consensus that successful large-group professional development sessions include the selection of a relevant needs-based focus, careful preparation, active engagement of all participants, and a plan for moving the work from one session forward into further professional development and/or practice.

While you may have read about effective practices for professional development, you may still view the organization and facilitation of a large-group professional development session as daunting tasks. There are questions about focus, participants, and content to be answered; there are materials to prepare; and there are logistical details to be finalized. In addition, you may be nervous about meeting the expectations of the participants, colleagues with whom you work on a daily basis. In this strategy, we draw on our own extensive experiences as facilitators of large-group professional development and on the work of others to provide you with a set of guidelines that will help you feel confident about delivering professional development in large-group settings.

How Do I Do It?

As educators, we've all attended a number of professional development sessions. Some have been excellent because they engaged us, offered practical applications, and helped us answer questions we had about our practice. Others may have frustrated us because presenters read from their PowerPoint presentations, seemed unprepared, or wasted time. How can you ensure that your professional development sessions fit into the excellent category? We suggest that thoughtful preparation and careful implementation are the keys to ensuring that your large-group professional development sessions run smoothly. Here are some tips that will help you accomplish your ultimate purpose—enhancing teacher knowledge and practice.

The Four Ps of Planning Powerful Professional Development

As a teacher, you knew that extensive planning was necessary to ensure that your instruction resulted in student learning. The same can be said for your work as a coach, except that in the case of professional development, you are focused on fostering adult learning. In this section, we discuss the four Ps of planning: purpose, participants, place, and preparation.

*P*urpose

Asking yourself the question "What is the purpose of this large-group professional development session?" is the first step of planning. In answering this question, keep in mind the principles of adult learning that we discussed in Chapter 1. Remember that adults are most interested in learning when the topic has immediate relevance to their jobs and when it is problem centered. Focusing large-group professional development sessions on building knowledge about the Common Core will certainly be relevant as the teachers in your school will need to tailor their instruction to help their students met the Common Core standards. Large-group sessions also might assist teachers in working through aspects of the Common Core that are problematic for students such as "How can we encourage the close reading of text?" or "How can we incorporate primary sources throughout our curriculum?"

Recalling the adult learning principle that adults want to be involved in the planning of their instruction, you want to be sure to involve others when determining the purpose of these large-group sessions. You could work with your school's leadership team or the teacher leaders to come up with a list of possible topics that the group believes would strengthen teachers' knowledge and practice related to the Common Core. To get wider input, you could then send out a survey to the teachers asking which of the topics they feel would be of most benefit to them. Selecting a purpose that teachers believe will enhance their practice means that they will arrive at the session eager to listen and participate.

Participants

Once you have set the purpose for the large-group session, determine who should participate. For example, a session focused on unpacking the standards as described in Strategy 5 might be appropriate for the entire staff. On the other hand, a session that focuses on an examination of the vertical alignment of the foundational skills of print concepts, phonological awareness, and beginning phonics and word recognition might include just the primary teachers and specialized professionals who work with students on those skills. Teachers are more likely to actively participate when they realize that you are being considerate of their time by matching participants to purpose.

Place and Time

Selecting an appropriate place, date, and time for the session is a third important element of planning. In terms of place, the following should be considered:

◆ Select a space that can be arranged so that all participants feel part of the learning community. For example, if you decide to arrange the tables in a U shape to facilitate face-to-face communication, be sure there is a chair at one of the tables for each participant.

◆ Make sure there is table space for each participant if you expect them to do any writing.

◆ If you are going to use any visual media (e.g., a video or PowerPoint presentation), be sure it can be easily seen by all participants.

◆ Regulate the temperature in the space. Participants can become distracted if the room is too cold or too warm.

It is easiest to schedule these large-group sessions during times that have already been designated for professional development (e.g., faculty meetings, early-release days, late-start days). In these cases, you want to check with the principal to ensure that the schedule gives you sufficient time to accomplish the session's purpose. If you are expected to schedule a session for a specific group of teachers (e.g., all primary teachers or all intermediate teachers) before or after school, you might want to survey the participants to see what day of the week would work best and whether the majority prefer meeting before or after school. Gathering this information from teachers shows that you are considerate of their busy schedules and may strengthen their commitment to participate.

Preparation

Now that you have determined the purpose, participants, place, and time of the session, it's time to prepare for the session itself. The following steps will ensure that you are well prepared.

1 Determine what activities will occur during the session. Think about how you will introduce the purpose, what activities will support that purpose, and how you will close the session. Carefully design how you will actively engage the participants. Small-group activities, such as those described in Strategies 2 through 6 of this part, can foster in-depth thought and conversation about critical aspects of the Common Core. For longer sessions, be sure to include an appropriate number of breaks.

2 Consider how the teacher leaders or other teachers might help you facilitate some of the activities. Meet with them to discuss your plans and revise those plans to incorporate their suggestions.

3 Develop an agenda that includes the purpose of the session and lists the main activities.

4 Prepare the materials that you plan to share with the group. If others are helping you facilitate the session, they could also help you prepare the materials.

- If you plan to use a PowerPoint, keep the text on each slide to a minimum and be sure the font size is large enough to be read easily. When possible, convey information through diagrams, charts, tables, and photos. Prepare handout versions of the PowerPoint for participants. Coaches have told us that, even when they put the PowerPoint on the shared drive after the session, participants like to have a copy so they can take notes while listening to the presentation.
- For small-group activities, design materials that will help the groups accomplish their task(s). Proofread your work twice, and be sure your printer or copy machine is working well when making copies of the materials. Participants can become distracted when materials are difficult to read (e.g., confusing layout, print too light to read easily, multiple misspellings).
- Develop an evaluation form for your session. If it's a short session related to the Common Core, you can give participants index cards and ask them to take 2–3 minutes to write two key ideas that they want to remember, one thing they might want to try with their students after attending this session, and one question they still have about the session's topic. For longer sessions, you may want to use the feedback form shown in Form 7.1.

5 Decide what snack you will share with the participants; make or purchase the snack. Snacks seem to foster a positive attitude among participants and, especially for after-school sessions, can give teachers the extra energy they may need to actively participate in the session.

6 Send a reminder about the date, time, and location to all participants and the principal.

7 Make arrangements for the technology to be at the location on the day of the session. Before the session begins, check that the technology works with the materials (e.g., PowerPoints, videos, Internet sites) you plan to use.

Clearly, there are many details involved in planning powerful professional development. The planning template in Form 7.2 will help you organize and address all of those details.

Five Tips for Implementing Powerful Professional Development

The day of the professional development session has arrived! You've completed the four Ps of planning and are confident that you and your co-facilitators are as prepared as you possibly could be. Now here are some tips to ensure that the session itself runs smoothly.

1 *Establish a set of working rules to foster a collaborative sense of learning.* At the beginning of the session, remind the participants of the working rules that have been established for professional development sessions. If your school has not established a set of working rules, you may want to use the following:

   ♦ We will maintain our focus on the topic/tasks throughout the entire session.
   ♦ We will share ideas and insights that are directly related to the topics/tasks.
   ♦ We will listen respectfully when others are talking and encourage all participants to share their ideas.
   ♦ We will respond to others with constructive, considerate comments.

2 *Clearly explain the purpose of the session and connect each activity to that purpose.* To start the session, share the purpose of the session and explain why this topic is relevant to the participants. For example, when introducing a session for intermediate teachers about strategies to help their students cite evidence from text to support their conclusions, you could note that many intermediate teachers had requested more information about this topic at the end of the last professional development session.

As the session progresses, clearly explain each activity and connect each activity to the purpose. For example, after giving a 5-minute introduction about the importance of being able to cite evidence from the text, you might say, " I just shared an overview of how citing evidence helps students focus specifically on the text when explaining answers to questions or drawing conclusions. Now, let's look at a video that shows two teachers using different strategies to help students cite evidence from the text." Notice how these two sentences make a clear connection between the two activities and link both activities to the session's purpose.

3 *Follow your agenda with flexibility.* Because of your careful planning, the purpose(s) of the session should be accomplished when you implement the session according to the agenda. During the planning stage, you probably designated a certain number of minutes for each activity on the agenda. Letting the participants know how much time they have for each small-group activity and notifying participants when they have a minute or two to finish up will help to keep the session on schedule. However, some activities may actually require a little less or a little more time than you had planned. Be ready to revise your schedule a bit to meet the needs of the participants, but be sure you are still able to complete all of the activities that are critical to meeting the purpose(s) of the session.

4 *Model the dispositions that you expect of the participants.* Having established the working rules for the group at the beginning of the session, it is essential that you model the behaviors specified in the rules. Your modeling provides all participants with clear examples of collegiality.

Tactfully handle comments that might take the discussion away from the session's purpose. You may find it helpful to think through, and even write down in your notes, possible responses to off-task remarks. For example, you might say, "That's an interesting point we could discuss further in a future session." Then you could restate the question or topic currently under discussion and ask for additional responses from the group.

Be an active listener. This can include connecting one participant's comments to the comments made by others, to articles that the group has read, and/or to previous professional development related to the Common Core. You can also exhibit active listening when you acknowledge how the session has enhanced your own learning by making comments such as "Larry's explanation really helped me understand the difficulty our students are having" or "Wow, that strategy Marisol uses is new to me and sounds like it might work with a wide range of students."

5 *End the session by sharing how the session topic will receive additional attention.* The layers of literacy coaching described in Chapter 2 suggest three ways of continuing the discussion. First, the group may determine that another large-group session is needed, suggesting specific ideas about what should be covered during the next session. Second, the group may decide to further explore the topic at grade-level meetings. In the case of helping students cite evidence, teacher leaders may work with their grade-level colleagues to select one or two strategies to try with their students. Then, at a subsequent grade-level meeting, teachers can share their experiences and refine strategies that appeared effective. Third, some participants may feel that they would benefit from additional individual coaching related to the session's topic. While they may not ask for such assistance during the whole-group session, you can present such an option by including, at the end of the session, something similar to the following comment: "If you'd like to talk about how to implement one of these strategies with your students, just stop by my office or drop me an e-mail."

FORM 7.1

Feedback Form for Large-Group Professional Development Sessions

Session Topic: _____

Please circle the title that describes your position:

Classroom teacher   Specialized professional   Paraprofessional   Administrator

Please rate the session based on the following scale:

SA	Strongly agree
A	Agree
D	Disagree
SD	Strongly disagree
NA	Not applicable to this session

The topic of the session strengthened my understanding of the Common Core.   SA   A   D   SD   NA
What key ideas will you remember from the session?

The topic will help me teach toward the Common Core.   SA   A   D   SD   NA
What ideas do you plan to try?

The purposes were clearly stated and addressed.   SA   A   D   SD   NA

The information was presented in a clear and organized manner.   SA   A   D   SD   NA

The pace and length of the session were appropriate.   SA   A   D   SD   NA

The session provided me with opportunities to be an active participant.   SA   A   D   SD   NA

Please write additional comments about the session and/or questions you may still have about the topic.

FORM 7.2

Planning Template for Large-Group Professional Development Sessions

Purpose	
Purpose of the session	
Rationale for selecting the purpose	

Participants	
Teachers	
Others	

Place, Date, and Time			
	Place	Date	Time
Set-up of room			

Preparation		✓ when done
List of co-facilitators		
List of activities, approximate time needed for each activity, and who will facilitate each activity		
Develop the agenda		
List of materials that need to be developed for whole-group presentation and small-group work and who will develop each one		
Snacks		
Arrangements made for technology		
Send out agenda to participants and principal		

PART THREE

Small-Group Coaching toward the Common Core

While large-group coaching activities serve many useful purposes as described in Part Two, they aren't sufficient to address all of the professional development needs of K–5 teachers as they update their teaching practices to meet the demands of the Common Core. By working with teachers in smaller groups such as grade-level teams or PLCs (DuFour et al., 2008), you can tailor coaching support to address the specific issues, challenges, and goals of the participating teachers. Furthermore, the small-group context provides many opportunities for teachers to pose questions, share ideas, dialogue with the literacy coach, and collaborate with their colleagues.

The three most common types of small groups involved in literacy coaching are grade-level teams, PLCs, and purposeful groups. Many schools are organized around grade-level teams that include all teachers in the school at a specific grade level. Generally, a teacher leader, who is an experienced and well-respected member of the team, will coordinate and facilitate grade-level meetings during common planning times. In PLCs, teachers work collaboratively to learn about a specific issue, topic, or goal such as teaching writing across the curriculum or differentiating instruction. PLCs may be composed of teachers from the same grade level, one teacher from each grade level, or an assortment of teachers who self-select or are assigned to be members of the specific PLCs. Finally, purposeful groups such as new teachers or teachers with clusters of English learners provide an appropriate context for literacy coaching related to the needs of the group. Embedding literacy coaching within any of these types of small groups is an ideal professional development approach to provide participating teachers with the information, support, and collaboration needed to enhance their teaching.

As we mentioned in Chapter 1, it is important to have a literacy leadership team at your school so that you are not the only person responsible for helping teachers move their teaching forward toward the Common Core. In addition to you and your principal, we recommend that the literacy leadership team include teacher leaders who work closely with you and with a small group of teachers to provide literacy coaching support. By meeting with you on a regular basis to review data, examine progress, and make plans, the teacher leaders are then able to facilitate grade-level meetings, PLC meetings, or purposeful group meetings. Many of the strategies described in Part Three can be implemented by you as the literacy coach, by a teacher leader, or by both of you working as a team.

Part Three contains five coaching strategies specifically designed for use with small groups of teachers. In Strategy 8, the focus is on coaching grade-level teams to develop implementation guides that determine the timeline and progression of instruction to meet specific standards. As you and the teachers in your school have probably already noticed, the CCSS focus on what students should be able to do at the end of the school year. Teachers, however, also want and need to know what to expect from students and how to sequence instruction across the entire school year. By helping grade-level teams develop implementation guides, you can assist those teachers with addressing the standards in their weekly or monthly instructional plans.

The ability to use assessment data to guide instruction is a hallmark of effective teaching, but many teachers have not had training or professional development related to this important process. Therefore, Strategies 9 and 10 both address using student assessments to plan and reflect on instruction. Strategy 9 provides information on how you can guide small groups of teachers to review assessment data to plan instruction aligned with the CCSS. Strategy 10 focuses on examining student work samples to clarify expectations, create or refine rubrics, determine the effectiveness of instruction, and plan instruction to address student needs.

Strategy 11 focuses on how you can guide small groups of teachers to review units of study to determine alignment with the Common Core and to promote collaboration and shared planning.

Finally, Strategy 12 describes how you can implement a manageable yet effective approach to lesson study. In this process, you will be able to help teachers plan, teach, observe, critique, and refine a lesson in order to improve their effectiveness.

As you implement the strategies in Part Three, you will be able to add a layer of small-group coaching by building on the outcomes of work with large groups of teachers (from Part Two). When you and the teacher leaders work with small groups, you can differentiate coaching support to address the specific needs and goals of participating teachers as they move their teaching toward the Common Core.

Developing Implementation Guides for the Common Core Standards

What Is It?

Teachers gain a tremendous amount of knowledge about the Common Core when they engage in large-group professional development sessions focused on unpacking the standards (see Strategy 5) and examining the vertical alignment of standards (see Strategy 6). When teachers unpack the standards, they learn that they will be helping students meet a total of 42 Reading, Writing, Speaking and Listening, and Language standards. When they examine the vertical alignment of the standards, they discover that many standards address more than one instructional element. Thus, while unpacking the standards and examining their vertical alignment enable teachers to be more confident about their basic understanding of the Common Core, these activities may raise concerns about how they can possibly address all of the elements of the 42 standards. One way some school districts have helped teachers deal with their concerns about the management phase of the Common Core is through the use of implementation guides.

Implementation guides establish parameters of what should be taught during specific time periods in order to ensure that all teachers address all of the expected learning objectives (David, 2008). The best implementation guides "focus on central ideas and provide links to exemplary curriculum materials, lessons, and instructional strategies" (David, 2008, p. 88). Implementation guides are not new. Districts that use core reading programs develop implementation guides to provide all teachers at the same grade level with a realistic time frame for completing each unit's instruction and assessment. Math is another area where implementation guides have become commonplace, often used to ensure that teachers have taught all of the concepts on which students will be tested during the spring high-stakes assessment (Au, 2007). In addition to ensuring that all key literacy or math strategies and skills are taught over the course of the school year, these implementation guides ensure curriculum continuity for students who change schools within the district.

While implementation guides can aid teachers in managing the instruction related to a large number of learning standards or objectives, they have their drawbacks. When teachers feel pressured by the time frames set forth in the implementation guides, they often reduce the amount of time for collaborative student activities, activities that provide the guided and independent practice necessary for mastering the learning standards (Willis & Sandholtz, 2009). Also, when teachers are expected to rigidly adhere to the implementation guides, they may no longer be able to include the review and reteaching activities that are often needed, especially by lower-performing students (Wills & Sandholtz, 2009). Thus, rigid adherence to implementation guides can negatively impact student learning, resulting in students who don't meet expectations on high-stakes tests and who don't have the foundation needed for learning more complex strategies and skills.

You can avoid the pitfalls of implementation guides by applying the adult learning principles you learned about in Chapter 1 as you work with small groups of teachers to develop implementation guides for teaching toward the Common Core. Remember that adults are motivated when they need to solve problems that are highly relevant to their positions. Certainly, that description represents teachers at your school who are questioning how they will fit all of the standards into their instruction. In addition, teachers want to be involved in professional development activities that will impact their instruction. Thus, teachers are more likely to follow the implementation guides that they—not publishers or district curriculum coordinators—develop, especially if they see the guides as flexible tools that can be revised if needed.

How Do I Do It?

The following steps outline a procedure that you can use to assist small groups of teachers in developing implementation guides for their grade-level standards.

1 Work with the teacher leaders or a representative from each grade level to design a template for the implementation guides. Using the same template across grades facilitates a schoolwide shared understanding of how the standards will be taught and assessed. The implementation guide template shown in Form 8.1 includes the following important components:

- ◆ *Grade-level standard.*
- ◆ *Essential questions that are addressed by the standard.* Essential questions establish the focus of the learning and should be stated in student-friendly lan-

guage. When students can answer the essential questions, they demonstrate their understanding of the knowledge, strategies, and skills that are important for a proficient reader, writer, listener, and speaker.

♦ *Elements of the standard that should be addressed during each specific time period.* That specific time period is typically a quarter or a trimester, corresponding to the school's report card cycle. Elements listed in an early time period are expected to be maintained or enhanced during subsequent periods so that, by the end of the year, students will have received the instruction and practice they need to successfully perform all elements of the grade-level standard.

♦ *Academic vocabulary that students will need to understand to achieve the standard.* Each standard includes specific terminology that students need to understand in order to master the standard. Listing these terms on the implementation guide reminds teachers that they need to explicitly explain the terms, use the terms when modeling and during discussions, develop activities that require students to use the terms repeatedly, and design assessments that include evaluating the students' understanding of the terms.

♦ *Instructional resources.* During the initial development of the implementation guides, teachers may want to keep the list of instructional resources quite general. Listing all of the possible resources can be time-consuming and take the focus away from the primary purpose of the implementation guide—determining when to address each element of the standards. To avoid spending too much time on this section, teachers should know that they can add instructional resources to their copies of the implementation guide as they teach and share those ideas with colleagues when they review the implementation guides at grade-level meetings. Giving teachers the following categories will help them develop the list of instructional resources.

   ○ Specific units from a core reading program or from the district's curriculum.
   ○ Titles of books that will be read aloud to the students.
   ○ Titles of guided reading selections.
   ○ Specific text exemplars from Appendix B of the Common Core standards (NGA & CCSSO, 2010).
   ○ Specific types of graphic organizers.
   ○ Interactive tools such as Photo Story, which can be downloaded for free from Microsoft, or tools found under Student Interactives at ReadWrite-Think (*www.readwritethink.org*).
   ○ Professional readings (articles, books, online documents) that provide the teachers with ideas for instructional strategies they can use to help students address the standards.

♦ *Assessments that will be used to determine if students have met the standard.* When developing an implementation guide for a set of related grade-level standards (e.g., Standards RL.1.1, RL.1.2, and RL.1.3 all focus on demonstrating an understanding of the main ideas and key details of literature), it is likely that one or two assessments will be sufficient for determining if the students have met expectations for that set of standards. Teachers can share the assessments they are already using to determine which ones could be used as common assessments. If new assessments need to be developed, those assessments should be noted on the implementation guide.

2 Meet with the grade-level team. Explain the purpose of an implementation guide and share the implementation guide template that will be used throughout the school. Collaborate with the teachers to select the standards they will focus on first. Often the standards within one category, such as Key Ideas and Details, are interrelated and, thus, it would be efficient to develop the implementation guide for all of the standards within that category at the same time.

3 Project an electronic copy of the template so that it is easy to view and revise during the discussion. Using a white board or chart paper would also work.

4 Guide the teachers to fill in the implementation guide template by following the steps described below. A completed implementation guide for Standards RL.1.1, R.1.2, and RL.1.3 is shown in Figure 8.1.

  a Write the grade-level standards in the appropriate boxes.
  b Assist the teachers in determining essential questions that will help students understand the purpose of their work. Asking a guiding question such as "What aspects of students' literacy development will be enhanced by engaging in the activities delineated in standards?" can help teachers formulate the essential questions. The first-grade teachers who worked with their literacy coach, Sabrina Rosenberg, to develop the implementation guide shown in Figure 8.1 concluded that meeting standards RL.1.1, RL.1.2, and RL.1.3 would enhance students' understanding of story elements and of author's purpose. They used those ideas to develop two essential questions. The teachers expected that the first essential question, "How can I understand the stories I read?" would elicit responses such as "I can tell about the characters, setting, and major events to show that I understand a story" and "I can answer questions to show I understand. I can ask questions to find out about characters and events I don't understand." They expected that students would answer the second essential question, "Why do authors write stories?" with responses such as "Authors write stories for us to enjoy and to give us lessons about how we should live our lives." Thus, just two essential questions were needed for those three standards.
  c Facilitate a discussion about which elements of each standard should be addressed during each time period. For example, in Figure 8.1, for standard RL.1.1, Sabrina and the first-grade teachers decided to focus on answering questions during the first and second quarters and then move the main focus to asking questions in the third quarter. They discussed how this process would ensure that, by the end of the year, the students would have received

instruction as well as guided and independent practice on all elements of that standard.

◆ During this step, the coach may ask the teachers if they need to clarify the expectations for any time period. For example, the first-grade teachers working on the implementation guide in Figure 8.1 wanted to be sure that their students learned that good retellings are told or written in sequence, and so they added the expectation of correctly sequencing key details under RL.1.2 for the last three quarters. They also added the concepts of problem and solution and the use of graphic organizers in RL.1.3.

d Assist the teachers in determining the academic vocabulary that students need to understand in order meet the standards. It is generally not necessary to break down these terms by time period. The academic vocabulary is typically used across the school year, first by teachers when giving explicit explanations and modeling strategies, and then by students during guided and independent practice.

e Help the teachers understand the range of instructional resources that could be used to address the standards. However, remind them not to be concerned about listing every possible resource. At this point, you just want them to be sure they know some specific resources they will use; they can always add to the list as they teach. If a team is developing an implementation guide for a related cluster of standards, the same resources can typically be used when teaching toward that cluster of standards. Consider the cluster of standards in Figure 8.1 as an example. Sabrina helped the teachers realize that, when first-grade students read any of the stories listed under Instructional Resources for Quarter 4, they can be expected to ask and answer questions about the story (RL.1.1); to give a retelling of the story (RL.1.2) that includes a description of the characters, setting, and major events (RL.1.3); and to explain the central message or lesson of that story (RL.1.2). Thus, it would be efficient to list all of the stories that students will read throughout the fourth quarter as instructional resources for the entire cluster of standards.

f Assist the teachers in determining a small set of assessments that will be used to determine whether the students have met the elements of the standard for each time period. Keeping the number of common assessments to a minimum leads to an efficient assessment process, in terms of administering and scoring the assessments. It is also efficient if an assessment, such as an oral retelling or a story map graphic organizer, can be used for multiple time periods, as was possible with some of the assessments listed in Figure 8.1. If some assessments and/or scoring rubrics still need to be developed, note on the implementation guide who will be responsible for developing the assessment/rubric and when that draft will be shared with the members of the team.

5 Make copies of the final implementation guide for all members of the grade-level team. Encourage the teachers to view the implementation guide as a work in prog-

Essential Questions: *How can I understand the stories I read? Why do authors write stories?*

Standards	Quarter 1	Quarter 2	Quarter 3	Quarter 4	Academic Vocabulary	Instructional Resources	Assessments
RL.1.1: Ask and answer questions about key details in a text.	Answer who, what, where, and when questions about key details in a text.	Same as Quarter 1	Ask who, what, where, and when questions about key details in a text.	Ask and answer who, what, where, and when questions about key details in a text.	◆ ask ◆ answer ◆ key details	**Quarter 1:** ◆ Read-alouds ◆ Shared reading stories from Units 1 and 2 ◆ Leveled readers—literary selections	**Quarter 1:** ◆ Unit assessments ◆ Oral retelling—score with retelling rubric (don't score central message section)
RL.1.2: Retell stories, including key details, and demonstrate understanding of their central message or lesson.	Retell stories orally, including key details.	Retell stories orally in correct sequence, including key details.	Same as Quarter 2. In addition, work with partner/ small group to determine central message or lesson of story.	Retell stories in correct sequence including key details, and individually demonstrate understanding of their central message or lesson.	◆ retell ◆ key details ◆ sequence ◆ central message ◆ lesson	**Quarter 2:** Same as Quarter 1 except use stories from Units 3 and 4	**Quarter 2:** ◆ Unit assessments ◆ Oral retelling—score with retelling rubric
RL.1.3: Describe characters, settings, and major events in a story, using key details.	Name main characters and major events in a story, using key details.	Name main and secondary characters, setting, and major events—including the problem and solution when appropriate, using key details. Complete appropriate graphic organizers.	With support, describe main and secondary characters, setting, and major events—including the problem and solution when appropriate, using key details. Complete appropriate graphic organizers.	Describe main and secondary characters, setting, and major events—including the problem and solution when appropriate, using key details. Complete appropriate graphic organizers.	◆ character ◆ main character ◆ secondary character ◆ setting ◆ major events ◆ key details ◆ problem ◆ solution	**Quarter 3:** Same as Quarter 1 except use stories from Units 5 and 6	**Quarter 3:** Same as Quarter 2
						Quarter 4: Same as Quarter 1 except use stories from Units 7 and 8	**Quarter 4:** Same as Quarter 2

FIGURE 8.1. Implementation guide for the category of key ideas and details of reading literature at grade 1.

ress. Suggest that, as they implement instruction related to the standards, they make notes right on the implementation guide. For example, they might jot down whether too many or not enough elements were covered during a particular time period. They might jot down additional instructional resources they found helpful, and they might list a new assessment they used and want to discuss with their colleagues.

6 You and/or the teacher leader should meet with the grade-level team to review the implementation guide at the end of each time period. At the meeting, the teachers will share student assessment results and the notes they made on their implementation guides. They will use the assessment data and notes to revise the implementation guide so that it more closely reflects actual practice.

Helping a grade-level team work through the entire process once or twice will provide them with the skills and confidence they need to develop implementation guides for other standards.

The Strategy in Action

Sabrina Rosenberg is a literacy specialist at a K–2 building that includes six teachers at each grade level. She spends half of her time coaching and half of her time providing instruction to students who struggle with reading. During one of the professional development days held prior to the start of school, Sabrina and the teacher leaders worked with the grade-level teams to develop implementation guides for the Reading and Writing standards; they plan to work on implementation guides for the Speaking and Listening and Language standards during the school's October professional development day.

Now that the first grading period has been completed, Sabrina wants the grade-level teams to review their implementation guides. To assist them in the process, she developed a protocol that all grade-level teams could use (see Form 8.2). The first-grade team wants to start their review by looking at the implementation guide for standards RL.1.1, RL.1.2, and RL.1.3 (see Figure 8.1). Sabrina will model the process so that Chanda Patel, the first-grade teacher leader, can facilitate future reviews.

The first-grade teachers brought their annotated implementation guides, unit assessments, and oral retelling rubrics to the meeting. When Sabrina asked them what the assessment results indicated, all six teachers commented that most of their students could answer the "who" and "what" questions but had some difficulty with "where" and "when" questions. They made a note in the second-quarter box for standard RL.1.1 that they should emphasize "where" and "when" questions. When examining the oral retelling rubrics, the teachers found that students generally included all characters, not differentiating main from secondary characters. The teachers noted that, during the second quarter, students should begin to make that distinction because the teachers plan to provide explicit explanations about main and secondary characters and use those terms during discussions of their read-alouds. The retelling rubrics also indicated that many students had difficulty retelling the key details of the stories in sequence. This reinforced the team's earlier decision to add the sequential element to the second-quarter focus for standard RL.1.2. The teachers concurred that the two assessments had been sufficient to determine whether the students had met the elements expected during the first quarter.

Sabrina asked the teachers to turn their attention to the Instructional Resources section and revise it to show what they had actually used during the first period. She then asked them to look forward to the second quarter. During the discussion, she noted that the students were expected to complete graphic organizers to show their understanding of story elements but that no such organizers were listed under Instructional Resources. She shared two possible graphic organizers with matching rubrics, discussing how they corresponded to the standard expectations for the second, third, and fourth quarters. The teachers suggested some minor revisions to one of the organizers and decided to use it with students during instruction and as a second-quarter assessment. This information was added to the second quarter of the implementation guide. Chanda, the teacher leader, also mentioned that she had recently found a story map that students can complete online and recommended that it be added to the Instructional Resources section for the second quarter. She offered to demonstrate the story map for her first-grade colleagues at the next grade-level meeting.

As the meeting wrapped up, the teachers commented that this session helped them see how the implementation guide could be a useful tool in developing data-driven instruction. After the meeting, Chanda thanked Sabrina for facilitating the meeting and said she felt confident that she could use the same protocol to facilitate future reviews of implementation guides.

Implementation Guide Template

Essential Questions:

Standards	Quarter 1	Quarter 2	Quarter 3	Quarter 4	Academic Vocabulary	Instructional Resources	Assessments
						Quarter 1:	Quarter 1:
						Quarter 2:	Quarter 2:
						Quarter 3:	Quarter 3:
						Quarter 4:	Quarter 4:

Protocol for Reviewing the Implementation Guide

Grade-Level Team: _____   Date: _____   Time Period Being Reviewed: 1   2   3   4

Standards Reviewed: RL _____   RIT _____   Writing _____   Speaking and Listening _____   Language _____

1. Did our students meet the elements of the standard expected for this time period? What evidence supports our conclusions?

2. Did our assessments provide sufficient information for us to determine whether the expectations had been met? If not, what assessments should we add to the list?

3. For elements where expectations were not met, what is our plan to address them in the next time period?

4. Did we use all of the instructional resources listed for this time period? For those we did not use, should they stay on the list or be removed?

5. Are there new instructional resources that should be added to the list for this time period?

6. As we look ahead to the next time period, are there instructional materials or assessments that need to be refined or developed? If so, who will take the lead in developing each one and when will these items be completed?

Reviewing Assessment Data to Plan Instruction

What Is It?

Assessment data are key ingredients of effective instructional planning (Paris, 2001). By reviewing assessment data, teachers are able to plan, deliver, and modify instruction to meet the needs of learners and to promote academic progress (Elish-Piper, Hinrichs, Morley, & Williams, 2012). Regardless of the types of assessment data reviewed, the purposes for reviewing the data must always be to change instructional practice (i.e., teaching methods, grouping patterns, curricular materials, instructional pacing, leadership support) in order to improve student achievement outcomes (McNulty & Besser, 2011).

Reeves (2008/2009) offers several key considerations to keep in mind regarding the use of assessment data to drive instruction (see Table 9.1). First, to be very effective, data review needs to be done on an ongoing regular basis—as often as several times per month. Second, addressing a specific question during the data review will save time and provide a clear focus. Third, going beyond just the numbers to consider factors such as curriculum, instructional practices, and teacher feedback will provide valuable insights about which factors are contributing to student success or failure. The most important idea to keep in mind is that

> the essence of a successful discussion about data is a commitment to examine not only the data, but also the stories behind the numbers. Only when we can articulate the 'why' behind the data and turn the lens on our own teaching and leadership behaviors can we understand how to move from drowning in data to improving professional practice. (Reeves, 2008/2009, p. 90)

The assessment review process has become even more complex and challenging for teachers as they now must also consider how to teach toward the Common

TABLE 9.1. Considerations for Using Assessment Data to Plan Instruction

Consideration	Explanation and examples
1. Review assessment data on a regular basis.	Plan to review data several times per month. Options include setting aside time at grade-level meetings, PLCs, or faculty meetings for data review. The coach may also meet with individual teachers to review specific assessment data.
2. Focus on a specific question to guide the data review process.	Sample questions include: • What are the greatest areas of strength shown in the data? • What specific skills are the weakest according to the data? • How did specific groups of students perform (e.g., English learners, students with individualized education plans, students who are gifted)? • Since we began targeting this aspect of instruction, how have students performed on the assessments in that area?
3. Go beyond just the numbers.	Consider the curriculum, pacing of instruction, instructional practices, and feedback to students, as well as demographic factors, that may help to explain the "why" behind the numbers.

Core standards. Literacy coaches and teacher leaders are uniquely qualified to help teachers understand what the assessments measure and how to interpret results, determine strengths and needs, and plan appropriate instruction—instruction that enables their students to meet the standards (Buhle & Blachowicz, 2008). Some schools have data teams in place to review assessment data on a regular basis (Allison et al., 2010). Literacy coaches are typically key members of such data teams. In addition to data teams, teachers may also meet in grade-level teams to review assessments such as writing samples, standardized tests, or unit assessments. Even if these processes are already in place in schools, adding literacy coaching can ensure that teachers have the support to develop the expertise needed to use data effectively to plan and modify instruction.

How Do I Do It?

If your school already has data teams in place, you may find that you or a teacher leader can jump right into the process of working with the teachers to review assessment data and plan instruction. However, if this process is new to your teachers, you may find that you will need to slow down, spend more time on some steps, and introduce the process over time.

Getting Started

1 Meet briefly with a grade-level team. Explain that you will be working together to review assessment data and examine curriculum and instructional practices so that you can make decisions about how to improve student learning.

2 Discuss the roles of participants and the norms for participation in data review meetings (see Figure 9.1).

3 Determine a day, time, and place to meet with a grade-level team to review assessment data. Generally at least 30 minutes will be needed, but if multiple assessments are being reviewed, an hour or more may be necessary.

4 Develop the agenda for the meeting. A sample agenda is provided in Figure 9.2.

5 Collect and chart the specific data to review. For groups that are new to the process, begin with a single source of assessment data such as unit test scores or standardized test data that your school already collects such as Measures of Academic Progress (MAP) or AIMSWeb data. The top portion of Form 9.1 can be used to chart data.

Facilitating the Data Review Meeting

1 Share the agenda.

2 Determine roles that each person will play and discuss norms for the meeting (see Figure 9.1).

3 Clarify the focal question for the meeting.

Roles and Responsibilities
- Facilitator: (Literacy coach or teacher leader)
  - Collect and chart data in advance.
  - Set meeting date, time, and place.
  - Facilitate meeting, promoting input and participation by all.
- Timekeeper
  - Monitor time and provide updates when half of the time is left, 10 minutes are left, and 2 minutes are left.
- Recorder
  - Write down all decisions and plans determined by the group.
  - Make and distribute copies of the record to all participants.
- Engaged participant
  - Listen, question, and contribute.

Norms for Participation
- Be on time.
- Stay on topic.
- All participants have an equal voice.
- Work toward consensus to make decisions.
- Be professional.

FIGURE 9.1. Data review meetings.

```
◆ Purpose setting/Focal question for meeting:
◆ What specific skill areas are the weakest according to the data?
◆ Review/Analyze/Interpret data.
◆ Review instructional practices and curriculum related to skill areas.
◆ Develop an action plan.
```

FIGURE 9.2. Data review meeting sample agenda.

4 Provide several minutes for each teacher to review the data on Form 9.1 individually.

5 Then ask them, "What do you notice?" Follow-up questions may include:

a "What does the assessment measure?"
b "In what area are the students doing best?"
c "In what area do the students need to improve?"

6 Shift the focus to the instructional practices (i.e., teaching methods, teaching strategies, curriculum, grouping, instructional pacing, instructional materials) that impact student outcomes for a specific area. Use open-ended questions such as those listed below to facilitate the discussion.

a "What are our current instructional practices related to this area?"
b "What teaching strategies are being used?"
c "How does the curriculum address this area?"
d "What type of grouping is being used to provide this instruction?"
e "What is the pacing for instruction in this area?"
f "What materials are being used for this instruction?"
g If students in one teacher's classroom are doing well in the area, ask, "What are you doing in your classroom that may have led to this outcome for your students?"

7 Move the discussion toward developing an action plan based on the review of assessment data and the discussion of curriculum and instruction. Prompts such as those listed below may be helpful to facilitate the discussion.

a "What should we do to improve student outcomes related to these findings?"
b "Who is responsible for implementation?"
c "How will we measure the impact?"
d "How and when will we follow up?"

8 As you work on the action plan, you may need to provide suggestions for research-based instructional strategies and offer to follow up with teachers regarding implementation.

9 Close the meeting by reviewing key findings and confirming the action plan. Clarify that the recorder will provide a copy of the meeting notes, including the action plan.

10 Thank the participants for their hard work and valuable contributions. Be sure to end the meeting on time.

Following Up

1 After the recorder has shared the meeting notes, review the action plan, paying special attention to who is responsible for each part of the plan. Follow up with those teachers who are responsible for implementing parts of the plan to offer support. Make sure that any parts of the plan for which you are responsible are completed in a timely manner.

2 Schedule the next data review meeting according to the action plan and begin preparing for that meeting.

The Strategy in Action

Kindergarten Team

Olivia Wojcinski is a reading specialist who spends about half of her time coaching K–2 teachers in her school and half of her time delivering reading intervention support for students in the primary grades. Her colleague Kate Curry-Walker is responsible for reading interventions and coaching in grades 3–5. Olivia is meeting with the kindergarten teachers to review assessment data from an assessment of vowel knowledge aligned with Standard RF.K.3 that states, "Associate the long and short vowel sounds with common spellings (graphemes) for the five major vowels." She has scheduled the meeting and prepared the agenda, including the focal question: "What vowel sounds are our students doing well with, and what vowel sounds are they struggling with?" Olivia has collected the assessment data and charted it using the format provided in Form 9.1. When the meeting starts, Olivia reminds the teachers of the purpose and since there are only two kindergarten teachers at her school, one takes the role of timekeeper and the other serves as the recorder. As they discuss the assessment data and reflect on their instructional practices and curriculum, Olivia is careful to let the teachers speak first so that they can share their ideas and take ownership for the data review process. She uses prompts such as "What else did you notice?" and "What are some options?" to invite the teachers to contribute to the discussion. At the end of the meeting, Olivia recaps their findings that the students are doing well with short vowels but are having difficulty with the vowel–consonant–silent *e* (VC*e*) long vowel pattern. The teachers discuss that they had just introduced this pattern and had not provided sufficient instruction or practice on it prior to the assessment. They discussed how they can provide explicit instruction through mini-lessons and practice opportunities through shared reading, shared writing, and literacy centers. They also identified certain students who need additional support with short vowels and planned how they will address that in the classroom. The team finalized their action plan and intends to meet again in 2 weeks to review new data related to this standard as well as to examine student performance for another foundational skill—sight-word knowledge.

Fourth-Grade Team

Kate Curry-Walker spends about half of her time coaching teachers in grades 3–5, and she spends the rest of her time providing small-group reading interventions. Kate has just met with the fourth-grade team to review student performance on reading fluency. There are four teachers on the team, and they were reviewing data from 1-minute oral reading fluency probes to examine student performance related to Standard RF.4.4, "Read with sufficient accuracy and fluency to support comprehension." During the review of data, one of the teachers, Meg, asked, "We know about their accuracy, rate, expression, and self-correction, but what other data do we have because these fluency probes don't really get at the heart of the standard—to support comprehension?!" Ivette explained that some of her students seem so focused on reading fast that they are not really even thinking about what they are reading. The other teachers agreed, and Kate quickly shifted the discussion to what additional data the teachers needed to determine student performance related to the entire standard. The teachers suggested that they could add comprehension questions to the reading fluency probes and also create a checklist to use when observing student reading behaviors associated with comprehension during guided reading groups. Their action plan focused on implementing the new assessment approach as well as ensuring that their instruction focused on fluency as a process that supports comprehension—not a race to finish a passage as quickly as possible! As she reflected on how the meeting went, Kate felt that even though the assessment data review process deviated from what she had planned, she was pleased that the teachers were so insightful about analyzing the data and offered such great ideas for the action plan. Shortly after the meeting Kate talked with Meg, the fourth-grade teacher leader, about taking over the facilitation of some of the assessment data review meetings in the future. Meg agreed, but she asked Kate to work with her on planning as well as being a participant in meetings when her schedule permits. Kate agreed and feels pleased at the way the fourth-grade team has taken ownership of the data review process.

Charting Assessment Data

Assessment: _____ **Date:** _____

Focal Question: _____

Teacher names	Number assessed	Number proficient	Percent proficient	Number not proficient	Names of students close to proficient	Names of students needing some additional support	Names of students needing extensive support

Reviewing Instructional Practices and Curriculum ◆ What are we doing? ◆ How is it working?	
Key Findings	
Action Plan ◆ What will we do? ◆ Who is responsible? ◆ How will we measure the impact? ◆ How and when will we follow up?	

························ **Strategy 10** ························

Examining Student Work

What Is It?

Teachers routinely examine their own students' work as part of the grading process. Many go beyond just grading the work and use the data to make appropriate changes to their instruction. This type of reflection about student work is certainly important for improving an individual teacher's practice. However, to ensure that students receive the instruction they need to perform well in relation to the standards, teachers must take collaborative responsibility for the learning of their students ("Examining Student Work," n.d.). One way to take collaborative responsibility is through the examination of student work beyond the individual teacher level. An in-depth look at student work within or across grade levels can positively impact the instruction of many teachers and, in turn, the learning of many students.

Purposes for the collaborative examination of student work vary. David Allen, one of the authors of *Looking Together at Student Work* (Blythe, Allen, & Powell, 2007), says that "most educators who look at student work in a collaborative process hope to learn about the effectiveness of their instruction, better understand students' learning and development, develop more effective curriculum and assessment, and find ways to help students do higher quality work" ("Teachers Learn," n.d.). More specifically, teachers often set one or more of the following purposes for their examination of student work:

◆ To determine if an assignment is meeting the learning goals or standards for which it was designed.

◆ To determine what aspects of a particular assignment students are doing well and what aspects are difficult for all students or for some students.

◆ To answer specific questions that a teacher or teachers have about the efficacy of an assignment.

◆ To understand a specific student's learning.

◆ To evaluate a piece of work according to a rubric.

When teachers share their students' work with colleagues, they often feel they are opening up their teaching for others to view and discuss. For some teachers, this may be an uncomfortable process. Protocols, such as those developed by the National School Reform Faculty (*www.nsrfharmony.org*), give a level of comfort to the process by providing a clear structure for the meetings and clear descriptions of each activity (e.g., introduction of purpose, setting of group norms, individual examination of the student work, group discussion of observations, and instructional recommendations). In addition, the consistent use of protocols by grade-level teams to examine students' academic needs has been linked to improved student achievement (Saunders, Goldenberg, & Gallimore, 2009). Coaches can contribute to the success of these small-group meetings by guiding teachers through the protocol in a timely fashion and by modeling the professional behaviors expected of all participants.

How Do I Do It?

When you meet with teachers to examine student work, your primary responsibilities are to help the teachers focus on the student work, ensure that all voices are heard, and facilitate the development of meaningful conclusions and future instructional steps. Tools such as the Protocol for Examining Student Work (Form 10.1) and the Student Work Examination Form (Form 10.2) will assist you in accomplishing these responsibilities. (If the purpose for examining student work is to collaboratively score student writing using a rubric, the protocol in Form 10.3 will be helpful.)

Preparation is critical to the success of any coaching activity, including a meeting to examine student work. Ask a teacher or teachers to provide you with a small sample of student work that represents the range of work submitted by the students (i.e., exemplary work, proficient work, developing work, and inadequate work). Make clear copies of the materials for each group member. Make copies of the Protocol for Examining Student Work (see Form 10.1) and the Student Work Examination Form (see Form 10.2) for each member too. The examination of student work will take about 30 minutes if you designate about 5 minutes to complete Steps 1–3 on the protocol, 10 minutes for the individual examination of the work (Step 4), and 15 minutes for the group discussion of the work (Step 5).

Purpose and Context

At the beginning of the meeting, pass out the Protocol for Examining Student Work (see Form 10.1) and the Student Work Examination Form (see Form 10.2), and state the purpose of the review session. Sometimes, the student work will represent an assignment that all teachers have completed with their students. At other times, the work to be examined will come from the students of just one or two teachers in the group. In either case, it is important to set the context for the student work and have the teachers record both the purpose and the context on the Student Work Examination Form (see Form 10.2).

Norms for the Group Work

Establishing the expected behaviors of participants is critical to the success of all group work and may be especially important when teachers are, in fact, revealing their teaching practices through the sharing of student work. The following norms include guidelines for the examination of student work and for the subsequent discussion.

- Examination of student work
  - Maintain a focus on the purpose as your examine the work.
  - Keep an open mind; don't begin to make conclusions until you've completed an initial examination of all work.
  - Be prepared to cite evidence for your observations, insights, and conclusions.

- Discussion
  - Be an active, but not dominating, participant.
  - Share observations, insights, conclusions, and recommendations in a supportive, professional manner.
  - Listen to others and carefully consider ideas that differ from your own.

Distribution of Student Work

Distribute the samples of student work and give the teachers time to examine them individually. Ask the teachers to write notes related to the five questions on the Student Work Examination Form (Form 10.2) about each piece of student work.

Individual Examination

Figures 10.1 and 10.2 present the materials related to a fourth-grade team's examination of student work. One fourth-grade teacher, Tanya Foster, asked Nick Giordano, the school's literacy coach, to facilitate a fourth-grade team review of the information collection chart (Figure 10.1). She had created the assignment and accompanying information collection chart to address standard RIT.4.9: "Integrate information from two texts on the same topic in order to write or speak about the subject knowledgeably." This was a new assignment in the biome unit, and the team wanted to discuss whether the assignment and chart had been effective in helping students meet the standard. Tanya collected all of the completed charts from the other two fourth-grade teachers and selected a representative piece of exemplary, proficient, developing, and inadequate work for the group to examine. Figure 10.1

I'm learning about *rain forests* by Student 1 [considered exemplary work by teacher]		
Information from Text 1 Text Title: Rain Forest Animals (2001) Author: Katie Billingslea Smith	**Also found in Text 2**	**NEW Information from Text 2** Text Title: Rain Forests (2001) Authors: Will Osborne and Mary Pope Osborne
1. Rain forests are close to the equator (big word). Equator is the middle of earth.	☐	1. Almost all rain forests get at least 6 feet of rain—that's 72 inches!
2. A tropical rain forest has four layers—forest floor, under story, under canopy, and emergent (big words).	☑	2. I drew a diagram of the rain forest on the back. This book uses different names—forest floor, understory, canopy, emergents (big words).
3. The largest tropical rain forest is the Amazon rain forest—it takes up 1/3 of South America.	☑	3. It's between 75 and 80 degrees in the rain forest.
4. It's about 80 degrees everyday in the rain forest.	☐	4. There are lots of strange plants in the rain forests. Like the pitcher plant. Each pitcher can hold 1/2 gallon of water! (I drew pitcher plant on the back of this paper.)
5. All rain forests get at least 80 inches of rain.	☐	5. Many rain forest animals use camouflage (big word) to stay alive. Some bugs look like leaves and hide in trees.
6. Fires and people destroy rain forests.	☐	6. Some animals are nocturnal (big word). That means they are wake at night. Like the night monkeys, vampire bats (scary picture), and click beetles.
7. Rain forests may disappear by 2050.	☐	7. You will die if you get shot by an arrow with poison arrow frog poison on it.
8. Jaguars, scarlet macaws (bird), sloths, mandrills, tree boas, and tree frogs live in the rain forest.	☐	8. A pangolin (big word) looks like a dinosaur but eats ants. I drew a picture of one the back of this paper.
9. Mandrills are big baboons. They have many colors on different parts of their body. They have very sharp teeth.	☐	9. Different groups of people live in the rain forest. Two groups are the Mbuti and the Yanomami (big words).
10. Jaguars are good swimmers—that's new to me.	☐	10. We get food and medicine from the rain forest.
11.		11. People are cutting down the trees in the rain forests. They want to have room for roads and houses. They want to have room for cattle.
12.		12. Some rain forest animals are endangered. Like the wooly spider monkey.

FIGURE 10.1. Integrating information from two texts: Completed information collection chart.

Prepare to examine the student work by writing notes about the following two areas:

Purpose(s) of the Examination (List the specific Common Core standard(s) related to the student work.)

To examine whether the Information Collection Form assignment is an appropriate method for helping students to integrate information from two informational texts on the same topic (RIT.4.9).

Context for the Student Work

This assignment was completed as part of the Social Studies unit on Biomes of the Earth. The teachers modeled the process using the topic of the tundra biome. Students then selected a biome of the earth and completed the Information Collection Chart while reading two texts about the biome. Students who read about the same biomes will later meet to combine their ideas and prepare a presentation for their peers (to meet the second part of RIT.4.9).

As you examine the student work, consider the following questions and write notes to prepare for the discussion with colleagues.

1. What does this work show that each student is doing well?

   Student 1—can select information from text; information is usually important; generally writes in complete sentences; doesn't sound like he copied the text; attempts to label duplicate information

2. What does the work show that each student could do better?

   Student 1—could more carefully check to see if the information he is writing for text 2 is repetitive of or very similar to text 1

3. What, if anything, surprised you about each student's work?

   Student 1—He spelled all of the content vocabulary correctly; he must have looked back at the text to do this! He defined some of the big words.

4. What questions do you have that you would like to discuss with your colleagues?

   Form seems to match expectations from first part of CCSS RIT.4.9.

   Two students from Rod's class labeled "big words." I did not model this or expect this from my students, but I think it's a great idea!

   Should we consider adding a first column where students write what they already know about the biome—or are we no longer considering prior knowledge to be important?

5. What changes to the task or instruction might improve student performance?

   Three of the four students seem to need more instruction in the marking of repeated information—and what repetitious means (does it have to be exact or just very similar).

   Two students had several spelling errors with content area vocabulary. Perhaps we need to remind all of our students that they should check the spelling of content area vocabulary by referring back to the text.

FIGURE 10.2. Partially completed Student Work Examination Form.

is an example of what Tanya submitted as exemplary work. Figure 10.2 presents a partially completed Student Work Examination Form (Form 10.2), showing how one fourth-grade teacher wrote notes about the purpose, the context, and Student 1's sample.

Group Discussion

When each teacher has completed an individual examination of the student work, use the five questions from the Student Work Examination Sheet (Form 10.2) to facilitate a discussion during which all members share their observations, questions, and insights. After this initial discussion, ask a question that allows the group to draw some final conclusions related to the main purpose of the review. For example, Nick Giordano, the literacy coach, asked, "What is the evidence that the assignment helped students meet standard RIT.4.9?"

Next, guide the teachers to make instructional recommendations related to the examination of student work and document all final recommendations. These recommendations might be related to the assignment itself, the directions for the assignment, or the instruction that enables students to successfully complete the assignment. If changes are needed to instructional materials, be sure to determine who will be responsible for making the changes. In relation to the assignment that incorporated the information collection chart (see Figure 10.1), the team concluded that students would be more likely to meet standard RIT.4.9 if the teachers more explicitly explained why it is important to designate repeated information, clarified the definition of *repeated information*, and required students to include content-related vocabulary on the chart, using the texts to find the accurate spelling of those terms.

Distribution of the Final Conclusions and Instructional Recommendations

After the meeting, compile the final conclusions and instructional recommendations into one document. Distribute the document to all group members. Even if the examination only focused on the work of students from one teacher, other members of the group may want to use a similar assignment in the future, and so the conclusions and recommendations document would be helpful as they plan their instruction.

Examination of student work can be a powerful way to enhance instruction that helps students meet the Common Core standards. By using the Protocol for Examining Student Work (Form 10.1) and the Student Work Examination Form (Form 10.2) when you facilitate the examination of student work with a grade-level team, you are modeling the process—making it highly likely that the team will be able to engage in future reviews of student work independently or with the assistance of the teacher leader.

The Strategy in Action

Nick Giordano has worked at Swanton Elementary School for 12 years—first as a fifth-grade teacher, then as a reading specialist, and for the past 3 years as a full-time literacy coach. At the beginning of the year, the three third-grade teachers asked Nick if he could help them revise their informational writing unit to align with the expectations of the Common Core Standard W.3.2: "Write informative/expository texts to examine a topic and convey ideas and information clearly." They wanted to begin with the development of the informational project assessment rubric, thinking that the assessment rubric would guide the revisions they needed to make to their instruction.

The third-grade implementation guide lists informational writing as the focus for the second quarter. So, during the first quarter, Nick worked with the third-grade team to develop an assessment rubric that was aligned with the expectations delineated in Standard W.3.2 (see Figure 10.3). They began with the district's four-level rubric template (i.e., Inadequate, Developing, Proficient, and Exemplary) and used the language from the standard itself to develop the Proficient descriptors. Then they wrote the Developing descriptors to indicate that the writing sometimes exhibited the expected characteristics, while the language of the Inadequate descriptors indicated that the writing generally lacked the expected characteristics. Nick suggested that they look at the expectations listed for fourth graders in standard W.4.2 to develop the Exemplary descriptors.

After a draft of the rubric had been developed, Nick recommended that they use their rubric to assess the third-grade informational writing sample from Appendix C of the Common Core standards. According to the introductory material in Appendix C, the student writing samples in that appendix "exhibit at least the level of quality required to meet the Writing standards for that grade" (NGA & CCSSO, 2010, Appendix C, p. 2). So, Nick explained, individual ratings of Proficient or Exemplary for the "Horses" informational writing sample from Appendix C would indicate that their rubric was valid. Nick guided them through the scoring process, and the teachers were pleased to see that their rubric ratings, as shown on Figure 10.4, indicated that "Horses" met or exceeded the expectations for standard W.3.2, except in the area of illustrations. This activity enabled them to be more confident that their rubric would serve as a good assessment tool. Nick distributed the final version of the rubric so that teachers could use it as they planned their instruction and when they introduced the project to the students.

At the end the second semester, the third-grade team set aside a meeting to begin scoring the informational writing pieces. Prior to the meeting, Nick asked Lorraine Hardy, one of the third-grade teachers, to provide him with four writing samples: one from a student whom she felt had produced an excellent project, one whom she felt had completed a fully acceptable project, one whom she felt had struggled to meet several of the expectations, and one whom she felt had failed to meet nearly all of the expectations. These would provide the teachers with a range of writing

Writing 3.2	Inadequate	Developing	Proficient	Exemplary
2a. Topic	Reader is unsure of the topic after reading the first section of the text.	Reader knows the topic after reading the first section of the text.	The text begins with a clear topic sentence/section.	The text begins with a clear, attention-grabbing topic sentence/ paragraph.
2a. Organization	Does not group related information together.	Groups related information together in some places.	Groups related information together.	Uses paragraphs to group related information together.
2a. Illustrations to aid comprehension	Illustrations are not included or do not aid comprehension.	Some illustrations are included when needed.	Illustrations are included whenever needed.	High-quality illustrations are included whenever needed.
2b. Development	Includes few to no facts, definitions, or details.	Includes some facts, definitions, or details but topic is not adequately developed.	Includes facts, definitions, and details to adequately develop the topic.	Includes facts, definitions, details, quotes, and examples to adequately develop the topic.
2c. Cohesion Expected linking words: *also, another, and, more, but*	No use of linking words and phrases.	Some use of linking words to connect ideas.	Uses linking words to connect ideas where needed throughout the text.	Uses grade-level and more sophisticated linking words (e.g., *because, for example*) to connect ideas throughout the text.
2d. Conclusion	The text does not have a concluding sentence/section.	The concluding sentence/section is poorly stated.	The text ends with a clear concluding sentence/section.	The text ends with a clear concluding sentence/section that refers to the information presented.
Language 3.2: Command of conventions of standard English capitalization, punctuation, and writing	Meets few grade-level expectations for conventions; errors distract the reader.	Meets some grade-level expectations for conventions; errors may distract the reader.	Meets grade-level expectations for conventions; errors are minor and do not distract the reader.	Exceeds grade-level expectations for conventions.

FIGURE 10.3. Rubric for informative/explanatory text.

Writing 3.2	Inadequate	Developing	Proficient	Exemplary
2a. Topic	Reader is unsure of the topic after reading the first section of the text.	Reader knows the topic after reading the first section of the text.	**The text begins with a clear topic sentence/section.**	The text begins with a clear, attention-grabbing topic sentence/ paragraph.
2a. Organization	Does not group related information together.	Groups related information together in some places.	Groups related information together.	**Uses paragraphs to group related information together.**
2a. Illustrations to aid comprehension	**Illustrations are not included or do not aid comprehension.**	Some illustrations are included when needed.	Illustrations are included whenever needed.	High-quality illustrations are included whenever needed.
2b. Development	Includes few to no facts, definitions, or details.	Includes some facts, definitions, or details but topic is not adequately developed.	**Includes facts, definitions, and details to adequately develop the topic.**	Includes facts, definitions, details, quotes, and examples to adequately develop the topic.
2c. Cohesion Expected linking words: *also, another, and, more, but*	No use of linking words and phrases.	Some use of linking words to connect ideas.	**Uses linking words to connect ideas where needed throughout the text.**	Uses grade-level and more sophisticated linking words (e.g., *because, for example*) to connect ideas throughout the text.
2d. Conclusion	The text does not have a concluding sentence/section.	The concluding sentence/section is poorly stated.	**The text ends with a clear concluding sentence/section.**	The text ends with a clear concluding sentence/section that refers to the information presented.
Language 3.2: Command of conventions of standard English capitalization, punctuation, and writing	Meets few grade-level expectations for conventions; errors distract the reader.	Meets some grade-level expectations for conventions; errors may distract the reader.	**Meets grade-level expectations for conventions; errors are minor and do not distract the reader.**	Exceeds grade-level expectations for conventions.

FIGURE 10.4. Completed rubric for the sample writing piece "Horses."

samples for the initial scoring activity. Nick made copies of the four samples for each teacher.

When the team met, Nick used the protocol in Form 10.3 to facilitate the process. After reviewing the purpose for the meeting and the rubric, Nick and the three teachers each scored and then discussed the four projects from Lorraine Hardy's students. The discussions about the differences in scoring helped them clarify exactly what each description meant, making it easier to differentiate a Proficient from an Exemplary rating, a Proficient from a Developing rating, and a Developing from an Inadequate rating. On the basis of their discussion, a few changes in the rubric language were made.

With time growing short, Nick helped the teachers develop a plan for completing the scoring. They decided that each project would be scored by the student's own teacher and one other teacher. To maintain a focus on the work itself, students' names would be removed from the copies and replaced with numbers. The teachers also decided that they wanted a hard copy of the rubric for each project so they could circle the ratings and write in explanatory notes where needed. They agreed to finish their individual scoring before their next grade-level meeting. Nick said that if they could turn the rubrics in to him on the day before the meeting, he would arrange to have a paraprofessional aggregate all of the results. Confident with their ability to use the rubric and having dealt with the logistics of the scoring, the third-grade teachers said they felt ready to score the projects and were looking forward to the next meeting where they would discuss the results and the corresponding instructional implications.

FORM 10.1

Protocol for Examining Student Work

1. **Purpose and context.** The facilitator clearly states the purpose for the examination of student work. The facilitator or teacher whose students completed the work provides the context for the assignment. Teachers write the purpose and context on their Student Work Examination Forms (Form 10.2).

2. **Norms for the group work.** The facilitator reminds the group of the norms or ground rules for the examination of the work and the subsequent discussion.

3. **Distribution of student work.** The facilitator distributes samples that have been previously selected to represent the range of work (i.e., exemplary, proficient, developing, inadequate) produced by the students.

4. **Individual examination.** Each teacher examines the student work and writes notes related to the questions on the Student Work Examination Form (see Form 10.2).

5. **Group discussion.** The facilitator leads the discussion where group members use the notes from their Student Work Examination Forms (Form 10.2) to share their observations, insights, and questions.
   - The group draws some final conclusions related to the purpose of the examination.
   - The group determines what changes might be beneficial for student learning. Depending on the type of review, changes may be made to the assignment itself, the directions related to the assignment, and/or the instruction related to the assignment.
   - The facilitator takes notes about the final conclusions and instructional recommendations.

6. **Distribution of conclusions and instructional recommendations.** After the meeting, the facilitator distributes copies of the final conclusions and instructional recommendations to all group members.

FORM 10.2

$tudent Work Examination Form

Prepare to examine the student work by writing notes about the following two areas:

Purpose of the Examination (List the specific Common Core standard[s] related to the student work.)

Context for the Student Work

As you examine the student work, consider the following questions and write notes to prepare for a discussion with colleagues.

1. What does this work show that each student is doing well?

2. What does the work show that each student could do better?

3. What, if anything, surprised you about each student's work?

4. What questions do you have that you would like to discuss with your colleagues?

5. What changes to the task or instruction might improve student performance?

Protocol for Scoring of Student Writing Assignments with Rubrics

1. **Purpose.** The facilitator clearly states the purpose for the scoring activity.

2. **Norms for the group work**. The facilitator reminds the group of the norms or ground rules for the meeting.

3. **Review of rubric categories.** The facilitator distributes the rubric to each member of the group and reviews the rubric categories.

4. **Developing consistent scoring.** The group scores some representative samples to develop consistency.

   - The facilitator distributes samples that appear to represent the range of work submitted by the students (i.e., exemplary, proficient, developing, and inadequate work samples).
   - Each member reads and scores the samples individually.
   - The members share their individual ratings.
   - The group discusses any differences in scoring and comes to a consensus about the final ratings.

5. **Scoring.** All of the writing pieces are scored.

   - Results will be more valid if two teachers score each sample. The two teachers can compare their scores and discuss any differences before agreeing on the final ratings.
   - If the scoring cannot be completed within one small-group meeting, teachers may decide to schedule a second meeting to finish the scoring or to finish the scoring on their own time.

6. **Discussion.** Teachers engage in a review of the final ratings and develop instructional recommendations.

   - Teachers may ask for their colleagues' assistance in examining pieces that they found difficult to score.
   - Teachers examine the results and determine what would help students improve their writing. For example, reteaching certain components of the writing type to the entire class or to small groups may be beneficial.
   - Teachers may also decide to modify the rubric language so that it more clearly describes the criteria.

7. **Follow-up.** After the meeting, the facilitator distributes copies of the instructional recommendations and, if applicable, the revised rubric to all group members.

Reviewing Units of Study

What Is It?

A unit of study is a set of related instructional activities that focus on a main topic and enable students to meet specific curricular objectives. Units of study are often developed by grade-level teams, and each unit is typically implemented by all teachers during the same time frame. In the area of language arts (Short, Lynch-Brown, & Tomlinson, 2013), teachers often develop units of study that focus on learning about specific genres of literature (e.g., realistic fiction, fantasy, biography), types of writing (e.g., narrative, informational, opinion), authors (e.g., Tomie dePaola, Eve Bunting, Gail Gibbons), or themes (e.g., survival, honesty, cooperation). These types of units definitely have the potential to focus on multiple Common Core standards.

Interdisciplinary units, where students use a variety of sources to develop disciplinary (i.e., content) understanding and enhance their literacy skills (Barton & Smith, 2000; Jones, 2000), also can help students meet the Common Core standards. Several of the instructional shifts associated with the English language arts (ELA) standards (EngageNY, 2012; Fisher et al., 2013) can be addressed through interdisciplinary units. More specifically, these units could require students to read multiple literary and informational texts, to write from sources, and to build their academic vocabulary.

After a unit has been implemented, a review of the unit will enable teachers to determine how well the students met the unit's learning standards and what changes would further enhance their learning. While individual reflection related to the implementation of a unit of study may be beneficial to a single teacher and his or her students (Larrivee, 2008), a collaborative review of the unit's objectives, instructional activities, and assessments will lead to improvements in teaching and learning across the grade level (Taylor, Pearson, Peterson, & Rodriguez, 2003; Vescio, Ross, & Adams, 2008). This collaborative review of units is critical when you consider (1) that teams of teachers spend a great deal of time developing such units, (2) that implementing the units generally consumes a large amount of instructional time, and (3) that the same units are often taught for multiple years.

The recent adoption of the Common Core standards makes the review of existing units even more important. Teachers must examine how their units are helping students meet grade-specific Common Core expectations across all four areas of literacy (Reading, Writing, Speaking and Listening, and Language) and make revisions as needed. For example, when reviewing and revising a unit on realistic fiction, teachers would want to ensure that students would be provided opportunities not only to read grade-appropriate realistic fiction texts but also to engage in in-depth discussions about those texts using conventions of standard English and to write narratives that incorporate the characteristics of realistic fiction using grade-appropriate conventions of standard English grammar and mechanics.

Interdisciplinary units of study also need to be reviewed to determine which Common Core standards are currently part of the unit and which ones should be added. For example, teachers can no longer simply present information about a topic through read-alouds or explicit explanation. Students are expected to read informational texts about the topic, share the information learned from reading during discussions and presentations, and write informational and/or opinion pieces that incorporate the main ideas and key details from their reading.

Coaches can be key players in the unit review process. When working with teachers who have little or no experience reviewing units of study, coaches can guide the entire process thereby helping teachers make appropriate revisions to essential questions, standards, instructional activities, assessments, and resources. Providing guidance with one or two unit reviews will help teachers become knowledgeable about the review process, so they can conduct future unit reviews independently or with the support of their teacher leader.

How Do I Do It?

As a coach, facilitating a unit review is most effective when you have a clear understanding of the unit's components and when you have seen teachers and students engaging in the unit's instructional activities. The following procedures outline how you can collaborate with teachers as they prepare to teach the unit, as they implement the unit, and as they review the unit.

Before the Unit

1 In many cases, you may work with a grade-level team of teachers to develop a new unit of study or to revise a previous unit so that it meets several of the Common Core standards. If you were not involved in the development or revision of the unit, you should read through the unit plan carefully and ask the teacher leader or a member of the grade-level team to clarify any questions you may have.

2 Facilitate a grade-level meeting before the unit begins.

   a Share the Unit Reflection Log (see Form 11.1) with the group. Explain that the log will enable them to document their observations, questions, and needs as the unit is progressing. These ongoing reflections will provide critical information that will lead to a productive end-of-unit review meeting.

   b Encourage teachers to use a copy of the unit plan to write notes about additional resources they used and changes or additions they made to instructional activities. These notes can be shared at the review meeting.

   c Ask teachers how you can support them in their teaching of the unit. You can offer to co-plan an instructional activity (see Strategy 15) with an individual teacher or with the entire team. If your coaching time corresponds to the time when the unit is being taught, you can offer to model (see Strategy 14) or co-teach (see Strategy 16) a lesson or to work with a group of students as they engage in one or more of the small-group activities.

During the Unit

1 While the unit is being taught, provide the support (e.g., co-planning, modeling, co-teaching, working with small groups of students) previously requested by teachers.

2 After the first week or so of the unit, check in with each team member to see how the unit is going. These casual conversations can occur before or after school or toward the end of a teacher's planning period. As you listen to the teachers' comments, you can encourage them to note their observations and insights on their reflection logs (see Form 11.1). In addition, you can inquire about ways in which you can support them as they implement the remainder of the unit.

3 If you are not involved in any modeling, co-teaching, or small-group work, try to observe in each classroom to see students engage in the different instructional activities. Make notes on your reflection log (see Form 11.1) about what seems to be working well, what seems to be difficult, and what questions you want to discuss with the team.

4 Even if you have to rearrange your schedule a bit to fit in these coaching activities, the effort will be worth it. These activities will provide you with a firsthand view of the unit in action, establishing a good foundation from which you can facilitate the unit review meeting.

After the Unit

1 You will facilitate a unit review meeting to determine what changes to the unit are warranted, especially changes that would improve the students' ability to answer the essential questions and meet the specific Common Core standards.

a. Remind teachers to bring their reflection logs and their annotated unit plans to the meeting.

b. As the teachers discuss the notes from their reflection logs, help them tie their comments directly to the unit plan:

  ◆ What essential questions, standards, instructional activities, and assessments do they want to keep? Why?

  ◆ What revisions or additions to essential questions, standards, instructional activities, and assessments do they feel are needed? Why? If applicable, who will be responsible for revising the instructional materials and assessments?

c. Offer ways that you can support the teachers. For example, if there is a standard that all students are struggling to meet, offer to co-plan a lesson with the team about that standard.

d. Determine who will update the unit plan. A teacher may volunteer to take on the task for this unit, with other teachers agreeing to do the same for future units they review.

2. Distribute the meeting summary and the updated unit plan to all members of the team. The teachers will rely on these documents when they teach the unit again.

The Strategy in Action

Nick Giordano is a full-time literacy coach from Swanton Elementary School. At the beginning of the year, he had worked with the fourth-grade team to revise their biome unit plan. He guided them in the development of essential questions and the selection of relevant Common Core standards from all four areas (i.e., Reading, Writing, Speaking and Listening, and Language). In addition, they agreed upon a set of instructional activities that would be implemented by all members of the team. The main components of the unit plan can be seen in Figure 11.1. Nick suggested that the teachers document their observations and questions on the Unit Reflection Log (Form 11.1) as they implement the unit. He also suggested that they write down additional resources they used and/or instructional activities they implemented on a copy of the unit plan. This ongoing reflection would enable them, when the unit had been completed, to conduct an efficient and effective review of the entire unit.

After the first week of the unit, Nick facilitated a fourth-grade team meeting in which the group examined one of the common assignments for the unit, the information collection chart. (Strategy 10 describes this process.) In addition to this examination of student work, Nick had an opportunity to collaborate with all three teachers as the unit was being taught. In Tanya Foster's and Rod Hildebrand's classrooms, he facilitated small-group discussions where students who had read about the same biome met to compile their information on a "Characteristics of the Biome" chart. He also helped Tim O'Halloran plan a demonstration of how students might use a Prezi (*http://prezi.com*) for their unit presentations. Finally,

Biome Unit: Fourth Grade—3 weeks*

Essential Question for Social Studies: What is a biome and how do biomes differ in terms of location, climate, animal life, and plant life?

Essential Questions for English Language Arts:
- ◆ How does reading a variety of informational texts help me learn about a topic?
- ◆ What do I need to do in order to present information to my peers in a clear and interesting way?

Common Core State Standards: (In some cases, only relevant elements of the standards, instead of the entire standard, are listed.)

RIT.4.9:	Integrate information from two texts on the same topic in order to write or speak about the subject knowledgeably.
RIT.4.4 and L.4.4:	Determine the meaning of general academic and domain-specific words or phrases in a text relevant to a grade 4 topic or subject, using a range of strategies (e.g., context, Greek and Latin affixes and roots, reference materials).
W.4.8:	Gather relevant information from print and digital sources; take notes and categorize information, and provide a list of sources.
SL.4.1:	Engage effectively in a range of collaborative discussions on grade 4 topics and texts building on others' ideas and expressing their own clearly. (Includes substandards SL.4.1a–4.1d.)
SL.4.4:	Report on a topic in an organized manner, using appropriate facts and relevant, descriptive details to support main ideas or themes; speak clearly at an understandable pace.
SL.4.5:	Add visual displays to presentations when appropriate to enhance the development of main idea or themes.
L.4.1 and L.4.2:	Demonstrate command of the conventions of standard English grammar and usage when writing and speaking and of capitalization, punctuation, and spelling when writing.

Instructional Activities
1. Individual—Each student selects a biome to study. At least two students need to choose the same biome. Each student reads two different texts about his or her chosen biome and completes the information collection chart (see Figure 11.1). *Teacher selects one biome to model the process.*
2. Small group—Students reading about the same biome meet to discuss the information they have gathered and combine their information using the Characteristics of the Biome chart. They engage in further research to gather specific information needed to complete missing pieces of the chart. *Teacher facilitates a fishbowl discussion with one group to model the process.*
3. Whole class—Students create a vocabulary word wall of vocabulary related to biomes that is organized to differentiate vocabulary about biomes in general and vocabulary specific to each biome.
4. Small group—Each group develops a presentation about its biome. *Teacher provides explicit explanation about presentation options (e.g., PowerPoint with embedded photographs, maps, and/or video clips; Glogster; trifold presentation boards; Prezi).*
5. Whole class/small group—Each small group gives its biome presentation to the other members of the class. Class members give positive feedback to and ask questions of the presenters. *Teacher and students work together to establish a protocol of Characteristics of Good Oral Presentations.*

Formative Assessments: Information collection chart; Characteristics of the Biome chart

Summative Assessment: Presentation rubric for the oral presentation; evaluates both oral and visual components

*The following additional items were included in the actual unit plan: titles of informational texts that students would read, websites, copies of blank charts that students would complete, copy of the summative assessment, and list of teacher resources.

FIGURE 11.1. Sample unit plan.

in each classroom, he watched one student presentation and the post-presentation discussion. These teaching, planning, and observation opportunities enabled Nick to document his own reflections, providing a good foundation for facilitating a productive unit review meeting.

The teachers came to the unit review meeting with their completed reflection logs and their annotated unit plans. Figure 11.2 shows Tim O'Halloran's reflection log. Knowing that they had a lot to discuss during the 40-minute meeting, Nick

---

Teacher Name: _Tim O'Halloran_

Unit Name: _Biomes_   Length of Unit: _2 weeks and 2 days_

As you teach the unit, think about the following questions and take notes whenever possible. Write additional notes after the unit has been completed. These notes will be valuable when you meet with your grade-level team to reflect on the unit.

Reflection Items	Comments and Questions
Observations • What did the students do well? • What was difficult for them? • What did I do to address those difficult areas?	_Did well—information collection chart; positive feedback on presentations_ _Difficult—finding missing information for the Characteristics of the Biome chart; managing group discussions independently_ _I helped groups individually when I saw the problem—not very efficient_
Questions • Are the essential questions appropriate for the unit? If not, what revisions would be beneficial? • Are all of the standards critical for the unit? Should additional standards be added? • What other questions about the unit (e.g., about activities, instructional practices, assessments, time frame) do you want to discuss?	_Questions okay—but need one about listening and speaking during small-group work_ _Standards are good for the unit—no more please!_ _Grouping was a problem in my class—self-selection of biome led to one very small group (of 2) and one very large group (of 7); also not good mix of levels in groups_
Needs • What additional instructional resources (texts, student charts, websites) are needed? • What additional support from the coach would be helpful?	_Need more materials about deciduous and coniferous forests_ _Need to include a map where each group labels its biome_ _Coach—to co-plan or model lesson about finding specific information_

Additional Insights and Comments to Share with the Team

How can we group the students so all biomes are covered and so all groups have a mixture of high, average, and low readers?

Do we need to assess the students on their understanding of all biomes?

FIGURE 11.2. Example of a completed Unit Reflection Log.

efficiently guided the teachers to share their observations about the students; their comments about the essential questions, standards, instruction, and assessment; and their needs when teaching the unit the following year. He took notes about the decisions made during the meeting (see the summary of the unit review meeting in Figure 11.3).

Nick helped the teachers see how their observations might lead to important revisions of the unit plan. For example, when discussing the instructional activities, all three teachers agreed that their students had the most difficulty working well together to complete the small-group tasks. Nick said that he, too, had noticed that the students understood the tasks but did not exhibit the listening, speaking, and organizational skills needed to complete the tasks efficiently. This discussion led to the creation of a new essential question, "How do listening and speaking with others help me learn about a topic?" and a decision to add an activity where the whole class participated in the development of small-group norms or working rules. Nick commented that this activity would strengthen the attention to standard SL.4.1. He also noted that they might want to use a set of norms that the fifth-grade teachers had developed to guide their work.

When Nick moved the group's attention to the essential questions and standards, the teachers felt that the standards were appropriate for the unit, but two teachers wondered if they had focused enough on the second part of the essential question for social studies. Students sometimes commented on similarities and differences across biomes during the postpresentation discussions, but teachers had not intentionally included such comparisons in all discussions or in another activity. Thus, they had little to no evidence that their students could explain how biomes differed. They discussed how they might be able to compile the information from all of the Characteristics of the Biome charts into one large chart that could be used to compare and contrast the biomes during a culminating discussion, and Tanya volunteered to create a template for such a chart.

As Nick listened to the group, he was always alert for ways that he could support the teachers in their efforts to improve the biome unit. Teachers said that they needed more resources about two types of biomes. Knowing that finding resources can be time-consuming and that the teachers were busy starting their next unit, he offered to work with the learning center coordinator to find additional texts and websites. Nick would preview materials that the coordinator had found and then share appropriate ones with the fourth-grade team. Nick was alerted to another coaching opportunity when two teachers noted that many students had difficulty using texts to locate specific information that was missing from their Characteristics of the Biome charts. Since the students would need to be able to locate specific information for other projects later in the year, Nick offered to model a mini-lesson (see Strategy 14) in Rod Hildebrand's class and to arrange coverage of the other fourth-grade classrooms so Tanya and Tim could observe the demonstration lesson as well.

Nick ended the meeting by reviewing all of the decisions made by the team. He said that he would send them each a copy of the meeting summary, and Rod volunteered to update and distribute the unit plan. Rod mentioned that he felt the ongoing reflection logs had led to a thorough review of the unit and he planned to use the log as he implemented other units. Tanya agreed and added that she was eager to see how the changes they had made would increase the ability of next year's students to answer the essential questions and meet the specified standards.

Grade Level: *4th*

Unit: *Biomes*   Date of Reflection Meeting: *November 2*

Essential Questions:

* Social Studies: Team not sure if the students could explain how the biomes differ. Decided to find a way to compile information from all Characteristics of the Biome charts. Tanya Foster volunteered to work on this.
* Added a new essential question for ELA: How do listening and speaking with others help me learn about a topic?

Common Core Standards:

* Requiring domain-specific words on the information collection chart and the word wall were helpful in addressing RIT.4.4 and L.4.4. Students consistently used appropriate terminology during small-group work and during presentations.
* Need to focus more on W.4.8 and SL.4.1 (see Instructional Activities).

Instructional Activities:

* Need to include specific instruction on how to find information that is missing from the Characteristics of the Biome chart (W.4.8).
* Need to develop norms that the students can use when working in small groups. Tied to SL.4.1 and new essential question. Nick will share norms used by the fifth-grade students.
* Decided to limit presentation types to PowerPoint and trifold presentation boards. It took too long to explain all four options; can add other options to projects they do later in the year.
* Grouping—Teachers will preview all of the biomes and have students list their first, second, and third choices. Teachers can then form groups that take student choice, size, and ability levels into consideration.

Resources:

* Additional resources used during the unit were shared.
* Nick Giordano will work with Carla Tremayne, learning center coordinator, to find additional resources about deciduous and coniferous forests.
* Decided to add "example of the food chain" to the Characteristics of the Biome chart. Rod Hildebrand will incorporate this into the chart.

Assessments:

* Charts and presentations provided evidence that students could gather, compile, and present main ideas and key details about the biome they had specifically investigated. The teachers discussed, but did not decide, whether the students should be assessed on their knowledge of all biomes. Will revisit this issue before teaching the unit next year.

Revision of Unit Plan:

* Nick will distribute the meeting summary. Rod Hildebrand will update the unit plan and distribute the updated unit plan to Nick and all members of the fourth-grade team.

FIGURE 11.3. Example summary of a unit review meeting.

FORM 11.1

Unit Reflection Log

Teacher Name: _____

Unit Name: _____ Length of Unit: _____

As you teach the unit, think about the following questions and make notes in the second column. Write additional notes after the unit has been completed. These notes will be valuable when you meet with your grade-level team to reflect on the unit.

Reflection Items	Comments and Questions
Observations ◆ What did the students do well? ◆ What was difficult for them? ◆ What did I do to address those difficult areas?	
Questions ◆ Are the essential questions appropriate for the unit? If not, what revisions would be beneficial? ◆ Are all of the standards critical for the unit? Should additional standards be added? ◆ What other questions about the unit (e.g., about activities, instructional practices, assessments, time frame) do you want to discuss?	
Needs ◆ What additional instructional resources (texts, student charts, websites) are needed? ◆ What additional support from the coach would be helpful?	
Additional Insights and Comments to Share with the Team	

Conducting a Lesson Study

What Is It?

Lesson study is a powerful, embedded approach to professional development that originated in Japan and started to spread in schools in the United States in 1999 (Lewis, Perry, Hurd, & O'Connell, 2006). In lesson study, small groups of teachers collaboratively plan, observe, and analyze lessons to examine instructional practices and student outcomes closely (Lewis, 2004). Lesson study follows a four-phase process. In the first phase, teachers study the Common Core standards and their curriculum and determine a focus for the study lesson. In the second phase, they collaboratively plan a lesson, usually called the research lesson, related to a specific aspect of the Common Core. They also develop an approach for collecting data on the effectiveness of the research lesson. In the third phase, one teacher teaches the research lesson while the others observe and collect data. In the fourth phase, the group reviews the data. The process generally continues for a second cycle wherein the research lesson is refined, taught by another teacher in the group, and reflected on by the group.

Lesson study leads to ongoing instructional improvement through seven key pathways (Lewis, Perry, & Hurd, 2004). Namely, teachers build:

1 Increased knowledge of subject matter.

2 Increased knowledge of instruction.

3 Increased ability to observe students.

4 Stronger collegial networks.

5 Stronger connections between daily practice and long-term goals.

6 Stronger motivation and self-efficacy.

7 Greater skill in planning effective lessons.

The positive effects of lesson study extend beyond just the research lesson, transferring to teachers' instructional practice in general (DuFour & Marzano, 2011). Furthermore, lesson study can be an effective approach for helping teachers align their instruction with new educational initiatives or standards (Benedict, Park, Brownell, Lauterbach, & Kiely, 2013) such as the Common Core. In short, through lesson study, teachers are able "to engage in close examination of their classroom practices and reflect meaningfully on the degree to which students are achieving content standards" (Benedict et al., 2013, p. 23).

When you hear the term *lesson study,* your initial response might be that it is not possible in your school because you've heard that it is very time-consuming and requires lots of substitute teachers, which can stretch already tight school budgets. While those concerns can be true depending on how you implement lesson study, we urge you to find a way to make lesson study work in your school due to the impressive, long-term outcomes on the quality of instruction. As Frank De La Cruz, the principal of a large elementary school told us, "lesson study has been the single most effective professional development we've done in our school during the 10 years I've been principal." He went on to explain the impact of lesson study in his school by saying, "It has transformed the way the teachers think about instruction, plan lessons, and collaborate."

How Do I Do It?

When teachers first begin to engage in lesson study, it is essential that they have a knowledgeable, supportive facilitator, and as the literacy coach, you can serve in that important role. As teachers become more familiar and comfortable with lesson study, a teacher leader may take over the role as facilitator. Eventually, as some teams embrace lesson study as an ongoing aspect of their professional work, they may even choose to rotate the role of facilitator among members.

We recommend using a streamlined model of lesson study if this approach is new to your school. In this model, the team will meet two times (for 45–60 minutes) during regularly scheduled grade-level or PLC meetings and then spend a half day engaged in delivering, observing, analyzing, revising, and reflecting on the research lesson and its outcomes. For the half-day portion of the process, teachers will need to have coverage for their classrooms from substitute teachers or other staff members.

Getting Started

1 Determine the grade-level team or PLC you will be working with for the lesson study.

2 Schedule a preliminary meeting to ensure that the teachers understand the purpose, structure, and phases associated with completing the lesson study process. Discuss the benefits of the lesson study process, including the seven key pathways

toward long-term instructional improvement (Lewis et al., 2004). Explain the four-step process and the scheduling for implementation. Clarify that the group will meet twice to engage in Phases One and Two and then spend a half day engaged in Phases Three and Four of the lesson study process. An overview of the lesson study process is provided in Table 12.1.

Facilitating Lesson Study Sessions

Phase One: Study and Preparation

1 Explain to the team members that they will be studying the Common Core standards and their curriculum to identify a key area to focus on for the research lesson. You may wish to use the needs assessment (Form 2.1 from Strategy 2) to determine an instructional shift on which to focus.

2 Use prompts such as those listed below to facilitate a discussion among the teachers regarding the specific target for student learning:

   a "What do we want our students to know and be able to do in relation to this instructional shift or standard?"

   b "How does our curriculum address this instructional shift or standard?"

   c "Are there specific lessons in the textbook or other curriculum resources that address this instructional shift or standard?"

TABLE 12.1. Lesson Study Implementation Overview

Phase	Schedule and tasks to be completed

Phase One: Study and Preparation	• One meeting to:
	  o Review the Common Core standards and curriculum.
	  o Determine lesson focus and desired outcomes for students.

Phase Two: Plan the Research Lesson and Data Collection Approach	• One meeting to:
	  o Plan research lesson.
	  o Develop data collection plan.

Phase Three: Teach the Research Lesson	• One-half day to: o Have one team member teach the research lesson in his or her classroom while other members collect data.

Phase Four: Review Data and Reflect	• Share data, reflect, revise the research lesson if appropriate so another team member can teach the revised lesson in his or her classroom (return to Phase Three)
	• Reflect on key learning about
	  o Student learning
	  o Teaching practice
	  o Implications beyond the research lesson

3 Determine and confirm the specific focus that the lesson study will address. For example, the second-grade team at Mr. De La Cruz's school focused their research lesson on Reading Literature Standard 3, "Describe how characters in a story respond to major events and challenges." Because this standard is addressed in their core reading program, they planned to start with a lesson from the teacher's manual as the basis for developing their research lesson.

Phase Two: Plan the Research Lesson and Data Collection Plan

If lesson study is new to the group, we recommend using a lesson plan from a teacher's manual or other curricular resource as a starting place. If the teachers will be planning an entirely new lesson, that process may require an additional meeting.

1 Review the specific focus of the lesson, including the Common Core standard(s) it will address.

2 Share copies of the lesson plan from the teacher's manual or curricular resource that the group will be using as a starting place for their planning. If possible, display an electronic copy of the lesson using a projector so it is easy to see and to make changes. If a projector is not available, chart paper or a white board can be used to display the lesson plan.

3 "Talk" the teachers through the lesson by saying things like "First, the teacher does this. Then, the students are expected to do that."

4 Stop periodically to ask the teachers, such as:

    a "Does this make sense?"
    b "Does this seem like it would work well with our students?"
    c "Will this provide enough support for our English learners?"
    d "Does this seem like the best way to work toward the target standard(s)?"
    e "Are there better ways to do this?"

5 Facilitate a discussion among group members regarding the changes they would like to make to the lesson. Encourage group members to support their suggestions with specific reasons so everyone understands the proposed changes.

6 As the group decides on changes, note them on the lesson plan so you have an accurate record of the revised lesson. If you are using a computer and data projector to display the lesson plan, you can type the changes right into the document. If you are using chart paper or a white board, you can write the changes on the lesson plan itself.

7 Review the entire revised lesson plan, "talking" the teachers through the process as noted above in Step 3.

8 Ask the teachers to suggest any final changes to the lesson plan.

9 Discuss what specific outcomes you will expect from the students in terms of reading and writing behaviors as well as knowledge. Facilitate a discussion and record the ideas that the group agrees upon.

10 Shift the focus to how group members will collect data to determine the effectiveness of the lesson and the quality of student learning. An Observation Template is provided in Form 17.1 (from Strategy 17).

11 Determine which group member will teach the research lesson. Generally, this responsibility is rotated around the group, but it is also appropriate to ask for a volunteer. Also determine who will teach the revised research lesson.

12 Confirm the date, time, and location for the half-day meeting when the group will engage in Phases Three and Four of the lesson study process.

13 Let the teachers know when they will receive copies of the research lesson plan as well as the Observation Template. Be sure to get those materials to the teachers as far in advance as possible.

Phase Three: Teach the Lesson

1 Meet with the group to confirm the procedures for Phases Three and Four of the lesson study process. Remind the members who will be observing to use the Observation Template (Form 17.1 from Strategy 17) to record their notes. Confirm that the purpose of the observation is to critique the lesson, not the teacher and his or her teaching. Finally, remind the member who will be teaching the lesson to follow the lesson plan explicitly. If, however, the teacher does deviate from the lesson, ask the observers to be sure to record that information so they can discuss it when the group engages in Phase Four of the lesson study process.

2 Provide several minutes for the member who will be teaching to get to the classroom and prepare for the lesson. This member should also make sure that the students understand that the other teachers will be arriving soon to observe the lesson, but they will not participate in the lesson. This member will also make sure enough chairs are placed in the classroom so that the teachers will be able to see the lesson but not interfere with its delivery.

3 Quietly lead the observing teachers to the classroom so they can get settled before the lesson begins.

4 Stay in the classroom, and observe the lesson, recording your notes on the Observation Template.

5 When the lesson is over, thank the teacher and students, and lead the group members from the room back to the meeting space. The member who taught the lesson should also leave the classroom once the substitute teacher or other staff member arrives to cover the class.

Phase Four: Review Data and Reflect

1 As soon as all of the group members are back in the meeting location, remind them that the lesson belongs to all of them and encourage them to use terms such as *our lesson* and to focus on the students and lesson—not on their colleague's teaching.

2 Ask the member who taught the lesson to begin the discussion by sharing any difficulties experienced during the lesson.

3 Ask the other members to share the evidence they recorded related to each of the four questions on the Observation Template (Form 17.1 from Strategy 17).

4 Facilitate a discussion about what worked well with the lesson and what should be changed. Ask the teachers to support their ideas with specific evidence they recorded while observing the lesson.

5 Display the lesson plan (using a computer and projector, white board, or chart paper) and ask the group members to suggest changes that the evidence warrants. After consensus is reached, revise the lesson plan to reflect these changes.

6 "Talk" the teachers through the revised research lesson plan, making sure that the group agrees that the revisions reflect the changes deemed necessary due to the evidence collected from the observation.

7 Review the Observation Template and determine whether any changes are needed to reflect the revised research lesson plan.

8 Quickly prepare copies of the revised research lesson plan and Observation Template for group members.

9 Ask the member who will be teaching the revised lesson to go to his or her classroom to get ready to teach. When that teacher is ready, repeat the steps in Phase Three of the lesson study process.

10 Finally, after the lesson has been taught the second time, engage the group members in Steps 1–4 of Phase Four of the lesson study process.

11 To provide closure, engage the teachers in a discussion of what insights they gained through the process. Questions such as those below may be helpful to facilitate this discussion:

    a "What new insights and understandings do you now have?"
    b "How might you use what you learned from this lesson study?"

c "What worked well with our lesson study process and what might we want to change for the next time?"

d "What are our next steps?"

e "What questions remain that we might address in future lesson study cycles?"

Following Up

1 Send the group members a note (via e-mail or in their office mailboxes) thanking them for their participation, summarizing the new insights and understandings the group identified as a result of the lesson study, and reminding them what the next steps for the group will be regarding lesson study. A sample message is provided in Figure 12.1. The message is from Allison Wagner, the literacy coach at Central Elementary School, where Frank De La Cruz is the principal.

The Strategy in Action

Frank De La Cruz is the principal at Central Elementary School, and Allison Wagner is the literacy coach. Frank is a big supporter of the lesson study approach to professional development; therefore, he has worked with Allison to create a model that is very efficient and effective.

Dear Second-Grade Teachers:

Thanks so much for your hard work and great collaboration during our lesson study on Reading Literature Standard 3. We all learned a great deal about building our students' understanding of characters and how they respond and change in relation to the major events and challenges in stories. Based on my notes from our discussion, the main things we learned were:

1. Thinking aloud worked well to model how readers can connect character actions and changes to story events.
2. Some of the students needed more support than just a story map to track the changes in a character across the story. Perhaps a graphic organizer that focuses on character change over time would be helpful. These students also might benefit from more explicit instruction and guided practice related to this standard during guided reading instruction.

We decided to discuss our next steps at our grade-level meeting next Monday afternoon.

Have a great day!

Allison

FIGURE 12.1. Follow-up message after lesson study process.

Frank explained:

"I ask each grade-level team to do a lesson study each quarter. I wish they could do it more often, and some grade levels do. At least if I ask them to do it quarterly, I know that every classroom teacher is engaged in this process four times per year. On lesson study days, we have two grade levels involved. One grade level does lesson study in the morning, and the other grade level does it in the afternoon. I get one set of subs and they spend half the day in one grade level and half of the day in the other grade level. When the research lessons are being taught, I even ask the subs to stay and watch so they understand the types of instruction we are trying to provide in our school. Lesson study days can be a bit hectic for Allison, but this structure has worked well for us."

Allison, the literacy coach, then went on to explain:

"We usually do a lesson study day about every 3 weeks. Mr. De La Cruz is right; lesson study days can be hectic, but in several of the grade levels, the teacher leaders are ready to take over with facilitating lesson study by the second quarter. In almost all the other grade levels, they take over by the third quarter. I still sit in on some of their meetings when my schedule allows, but the teams take ownership and control over the process. Mr. De La Cruz also likes to sit in on some of the lesson study meetings too, mainly to show his support and to stay informed about what the teachers are addressing. While the process seemed overwhelming to me in the beginning, we have found that we have our most meaningful conversations and truly enhance our understanding of instruction through lesson study."

PART FOUR

Individual Coaching
toward the Common Core

When many educators hear the term *literacy coaching* they envision a literacy coach working with an individual teacher. That image is accurate because supporting individual teachers is a cornerstone of literacy coaching (Toll, 2005). By working with an individual teacher, the coach can tailor coaching support to meet the specific needs and goals of that teacher. As noted earlier in this book, an effective literacy coaching program includes three layers of coaching support—large-group coaching, small-group coaching, and individual coaching. While it is true that individual coaching is time intensive, it is also highly effective in terms of helping teachers enhance their classroom literacy environments (De Alba-Johnston et al., 2004), implement best practices and new instructional strategies effectively (Blachowicz, Obrochta, & Fogelberg, 2005), and accept change in a positive manner (Symonds, 2003). Furthermore, research shows that individual coaching support can contribute to meaningful literacy gains for students in those classrooms (Biancarosa, Bryk, & Dexter, 2010; Elish-Piper & L'Allier, 2011).

Because individual literacy coaching is time intensive, it is important to ensure that time spent working with individual teachers is purposeful and effective. To that end, we offer six research-based coaching strategies (L'Allier, Elish-Piper, & Bean, 2010) to support individual teachers as they enhance their teaching to meet the demands of the Common Core. We anticipate that due to the intensity of these strategies, they are most appropriately implemented by the literacy coach, who will have time in his or her schedule designated for working with individual teachers. If your school provides release time for teacher leaders to work with other teachers, then they may be able to implement some of these strategies with their colleagues.

The six strategies in this part are presented separately, and it is appropriate to implement a single individual coaching strategy with a teacher. It is also important to note that Strategies 13 (Setting Goals), 14 (Modeling), 15 (Co-Planning), 16 (Co-Teaching), and 17 (Observing) can be linked together to implement a complete coaching cycle. This cycle is described in Strategy 18.

Setting instructional goals is key to effective planning and teaching. In Strategy 13 we illustrate how you can help individual teachers determine and set goals to provide focus for enhancing their instructional practice. When implementing a new initiative such as the Common Core, teachers may be overwhelmed with trying to address so many different aspects of the standards all at the same time. By helping teachers set specific goals and develop plans to move toward those goals, literacy coaching can help individual teachers enhance their teaching toward the Common Core.

At times teachers may struggle to envision or enact new instructional strategies into their teaching. By having the literacy coach model the instructional strategy, that teacher can see it in action with his or her own students. In Strategy 14 we describe how the literacy coach can support individual teachers through modeling instructional strategies. A key aspect of modeling includes conferencing with the teacher before and after the modeled lesson to help the teacher develop a thorough understanding of the instructional strategy and its implementation.

Co-planning (Strategy 15) provides a purposeful setting for the literacy coach and an individual teacher to work side by side to discuss instructional planning, select instructional materials, and determine anticipated student outcomes as they plan a lesson. Co-teaching (Strategy 16) is a coaching strategy that allows the coach and an individual teacher to collaboratively teach a lesson in the teacher's classroom. In co-teaching, the coach and teacher determine in advance which parts of the lesson each will lead. An important aspect of co-teaching is the conferencing that the coach and teacher do before and after the lesson to prepare for and reflect on the lesson. Strategies 15 (Co-Planning) and 16 (Co-Teaching) are often linked as the literacy coach works with an individual teacher to co-plan and then to co-teach the lesson.

Strategy 17 focuses on the coach observing an individual teacher to offer supportive feedback and insights. Generally, the teacher identifies specific questions or concerns to guide the coach's observation. The coach observes as a helpful peer to offer support, encouragement, and useful suggestions.

Finally, Strategy 18 describes the literacy coaching cycle. In the literacy coaching cycle, the coach works with an individual teacher over an extended period of time (from several days to several weeks) to move through the entire process of setting goals (Strategy 13), modeling (Strategy 14), co-planning (Strategy 15), co-teaching (Strategy 16), and observing (Strategy 17). If their schedules permit, a coach and teacher may go through several coaching cycles as they work together to address specific aspects of instruction, student learning, and standards.

While all of the teachers in your school will not request or require individual coaching, this layer of coaching is essential for an effective literacy coaching program. By implementing the individual coaching strategies in Part Four, you will be able to provide the types of support that some teachers will need as they update their instructional practices to address the Common Core standards.

··············· **Strategy 13** ···············

Setting Goals

What Is It?

Goal setting is an essential component of professional development for teachers. Lyons and Pinnell (2001) argue that teachers tend to be goal oriented. "They generally have a set of goals and/or issues they are facing at a particular time, and they want to resolve these problems or issues *now*" (p. 3). When literacy coaches help teachers to determine and set specific goals for enhancing their instructional practice and their students' literacy learning, those goals can serve to motivate and guide teachers' professional learning (Bandura, 2001).

Goal setting is especially important when teachers are faced with initiatives that require new professional learning and changes to their practice (May, 2010). As we discussed in Chapter 1, change can be frustrating and overwhelming for teachers. According to the concerns-based adoption model (CBAM), when teachers enter the personal and management phases of the change process, they are concerned about how to enact new practices in their teaching (Hall & Hord, 1987; see Chapter 1, Figure 2, of the current book). These are the stages of the change process where many teachers "get stuck" because these stages involve the complexity of teaching and learning in classrooms such as varied student needs and organization and management issues, as well as increasing expectations and standards for student learning. Given the scope of the Common Core and the related instructional shifts, it is not surprising that some teachers might not know where or how to begin to change their instructional practices to address the CCSS. Working with the literacy coach to determine and set specific goals can be a productive way to help these teachers focus their efforts and move their teaching intentionally toward the Common Core.

An effective approach to setting goals is the use of the SMART goal format (DuFour, DuFour, Eaker, & Many, 2010). The characteristics of SMART goals are provided in Figure 13.1.

```
SMART Goals are:

Specific:      They identify exactly what the teacher is going to do.

Measurable:   They include criteria for measuring progress toward the goal.

Attainable:    They focus on a goal that is challenging and meaningful yet "do-able."

Relevant:      They address a practical issue that aligns with district and school priorities.

Timely:        They set a timeline for completion during the school year.
```

FIGURE 13.1. SMART goals.

A main benefit of SMART goals is that they provide sufficient detail and direction to guide teachers' professional learning. While there are other ways that coaches can help teachers set goals, we recommend the SMART goal-setting approach in this strategy.

How Do I Do It?

After implementing some of the large- and small-group coaching strategies outlined in Chapters 3 and 4, you may find that certain teachers in your school are overwhelmed by the number of standards and the associated instructional shifts. Working with those teachers to set specific goals for their instruction is an effective way to help them focus their attention and efforts. In this strategy, we address setting goals as a stand-alone coaching activity; however, you may find that setting goals with a teacher can lead to other individual coaching strategies such as modeling (Strategy 14), co-planning (Strategy 15), co-teaching (Strategy 16), and observing (Strategy 17), as well as follow-up meetings to discuss progress toward goals. However, for some teachers simply providing support to help them set goals may be sufficient to move their teaching forward toward the Common Core.

1 Set a time to meet with the teacher. Generally 20 minutes is sufficient for a goal-setting conference. Meet in the teacher's classroom or in the space where the teacher plans lessons so instructional materials, assessments, lesson plans, calendar, copies of the CCSS, and other planning tools are handy.

2 To begin the goal-setting conference, discuss the prompts provided in Figure 13.2.

3 Share the SMART goal characteristics from Figure 13.1, emphasizing that SMART goals are specific, measurable, attainable, relevant, and timely.

4 Show the teacher the SMART Goal-Setting Template (Form 13.1). Talk through the template with the teacher to guide the goal-setting process. Use prompts such as "What else are you thinking?" and "What questions do you have?" to keep the conversation going.

5 After you and the teacher have completed Form 13.1, review the SMART goal to ensure that the teacher is comfortable with it and that it is specific, measurable, attainable, relevant, and timely. If necessary, make changes to the goal or template to reflect your conversation.

6 Make a copy of the template for yourself so you and the teacher each have a copy.

7 Follow up with the teacher to provide coaching support as described on Form 13.1 in the box "Coaching Support Needed to Work toward the Goal."

The Strategy in Action

Jessica Rivers is a reading specialist who spends about 25% of her time coaching teachers, 25% delivering push-in reading instruction in classrooms, and 50% providing small-group reading interventions for K–2 students. After participating in several large- and small-group coaching strategies, Anne Marie Miller, a kindergarten teacher with 3 years of experience, approached Jessica saying, "I have learned so many good ideas about how I can help my students meet the Common Core standards, but I just don't know what to do first. I feel overwhelmed and pulled in so many different directions! Since my kindergarten classes only meet for a half-day, I just don't know where to begin." Jessica responded, "Anne Marie, I understand completely. It might help for us to meet to set a SMART goal so you can focus your efforts toward a specific aspect of the Common Core. What do you think? Would you like to meet to work on setting a goal?" Anne Marie responded, "Yes, I'd love to meet so I can sort out my ideas and develop a plan!" She and Jessica identified a time later that week when they could meet. Jessica started the meeting

---

- ◆ "Do you have specific concerns related to student performance on recent assessments?"
  - • "If so, what are your concerns?"

- ◆ "Are there specific standards or clusters of standards that you want to address in your teaching?"
  - • "If so, what are they?"

- ◆ "If your grade-level team has prepared pacing guides, do they raise any concerns for you in terms of instruction or student progress?"
  - • "If so, what are those concerns?"

- ◆ "As you look at the ideas from above, are there any patterns or connections?"
  - • "If so, what are they?"

FIGURE 13.2. Discussion prompts for a goal-setting conference.

by sharing the information on what a SMART goal is from Figure 13.1. She then engaged in a conversation with Anne Marie, using the prompts from Figure 13.2. Anne Marie discussed concerns about her kindergarten students' vocabulary. She explained, "Many of the students seem to have limited vocabularies. They are not familiar with words I think they should know such as *above*, *before*, and *rule*. I know how important having a strong vocabulary is to being successful in school." From their conversation, they agreed that Anne Marie would focus her smart goal on Language Standards 4, 5, and 6 that address vocabulary acquisition and use. They completed Form 13.1 together; a copy of that completed template is provided in Figure 13.3. Jessica and Anne Marie also compared their schedules to set meeting times to ensure that they will be able to meet as outlined in the plan. At the end of the meeting Anne Marie shared, "I am so excited: This SMART goal will really focus my teaching on my students' vocabulary needs. I think that after I get used to doing this in my practice, I will be able to shift my attention to addressing another of the instructional shifts. It really helped having you walk and talk me through the SMART goal-setting process!"

SMART Goal Considerations	My Plans
SPECIFIC	General focus: *Language*
	Specific Common Core standard(s) to be addressed by the goal: *Language 4, 5, and 6 at kindergarten level*
	Tells exactly what I will do: *Yes :) See below.*
MEASURABLE	How will I be able to demonstrate my progress toward this goal? *Weekly lesson plans will specify words, instructional activities, and practice/application opportunities provided. I will also use informal assessment to document student vocabulary growth. I will work with Jessica to set expectations, but I plan to target at least 80% of the students knowing and being able to use all 10 of the words from the week.*
ATTAINABLE	Is my goal challenging and meaningful, yet "do-able"? *Yes, by focusing on one week at a time with 10 words per week, I only have to teach 2 new words per day, but that will total 90 words per quarter or 360 words per year!*
RELEVANT	My goal aligns with district and/or school priorities because . . . *We are working on the CCSS, and these language standards are especially important for kindergarteners. Our school has selected the "academic vocabulary" shift as one of our schoolwide priorities because we have so many low-income and EL students in our school who do not have well-developed vocabularies.*
TIMELY	Timeline for meeting my goal: *I will begin to implement my action plan within 2 weeks. I will implement the plan for the entire quarter. If it goes well, I will make this approach an ongoing part of my teaching and move on to another SMART goal.*
Strategies to Work toward the Goal	My action plan to work toward this goal: ◆ *Daily read-alouds to introduce words* ◆ *Strategies from Beck, McKeown, and Kucan (2013)* ◆ *Daily practice/application opportunities* ◆ *Weekly informal assessment*
Coaching Support Needed to Work toward the Goal	The literacy coach will do these things to support my work toward this goal: ◆ *Jessica will meet with me this week to:* • *Select words for the first month of instruction and to identify resource materials.* • *Select or develop the informal vocabulary assessment I'll use and determine expectations for student performance.*

Summary of My SMART Goal: *I will develop my expertise with teaching Tier Two vocabulary so I can teach 8–10 new Tier Two words each week using specific strategies from* Bringing Words to Life *(Beck et al., 2013). My instruction will address CCSS Language Standards 4, 5, and 6 at the kindergarten level. I will also plan and provide multiple opportunities for students to use these words in their reading, writing, listening, and speaking. I will informally assess student progress weekly to determine if my instructional approach needs to be modified to be more effective.*

FIGURE 13.3. SMART Goal-Planning Template completed with Anne Marie Miller.

SMART Goal-Setting Template

SMART Goal Considerations	My Plans
SPECIFIC	General focus: Specific Common Core standard(s) to be addressed by the goal: Tells exactly what I will do:
MEASURABLE	How will I be able to demonstrate my progress toward this goal?
ATTAINABLE	Is my goal challenging and meaningful, yet "do-able"?
RELEVANT	My goal aligns with district and/or school priorities because . . .
TIMELY	Timeline for meeting my goal:
Strategies to Work toward the Goal	My action plan to work toward this goal:
Coaching Support Needed to Work toward the Goal	The literacy coach will do these things to support my work toward this goal:
Summary of My SMART Goal:	

Modeling

What Is It?

In effective schools, teachers and allied professionals have a shared vision of good teaching. By modeling lessons, literacy coaches can make teaching and learning visible so that a common vision of effective instruction can be developed across the school. That common vision can then serve as a road map for ongoing professional development efforts (Wagner, 2003). This process is especially important as teachers work to update their teaching to address the Common Core and the related instructional shifts. When literacy coaches model an instructional strategy or approach in a teacher's classroom, he or she can see the coach "interacting with students, managing behaviors, juggling instructional materials, pacing the lesson to keep students engaged, checking for understanding, and making necessary adjustments" (Casey, 2011, p. 24). By seeing the instruction in action with their own students, teachers are more able to understand how to implement the strategy or approach into their own practice (Knight, 2009a).

Modeling is well aligned with the principles of adult learning theory discussed in Chapter 1 (Knowles, 1970). In addition, modeling addresses some of the most challenging aspects of the change process as outlined in CBAM (Hall & Hord, 1987; see Chapter 1 of the current book). Namely, modeling addresses the personal and management stages of the change process wherein teachers are most concerned about how they plan to implement new instructional approaches, organize their schedules, and deal with other logistics of teaching.

To be effective, modeling must be purposeful and planned so that the modeled lesson is designed to address the specific issues, methods, and concerns about which the teacher wants to learn more. Furthermore, the teacher's observation of the modeled lesson must also be purposeful so it ensures that the teacher is engaged and focused on the key aspects of the instructional practice, as well as related management and organizational issues (Darling-Hammond & Richardson, 2009).

How Do I Do It?

After a large- or small-group coaching activity, a teacher may approach you and ask, "What does that strategy look like in the classroom?" or "I can't figure out how to implement this strategy with my students in my classroom. Can you help?" This is a great opportunity for you to work with an individual teacher to model the strategy or approach in his or her classroom; however, you need to make sure that the modeling is purposeful and planned. Therefore, this strategy includes a preconference and a postconference to ensure that you and the teacher set the specific purpose for the modeled lesson and then debrief and reflect on the lesson after it has been taught. An extra benefit of modeling instruction is that it gives you an opportunity to demonstrate that you are a capable teacher and are willing to take a risk and grow professionally (Casey, 2006). These things contribute to the sense that you are a professional learning partner for the teacher.

Before the Conference

1 Schedule a short meeting with the teacher to discuss what he or she would like to see modeled.

2 Determine the purpose for the modeled lesson. A planning template is provided in Form 14.1 to ensure that the purpose and plan for the modeled lesson are clear to both the coach and the teacher.

3 Develop an observation form for the teacher to use to focus his or her observations during the modeled lesson. The observation form should be aligned directly with the purpose of the modeled lesson. An observation form template is provided in Form 14.2.

4 Discuss that the teacher's role during the modeled lesson is to observe, not to co-teach or to participate. Talk to the teacher about how one of you will explain the teacher's role as observer during the modeled lesson to the students.

5 Work with the teacher to fill in the top of the observation template (Form 14.2), as well as the left column, prior to the lesson. Doing so will ensure that the teacher is prepared to focus his or her attention on how the modeled lesson addresses the specific CCSS or instructional shift.

6 Set the date and time for the modeled lesson. Be sure that there is sufficient time for the coach to plan the lesson as it is essential that modeled lessons be well planned and directly aligned with the teacher's stated purpose.

7 Set the date and time for the postconference. If possible, it should be scheduled later the same day as the modeled lesson or the next day so that the lesson is still fresh in the minds of both the teacher and coach.

Preparing for the Modeled Lesson

1 After meeting with the teacher, plan the lesson so that it aligns directly with the purpose set by the teacher as well as the target Common Core standards or instructional shifts.

2 Prepare materials and gather necessary supplies for the lesson.

3 Confirm the date and time for the lesson with the teacher. Also provide the teacher with a copy of the lesson plan as well as the observation form you developed during the preconference.

The Modeled Lesson

1 Arrive a few minutes early to organize your materials and ensure that the teacher has an appropriate place from which to observe the lesson. The location should allow the teacher to see the coach and the students. The teacher will need a chair and a desk, table, or clipboard to aid with note taking. Also, be sure the teacher has a copy of the observation template (Form 14.2).

2 Explain the format for the modeled lesson to the students. You may say something like:

> "Students, today I will be teaching a lesson on close reading. Your teacher will be watching me teach the lesson. She will be taking notes as an observer, but she will not be participating in the lesson. You will need to think of me as your teacher for this lesson. That means you will need to pay attention to me, ask me any questions, and pretend that your teacher is not here during the lesson. At times, I may need to talk to your teacher about the lesson. I will say 'Push *pause*' like on a DVD player so I can talk to your teacher for a few seconds. When I am done talking to your teacher, I will say 'Push *play*' so we can get back to the lesson."

If this format is new to students, you may want to practice this format for a moment, or you may want to ask if they have questions before beginning the lesson.

3 Provide time for the teacher to move to the observation location before beginning the lesson.

4 Teach the lesson, making sure to follow the plan as closely as possible.

5 If you need to modify the lesson based on student response or understanding, use the "push *pause*" technique to ake a moment to tell the teacher what you are doing and why. As soon as you are done, use the "push *play*" technique to resume the lesson.

6 You may also want to use the "push *pause*" technique to draw the teacher's attention to a specific aspect of the lesson or to clarify the purpose of an aspect of your instruction.

7 At the end of the lesson, tell the students that their teacher will now be coming back to his or her role as teacher. Clarify that the students need to resume paying attention to their own teacher.

After the Conference

1 Begin the conference by reviewing the purpose of the modeling.

2 Ask the teacher to share his or her notes from the observation form.

3 Discuss the teacher's observations and comments, sharing your own insights as well.

4 Discuss whether the teacher feels that the purpose of the modeled lesson has been met.

5 Ask the teacher if he or she would like any additional coaching support related to the instructional strategy or approach in the modeled lesson. For example, some teachers may request that the coach co-plan and co-teach a lesson to ensure that they are comfortable incorporating the strategy into their own practice. Some teachers may request a follow-up conference in a week or two after they have tried to implement the strategy into their own practice. And other teachers may decide that they do not need additional coaching support because the modeling and postconference addressed all of their questions.

The Strategy in Action

Focus on Planning for the Modeled Lesson in Grade 5

Christine O'Malley is a reading specialist who spends about a third of her time coaching. She devotes the remainder of her time to providing small-group reading interventions for struggling readers in grades K–5. After a recent grade-level team meeting focused on developing an implementation guide related to Reading Standard 1, Patti Guzowski, a fifth-grade teacher, approached Christine and explained, "I understand the implementation guide we developed, but I am not sure what a lesson would look like related to Reading Standard 1." Christine responded, "Patti, I could come in and model a lesson designed around Reading Standard 1. We could have a preconference to plan the lesson, I'd model the lesson, and then we can have a postconference to talk through what you observed and the questions you have about the lesson. Do you think that would be helpful?" Patti responded, "Yes, that would be great!"

At their preconference meeting, Christine and Patti worked through the planning template (Form 14.1). The template they filled out is provided in Figure 14.1. They discussed the purpose for Patti's observation of the lesson and prepared an observation form for use when the lesson was being taught. Christine planned and modeled a lesson using a two-page segment of the new social studies textbook. The lesson included a think-aloud and guided practice on how to quote accurately from the text to explain what the text said explicitly, as well as to make logical inferences. Because Patti's students enjoy small-group discussions, Christine included several opportunities for students to talk in small groups to formulate their responses before sharing with the whole class. After Christine modeled the lesson, they had their postconference, focusing on the comments Patti had written on her observation form. At the end of their conference, Patti commented, "That was so helpful! I get what close reading means now! Seeing you model the lesson in my classroom with my students made all the difference in the world."

Purpose for Modeling	◆ I want the coach to develop and model a lesson that will allow me to learn . . . *what close reading looks like with informational text. I want to learn about how to help kids quote from the text to support their responses.* ◆ Specific questions or concerns I have are . . . *I don't want to quiz the kids when I'm teaching . . . "What is this?" or "What quote supports that?" I'm also concerned about how to model my thinking related to close reading.*
Common Core Standards	◆ What Common Core standard(s) will the modeled lesson address? *RIT.5.1 "Quote accurately from a text when explaining what the text says explicitly and when drawing inferences from the text."* ◆ What do I want to see in the lesson related to the standard(s)? *I want to see this process modeled for students. What do I say and do to get students quoting accurately from a text? How do explain or model the process for them?*
Lesson Ideas	◆ What is the objective for the lesson? *The students will quote accurately from a social studies text to respond to questions about: (1) What the text says explicitly and (2) inferences that can be drawn from the text.* ◆ Are there specific materials the coach should use in the lesson? If so, what are they? *I'd like to address this standard with the new social studies textbook.* ◆ What is the grouping for the lesson—whole group, small group? *Social studies is taught to the whole group so I'd like to see a whole-group lesson.* ◆ Are there other considerations that the coach should have in mind when planning the modeled lesson? *There are several ELs in my classroom that may not have background knowledge or the vocabulary knowledge related to the topic. I also have one student who has an IEP for a learning disability in reading. My students are pretty talkative, and they enjoy whole-group and small-group discussions.*

FIGURE 14.1. Sample Modeling Planning Template for RIT.5.1.

Focus on Teacher Observation of the Modeled Lesson in Grade 1

Alexis Barnes is a full-time literacy coach, and Paul Shepherd is an experienced first-grade teacher. After a recent lesson study (see Strategy 12), Paul explained:

"I really learned a lot from working on close reading during the lesson study. I have tried to incorporate close reading into my instruction. Unfortunately, I feel like I'm just asking a series of questions rather than having a discussion about a book. I don't think the students are really reading closely. I also worry that I'm not providing enough instruction for my students to ask questions. Could you come in and do a lesson to model what close reading of literature looks like in first grade?"

Teacher: *Paul Shepherd*   Date: *October 22*

Lesson Description: *Close reading with Nothing Like a Puffin (Soltis, 2011) to model how to ask and answer questions about key details in the story. This will be a small-group guided reading lesson with five students.*

Common Core Standard(s) Addressed: *RL 1.1: "Ask and answer questions about key details in a text."*

Teaching Practice	CCSS or Instructional Shift	Observed	Comments
Modeling how to answer questions about key details in the story	*RL.1.1* *Close Reading*		
Modeling how to ask questions about key details in the story	*RL.1.1* *Close Reading*		
Thinking aloud	*RL.1.1* *Close Reading*		
Explicit explanations of processes associated with close reading	*RL.1.1* *Close Reading*		
Guided practice	*RL.1.1* *Close Reading*		
Other observations, issues, or questions:			

FIGURE 14.2. Sample Observation Form for RL.1.1.

Alexis agreed and they had a preconference to determine the purpose for the modeled lesson as well as the purpose for the observation. Because Paul had so many specific things he wanted the modeled lesson to address, he and Alexis spent most of their preconference discussing the purpose for the observation and the development of the observation form (see Figure 14.2). Paul would then use the observation form as he watched Alexis teach the lesson, and they would discuss his observations at the postconference.

Modeling Planning Template

Purpose for Modeling	◆ I want the coach to develop and model a lesson that will allow me to learn . . . ◆ Specific questions or concerns I have are . . .
Common Core Standards	◆ What Common Core standard(s) will the modeled lesson address? ◆ What do I want to see in the lesson related to the standard(s)?
Lesson Ideas	◆ What is the objective for the lesson? ◆ Are there specific materials the coach should use in the lesson? If so, what are they? ◆ What is the grouping for the lesson—whole group, small group? ◆ Are there other considerations that the coach should have in mind when planning the modeled lesson?

FORM 14.2

Observation Form Template for Modeling

Teacher: _____ Date: _____

Lesson Description: _____

_____

_____

Common Core Standard(s) Addressed: _____

_____

Teaching Practice	CCSS or Instructional Shift	Observed	Comments
Other observations, issues, or questions:			

Co-Planning

What Is It?

A literacy coach is often referred to as someone with whom teachers can think and problem solve. Co-planning provides the perfect opportunity for this type of interaction. Whether co-planning a lesson, a series of lessons, or even an entire unit, the teacher and coach think together, making decisions about purpose, instruction, materials, and assessment (Harrison & Killion, 2007; Murawski, 2012). They are, in effect, putting the planning process into slow motion so that they have time to examine relevant student data and address the critical components of the lesson before actual teaching begins. Careful planning that leads to purposeful instruction results in enhanced student learning (Stronge, 2007).

Co-planning can be initiated for a variety of reasons. Teachers may want to co-plan instruction about an aspect of literacy with which their students are struggling (Moran, 2007). When, for example, a teacher has taught several lessons about making inferences from text but informal assessments show that many students are still unable to make inferences on their own, he or she may be unsure of what additional instruction would be beneficial. Meeting with the literacy coach to discuss the previous lessons and co-plan the next lesson provides that teacher with the assistance needed to move forward with purposeful instruction. Teachers also may find it helpful to co-plan when they are preparing to teach a strategy or skill for the first time (Moran, 2007), which may be the case as they adapt their instruction to address the Common Core standards. A fourth-grade teacher, for example, may seek the help of the literacy coach to think through a lesson that addresses standard RIT.4.8: "Explain how an author uses reasons and evidence to support particular points in a text," a skill that he or she has not taught in previous years.

Co-planning can be effective in enhancing teacher practice when used as a stand-alone coaching activity or as a part of a coaching cycle. As a stand-alone activity, it can easily fit into the schedules of coaches because they can hold co-planning meetings with teachers before or after school or during a teacher's planning period. Co-planning, classified by Moran as a relatively "less intrusive" (2007, p. 13) coaching activity, may also appeal to teachers who would like support with their teaching but are hesitant to have coaches come into their classrooms to observe or co-teach. However, co-planning is often linked to other coaching activities (Casey, 2006). The coach and teacher may co-plan a lesson that they will then co-teach (see Strategy 16) or that the coach will observe (see Strategy 17). Regardless of the context, opportunities to co-plan enable teachers to develop and enhance the decision-making skills related to instructional planning.

How Do I Do It?

As you co-plan lessons, you will find that teachers differ in the amount of assistance they need. Think back to the discussion of coaching stances in Chapter 2 as you prepare for your co-planning sessions. Some teachers may have developed lessons that they want to share with you; they are looking for confirmation that they are moving in the right direction or they may want to refine specific aspects of their lessons. With these teachers, you generally will take the facilitating stance, paraphrasing what you hear and asking clarifying questions. Other teachers may have some ideas for their lessons but want to gather more information. In these cases, you often will take the collaborative stance where you and the teacher will exchange ideas about instruction, assessment, and materials as you co-plan the lesson. Finally, some teachers will tell you they are at a loss as to how to approach the teaching of a particular strategy or skill. With these teachers, you likely will begin with the consulting stance, where you take the lead in the co-planning process by explaining each step of the process and offering specific suggestions as needed.

Regardless of the stance you take during the co-planning process, using a lesson planning template (see Form 15.1) will enable you to move through the process efficiently. It will also provide teachers with a procedure they can use in the future when they co-plan with colleagues or independently.

Preparing for the Co-Planning Session

1 Schedule a time and place for the co-planning meeting. You can generally co-plan a single lesson in 20–30 minutes. If possible, schedule the meeting in the teacher's classroom so materials related to the lesson will be easy to access.

2 When you set the time for the meeting, confirm the purpose of the lesson so that you can begin thinking about what you need to do to prepare for the meeting. For example, you may want to think about instructional strategies that could be incorporated into the lesson. You may also want to locate some texts that the teacher could use during the lesson.

3 Gather any materials you need for the meeting (e.g., resources, professional books

that describe strategies, copy of the CCSS) and make a copy of the Co-Planning Template (Form 15.1).

Facilitating the Co-Planning Session

1 Arrive at the meeting on time. This shows that you value the opportunity to work with the teacher and that you respect his or her busy schedule.

2 Share the Co-Planning Template and explain how it will assist the two of you in completing the lesson planning in a timely fashion.

3 Review the purpose or objective of the lesson and write it on the lesson plan template. This can be stated in general terms. For example, Meg Bloomfield, a first-grade teacher, told Tricia Jimenez, the coach, that her students could not tell her which character was speaking when they read dialogue, and she wanted to plan a lesson to help her students figure out who was talking.

4 Guide the teacher in using the purpose to develop a more precise explanation of what the students will be expected to do as a result of the lesson. With the first-grade lesson that Tricia and Meg were co-planning they decided that, by the end of the lesson, Meg's students should be able to identify the characters represented by the pronouns *she*, *he*, *I*, and *they* when they are used in phrases that are attached to dialogue in literature (e.g., "She said," "He yelled," "I asked").

5 Discuss which Common Core standards the lesson will address. Many teachers are just beginning to align their daily instruction to the Common Core standards and will appreciate your helping them pinpoint one or two standards that are most closely related to the purpose of the lesson.

6 Think through the academic vocabulary that the students will need to know in order to understand the lesson. Because it is important to provide multiple opportunities for the teacher and the students to use that vocabulary during the lesson, it is crucial to identify the specific terms before moving on to planning the instructional steps. You can point out that sometimes the academic vocabulary can be found right in the Common Core standards, but that teachers need to carefully consider what additional terms may need to be listed. For example, while Tricia and Meg agreed to list the word *identify* from standard RL.1.6, Meg suggested that *dialogue* be added and Tricia explained why they might also want to include the term *pronoun*.

7 The instructional steps are the heart of lesson planning. The template includes space for you to list both teacher and student activities.

   a Work together to develop the teacher's instructional steps. Help the teacher align the instruction with the gradual release-of-responsibility model that includes explicit explanation, modeling, guided practice, and independent practice (Fisher & Frey, 2008).

◆ Remind teachers that most lessons begin with an explicit explanation about the purpose of the lesson. Share how you would provide that explicit explanation to the students. Jot down some of the key phrases on the planning template as a reminder for the teacher.

◆ Discuss ways the teacher could model the strategy so students know exactly what is expected of them. "Think-alouds," where teachers explain their thinking as they work through the strategy, have been found to be an effective method of modeling (Block & Israel, 2004).

◆ Next, help the teacher decide how the students will apply the strategy themselves, with the support of the teacher and/or peers. This guided practice is an essential component of the learning cycle; explicit explanation and modeling are not sufficient for students to move on to independence.

◆ Guide the teacher in developing a meaningful closure to the lesson. For example, the teacher can help the students summarize what they have learned and how the activities in which they engaged help them become better readers (or writers or listeners or speakers).

b For each instructional activity listed on the teacher side of the chart, discuss what the teacher will be expecting the students to do. "Actively listen" might be written next to the explicit explanation and the modeling activities. "Partner reading of text" or "small-group completion of graphic organizer" might apply to some of the guided practice activities.

8 Develop a complete list of the materials needed for the lesson so that the teacher can be sure he or she has gathered all of the necessary materials before starting to teach the lesson. Include texts that students will read as well as texts that teachers will use when modeling. Graphic organizers, maps, globes, and technology should also be listed. Circle any materials (e.g., graphic organizers, anchor charts) that need to be developed.

9 Carefully consider what evidence will be used to determine whether the students have met the expectations described in the second section of the template. Informal assessments (anecdotal notes, class checklists, completed graphic organizers) will generally provide the necessary data. You may need to explain possible assessments and/or help the teacher develop the assessment. For example, you can show the teacher how to use a class checklist to designate the level of teacher support (i.e., a lot, some, none) that each student needed to accomplish the purpose. Explain how checklists like this can help determine what additional instruction is needed by the whole class or by specific students.

10 Ask the teacher how you can provide support as he or she implements the lesson. Some teachers may feel that the co-planning session has prepared them to teach the lesson; therefore, they need no additional support. Others may ask if you could teach part of the lesson—perhaps the part that they see as most challenging (see Strategy 16). Still others may ask if you could come in and observe the lesson. If

that happens, you will want to set specific purposes for the observation (see Strategy 17).

11 Regardless of whether you are involved in the implementation of the lesson, you should schedule a time to discuss how the lesson went. This meeting should take place when the lesson is fresh in the teacher's mind, preferably on the same day that the lesson was taught or on the next day.

After the Co-Planning Session

1 Meet according to the plan specified on the Co-Planning Template (Form 15.1). If you are meeting briefly to discuss a lesson that the teacher taught independently and that you did not observe, the following questions will encourage teacher reflection:

- ◆ "Did the plan enable the students to meet the purpose/standard(s)? How do you know?"
- ◆ "What changes did you make to the lesson and why did you decide to make those changes? Were the changes effective?"
- ◆ "Are you planning to continue teaching about this aspect of literacy? If so, what might you do next?"

These questions help teachers establish a pattern of reflection that they can use after teaching other lessons. If you are meeting to discuss a lesson that you co-taught or observed, ideas for the postlesson conference can be found in Strategy 16 and Strategy 17.

2 Ask the teacher how you can provide support as he or she moves forward with this instructional focus or with a new focus.

Strategy in Action

Tricia Jimenez is a reading specialist in a K–5 elementary school. She spends about a third of her time coaching and the rest of her time providing interventions to students. At the end of a third-grade team meeting, the teachers took a few minutes to update one another about the narrative writing pieces that their students had just begun. They all agreed that most of their students were progressing nicely with their first drafts, but Luke Harris said he was dreading the revision stage. He commented, "I never know how to help my students make substantive changes; they always seem to end up editing instead of revising." One of his colleagues shared how she explained revision to her students, but it appeared to Tricia that Luke was looking for more specific ideas. So, later in the day, Tricia stopped by Luke's classroom and offered to co-plan a revision lesson with him. He immediately accepted, and they set a date and time for the meeting.

At the beginning of the meeting, Tricia took a facilitating stance when she asked Luke what he was noticing in the students' first drafts. Luke responded,

"I am a little surprised at how many of the students are not writing their stories in a logical sequence. Sometimes it seems that when they realize they have forgotten something, they just add that event right where they are at—in spite of the fact that the event actually belongs much earlier in the story. And, of course, many of the stories are just a set of events without much descriptive detail."

Luke showed Tricia several drafts that exhibited the characteristics he had mentioned. Tricia and Luke agreed that a revision lesson that focused on sequential organization and descriptive details might be beneficial for the whole class.

Having determined the focus of the lesson, Tricia and Luke discussed the details of the lesson and documented their decisions on the Co-Planning Template (see Figure 15.1). Because Luke had earlier said that he was struggling to come up with a lesson, Tricia took on a consulting stance when they begin to discuss instructional steps. She suggested a resequencing technique (Spandel, 2013) that she had read about and used with her own students. She carefully explained what the entire lesson might look like, highlighting how each step fits into the gradual release-of-responsibility model. As she explained, Luke asked questions. Luke also contributed to the development of the plan by providing information about books the students had recently read, his use of small guided writing groups, and his use of technology.

Luke had originally planned to teach the revision lesson on his own. However, when Tricia asked how she could support him with the lesson, Luke said, "As I look at the guided practice activity for Day 1, I think it might be hard for me to touch base with each partner group during the work time. Would you be free to come in during that part of the lesson to provide additional support?" After checking her schedule, Tricia said she was free and would be happy to come in for the partner work. She also said she would be willing to work with a small guided writing group on Day 2. As they ended the meeting, Luke thanked Tricia and said, "I'm no longer dreading talking about revisions with my students. In fact, I'm looking forward to it!" Tricia was pleased that the co-planning had gone well and that this session had opened the door for future interactions with Luke and his students.

Teacher: *Luke Harris*	
Purpose or objective of lesson: *To help students revise their narratives in terms of organization and detail*	
What do you expect the students to be able to do as a result of the lesson? *Students will revise their narratives so they are correctly sequenced and include more descriptive details to explain the main events.*	
Common Core standards to be addressed: *W.3.5 and W.3.3; also RL.3.5*	
What academic vocabulary will be emphasized during the lesson?	

revise   *narrative*   *organization*   *sequence*   *descriptive details*   *events*

Instructional Steps by Teacher and Students
Label explicit explanation (EE), modeling (M), guided practice (GP), and independent practice (IP).

Teacher	Students
1. EE—*Why revision in terms of organization helps us create better narratives; how descriptive details add interest for the reader.* ♦ *Use story map from* <u>The Raft</u> *(LaMarche, 2000) to show good sequential organization.*	1. *Actively listen; answer questions.*
2. M—*Model revision process—Day 1: Use cut-up first draft of narrative from previous year; think aloud putting the strips in order and noting where more detail would be helpful; compare with first draft.* *Day 2: Model how to add descriptive details to events.*	2. *Actively listen.*
3. GP—*Day 1: Provide assistance as students go through sequence and marking activity with a partner.*	3. *Day 1: Partner work—reassembling partner's narrative in correct sequence and writing notes where additional details are needed; comparing difference between original draft and reassembled piece.*
4. GP and IP: *Day 2 and Day 3: Work with small groups of writers to help them add descriptive details; start with struggling writers.*	4. *Day 2 and 3: Most students work independently to add descriptive details to narratives. Small groups work with teacher.*
5. Closing—*Day 1 and Day 2—Help students articulate purpose and benefits of the day's work.*	5. *Students include academic vocabulary in their explanations of the purpose and benefits.*

What materials are needed? <u>The Raft</u> *(LaMarche, 2000); story map of* <u>The Raft</u>*; original and cut-up versions of narrative for modeling and of each student's narrative; computer, projector, and smartboard; colored pencils for students to use to mark parts that need expansion.*
Assessment: How will you know that the students have met the expectations? *Revised drafts will show appropriate changes in sequence and some additional descriptive details in places recommended by peer.*
How will the coach support you with this lesson? *Day 1: Tricia will help during Guided Practice portion—checking on resequencing by peers and helping students note places where descriptive details should be added.* *Day 2: Tricia will work with a guided writing group to help them add descriptive details.*
When will you and the coach meet to discuss the lesson? *For 10 minutes after school on October 21 (Day 1); during Luke's planning time (1:45–2:15) on October 25—after Luke's had time to review the revisions.*

FIGURE 15.1. Completed Co-Planning Template.

Co-Planning Template

Teacher:

Purpose or objective of lesson:

What do you expect the students to be able to do as a result of the lesson?

Common Core standard(s) to be addressed:

What academic vocabulary will be emphasized during the lesson?

Instructional Steps by Teacher and Students

Label explicit explanation (EE), modeling (M), guided practice (GP), and independent practice (IP).

Teacher	Students

What materials are needed?

Assessment: How will you know that the students have met the expectations?

How will the coach support you with this lesson?

When will you and the coach meet to discuss the lesson?

······················ **Strategy 16** ······················

Co-Teaching

What Is It?

Co-teaching refers to the instructional delivery model where "two colleagues work collaboratively to enrich the educational experience for all students in a classroom" (Moran, 2007, p. 20). Literacy coaches and teachers co-teach for a variety of reasons (Moran, 2007; Toll, 2006). In general, these reasons fall into one or more of the following categories:

◆ To provide students with evidence-based instruction related to areas of need.

◆ To enhance the gathering of data about student participation and learning.

◆ To build teacher capacity by supporting the teacher in trying something he or she would not be willing to try independently.

◆ To share a common experience that serves as the basis for future instructional discussions and collaborations.

More specifically, co-teaching is a way to support teachers in their efforts to teach toward the Common Core. For example, lessons that are co-taught can focus on one of the instructional shifts, on a Common Core standard that students are struggling to meet, or on a Common Core standard that is new to the teacher. By working with the coach to co-teach these lessons, teachers receive the support they need to make the instructional changes that will help their students meet the Common Core standards.

In terms of Moran's continuum of literacy coaching (2007), co-teaching is considered one of the more intrusive activities as teachers are not only inviting coaches to teach in their classrooms but are also allowing their teaching to be viewed by their coaches. Thus, co-teaching requires a trusting relationship so that teachers feel comfortable sharing their teaching, ideas, and concerns. Coaches can do their part to develop the relationship by exhibiting the five faces of trust (Hoy & Tschannen-Moran, 1999): benevolence, honesty, openness, reliability, and competence. Benevolence is more than mere kindness; coaches who are benevolent always act in the best interests of the teachers and their students. Coaches who exhibit honesty are frank but considerate when discussing their observations of student learning and their recommendations for improving that learning. Coaches who are open value teachers' ideas and their styles of teaching. Reliability implies that coaches can be counted on to complete what they've agreed to do, including careful preparation for the co-taught lessons and adhering to the co-teaching schedule. Finally, teachers will be more likely to share their teaching responsibilities when they know that coaches are competent teachers. In addition to a trusting relationship, co-teaching necessitates commitment on the part of both coaches and teachers—especially in terms of a commitment to devote the time needed to co-plan, co-teach, and discuss the co-taught lesson(s).

How Do I Do It?

While you will often co-teach in conjunction with co-planning (see Strategy 15) or as part of an entire coaching cycle (see Strategy 18), you may also co-teach a single lesson. For example, teachers who are participating in a book-study group may want to co-teach a strategy they have read about, but don't feel they could implement on their own. Other teachers may want to co-teach a lesson that will focus on a common student need or will help them address a specific Common Core standard. Even the co-teaching of a single lesson requires commitment from you and the teacher, as you must meet before you co-teach to plan the lesson and after you co-teach to discuss how the lesson went. The following procedures will help you and the teacher plan, implement, and reflect on a co-taught lesson.

Before Co-Teaching

1 Schedule a time to plan the co-teaching lesson. For most lessons, 30 minutes will be a sufficient amount of time.

2 Co-plan the lesson. Begin the co-planning conference by moving through the co-planning process described in Strategy 15. As you plan the instructional steps, determine who will teach which activities. Write the name or initials of the "teacher" next to each activity on Form 15.1. In a single co-taught lesson, the teacher generally teaches the more familiar parts of the lesson, while you take on the more challenging or new aspects. By taking on the more familiar activities, the teacher feels more comfortable having you observe his or her teaching, and that level of comfort also allows the teacher to concentrate on your teaching of the more challenging parts. When you teach those more difficult parts, you are, in fact, modeling for the teacher, enabling the teacher to understand the instructional strategy/approach and how to incorporate it into his or her future practice.

3 In addition to completing the Co-Planning Template (see Strategy 15, Form 15.1), discuss how you will deal with logistic and communication issues related to co-teaching. Form 16.1 can guide this discussion.

a Consider whether changes will be needed to the classroom arrangement. There should be sufficient space in the teaching area for both of you. If more space is needed, determine what tables, desks, or charts could be moved temporarily.

b If this is the first time you have co-taught with the teacher, decide how to explain the activity to the students. For example, when Leslie Simmons, the literacy coach, co-taught a reading lesson with Jeremy Wilton, Jeremy told his students,

> "For our reading lesson today, you will have not one, but two, teachers. That's right—Mrs. Simmons and I will be teaching together. Sometimes, I will be teaching and Mrs. Simmons will be watching. Sometimes, Mrs. Simons will be teaching and I will be watching. Your job is to continue to be responsible, respectful students as described on our class behavior chart. Let's read through the chart together so Mrs. Simmons knows exactly how students in our classroom demonstrate good listening, speaking, and thinking behaviors."

c To help the lesson flow smoothly, determine what language you will use to transfer the teaching from one person to the other. Leslie Simmons and Jeremy Wilton used phrases such as "Now, Mrs. Simmons will show us how . . . " or "Next, I know you will listen carefully as Mr. Wilton explains. . . . "

d Decide where the person who is not teaching will be sitting or standing. We recommend that the person sit in close proximity to the teaching. Standing near the person who is teaching can be distracting and standing to the side or the back of the room impedes smooth transitions. Discuss what you should be doing while the teacher is teaching. You may simply observe the teaching or you may take observational notes on specific students selected by the teacher. When you are teaching, the teacher should be observing you. Some teachers find it helpful to write comments, questions, and observations about your instruction as they watch; others prefer to make mental notes that they write down immediately after the lesson.

e In most co-teaching situations, the nonteaching person is welcome to add a comment or example when the other person is teaching. For example, a teacher may want to make a connection between what you are teaching and something the students had learned earlier. Or you may want to offer a clarifying example when the teacher has taken on the teaching role. Therefore, it's a good idea to agree upon some sort of signal that the nonteaching person can use to indicate that he or she wants to participate. Raising a hand can work but the person who is teaching may be focusing more on the students and not see the hand. In that case, the nonteaching person may stand up and wait to be recognized by the person who is teaching.

f Even though you have carefully co-planned the lesson, it is sometimes necessary to change those plans based on student responses or understanding. If you or the teacher makes a change that will impact what the other person is planning to do next, you'll want a moment to discuss the change. Consider using the "Push *pause*/Push *play*" technique described in Strategy 14 to take a moment to discuss the change. Another option is to provide the students with a think–pair–share question related to the lesson so that you and the teacher can discuss the change while the students are sharing their thinking with a peer.

4 Decide how you will take reflective notes about the lesson. Consider using a Co-Teaching Reflection Form such as the one shown in Form 16.2.

5 Schedule a postlesson conference. Details of the lesson will be easier to recall if you schedule the conference on the same day as the co-taught lesson or on the following day.

6 After the co-planning meeting, take time to prepare for the lesson and to create any materials you will need.

During the Co-Taught Lesson

1 Arrive in the classroom 5 minutes before the lesson is scheduled to begin. Organize all of your materials and place them within easy reach.

2 Introduce the co-teaching format to the students according to the plan described on the Co-Teaching Decision Form (Form 16.1).

3 Remember that you are teaching in a colleague's room and need to adhere to the behavioral expectations that have been established in the room.

4 Stick to the plan if possible. Make changes only when they are needed to improve student understanding and practice.

5 If you make comments, clarifications, or ask questions when the teacher is teaching, be sure they are necessary to improve student understanding. Too many interruptions may frustrate the teacher, confuse the students, and extend the lesson beyond its scheduled time frame.

After the Co-Taught Lesson

1 As soon as possible after the lesson, you and the teacher should write reflective notes on the Co-Teaching Reflection Form (Form 16.2). Be sure to include specific examples to support your conclusions.

2 Meet with the teacher to discuss the lesson.

a Discuss how the instruction helped the students meet the designated objectives(s). Notes from the reflection forms can guide discussion about what students were able to do well, what was difficult for them, and what changes were helpful.

b Take time to talk about the comments or questions written in the "Aspects I Want to Discuss" column of the Co-Teaching Reflection Form.

c Discuss where the teacher plans to go next with his or her instruction. Ask how you can support these next steps. Some teachers will want to co-plan and co-teach another lesson where they take on the more challenging parts; some will want to co-plan the next lesson but teach it themselves; and others will feel ready to plan and teach the next lesson without any coaching support.

Professional Dispositions for Co-Teaching

When you and a teacher have developed a trusting relationship and made a commitment to co-teach, you have taken the first steps to a successful collaboration. Exhibiting the professional dispositions listed in Figure 16.1 will help to ensure that the entire process of co-planning, co-teaching, and debriefing runs smoothly.

The Strategy in Action

Leslie Simmons has been a full-time literacy coach for 3 years at Big Creek Elementary School. Prior to becoming a literacy coach, she served as the school's reading specialist for 5 years. Jeremy Wilton is in his second year of teaching at Big Creek; he is a member of the fifth-grade team. Leslie began working with Jeremy during his first year of teaching. She helped him set up his reader's workshop, modeled

---

1. Follow through with your commitment to co-teach.
   - Work with the teacher to schedule the co-teaching activities (i.e., co-planning conference, co-teaching lesson, and postlesson conference).
   - Adhere to the plan. The scheduled co-teaching activities should take priority over new requests for your time.
   - Carefully prepare your part of the lesson.

2. Respect the teacher's ideas throughout the co-teaching process.

3. Respect the teacher's style of teaching. Don't expect him or her to imitate your teaching style.

4. When you are co-teaching . . .
   - Show the students that you respect their teacher. Don't try to "outshine" the teacher.
   - Expect students to follow the behavioral expectations that have been set by the teacher.
   - Remain positive even if everything doesn't go as planned.

FIGURE 16.1. Professional dispositions for co-teaching.

several reading lessons that addressed Common Core standards, and co-planned several reading lessons with him. This year, Leslie worked with the entire fifth-grade team, including Jeremy, to develop a biography unit that incorporated informational writing. As a result of these coaching activities, Leslie and Jeremy have developed a trusting relationship.

As Jeremy reviewed the fifth-grade implementation guide at the beginning of the third quarter, he noticed that he was supposed to focus on metaphors and similes to help students address RL.5.4: "Determine the meaning of words and phrases as they are used in a text including figurative language such as metaphors and similes." While he knew what metaphors and similes were, he was not sure how to teach his students about these types of figurative language. When he stopped by Leslie's office after school to ask her if she would model a lesson on metaphors and similes for him, she replied, "Oh, Jeremy, I would love to work with you again. Remember last year when we co-planned those reading lessons? Why don't we co-plan and then co-teach a lesson on figurative language? As we plan, we can decide who would teach each part of the lesson." Remembering how much he had learned from co-planning with Leslie, Jeremy agreed to her suggestion.

During the co-planning conference, Leslie and Jeremy examined materials that the students had been reading. They found several examples of metaphors and similes in the historical fiction novels that the students were reading in conjunction with their World War II unit. They decided to use those novels during the lesson and to begin with a focus on similes. As they planned (see Figure 16.2), Leslie asked Jeremy which parts he would like her to teach. He said, "I'd love for you to do the explicit explanation and modeling parts because, even though we've talked through those activities, I am not totally sure about how to teach them. If you teach those parts, I could take on the group work and closing." At the end of the co-planning session, they completed the Co-Teaching Decision Form. The decisions they made can be seen in Figure 16.3.

The co-teaching lesson was implemented as planned. While Leslie made some minor changes to her think-aloud, none of the changes affected the part of the lesson that Jeremy was going to be teaching. After the lesson, they each completed a Co-Teaching Reflection Form (Form 16.2) so they would be ready for their postlesson conference. Leslie's reflections are shown in Figure 16.4. As they talked about the lesson, they both agreed that the student pairs did a good job discussing and writing down an explanation of the similes on their instructional sheets. However, when asked to reread a specific page from their historical novels and find a simile, only about half of the students had been successful. Clearly, they needed more guidance in recognizing similes in the material they were reading. Leslie also noted that, of the three students she closely observed, only Hannah was able to appropriately respond to a question. All three let their partners do the writing on the simile instructional sheet. Jeremy said that he would give them more practice by teaching a follow-up lesson with a small group of students that included Hannah, Simone, and Nathan.

Leslie asked Jeremy where he planned to go next. He said that he had earlier taught students how to find specific information within a text and that he would

Teacher: Jeremy Wilton	Coach : Leslie Simmons

Purpose or objective of lesson: To help students understand what a simile is and explain the meaning of similes.

What do you expect the students to be able to do as a result of the lesson? Students will define a simile, explain similes that come from their reading, and find similes in texts they have read.

Common Core Standards to be addressed: RL.5.4; L.5.5

What academic vocabulary will be emphasized during the lesson?
figurative language   simile   comparison (compares)

Instructional Steps by Teacher and Students
Label explicit explanation (EE), modeling (M), guided practice (GP), and independent practice (IP).

Teacher	Students
1. Explicit explanation of simile and how similes can enhance comprehension. Use examples from Skin Like Milk, Hair of Silk (Cleary, 2011). Simmons	1. Actively listen.
2. Think aloud to model how to explain the meaning of similes. Use examples from The Yellow Star (Deedy, 2000). Simmons	2. Actively listen.
3. GP—Whole class—Guide students as they explain two similes from a recent read-aloud. Wilton	3. Contribute to class discussion; listen to peers' comments.
4. GP—Give directions for the partner work. Wilton	4. Actively listen; ask clarification questions.
5. GP—Provide assistance to partner groups as needed. Willton and Simmons	5. Partner work (partners have read same historical fiction novel)—Discuss and then write explanations of similes on the instructional sheet. Locate simile on specific page of novel, write simile on instructional sheet, and write explanation.
6. Closing—Ask students to define a simile and explain why authors use similes. Wilton	6. Contribute to discussion about definition and importance of simile; listen to peers' comments. Use academic vocabulary.

What materials are needed? Skin Like Milk, Hair of Silk; The Yellow Star, historical fiction novels the students are reading; projector and document camera; simile instructional sheet; pencils
Jeremy will develop a simile instructional sheet with examples from each of the four historical novels and will find a page from each novel that includes an additional simile.

Assessment: How will you know that the students have met the expectations? Accurate completion of the simile instructional sheet will show whether students met expectations when working with a peer. Observations during partner work will add data about students' contributions to the partner discussions.

How will the coach support you with this lesson? This lesson will be co-taught. The person responsible for teaching each part of the lesson is noted under Instructional Steps.

When will you and the coach meet to discuss the lesson? After school on the day that the lesson is taught.

FIGURE 16.2. Completed co-teaching lesson plan.

Teacher: *Jeremy Wilton*   Coach: *Leslie Simmons*

1. What adjustments to the classroom arrangement will need to be made to accommodate the co-teaching lesson?
   - *Need to move the chart stand to the back of the room*
   - *Need to put a teacher chair at the front of the room—to the left of where the person teaching will be standing*

2. How do we plan to explain the co-teaching process to the student?

   Jeremy will explain it to the students using language similar to this:

   "For our reading lesson today, you will have not one, but two, teachers. That's right—Mrs. Simmons and I will be teaching together. Sometimes, I will be teaching and Mrs. Simmons will be watching. Sometimes, Mrs. Simons will be teaching and I will be watching. Your job is to continue to be responsible, respectful students as described on our class behavior chart. Let's read through the chart together so Mrs. Simmons knows exactly how students in our classroom demonstrate good listening, speaking, and thinking behaviors."

3. What language will we use when transferring the teaching responsibility from one person to the other?

   Now, Mrs. Simmons will . . .

   For the next part of the lesson, Mr. Wilton will . . .

   Let's watch how Mr. Wilton . . .

   Let's listen to Mrs. Simmons . . .

4. Where will the person who is not teaching be standing (or sitting)? What will he or she be doing?
   - *The nonteaching person will be sitting in the teacher chair that has been placed to the left of person who is teaching.*
   - *When Mr. Wilton is teaching and during partner work, Mrs. Simmons will observe Nathan, Simone, and Hannah and document their responses to questions and their contributions during the partner work.*
   - *Mr. Wilton will watch Mrs. Simmons teach; he will not take notes while she teaches.*

5. How will the nonteaching person indicate that he or she wants to share an example or ask a question during the lesson?

   Raising a hand or standing up.

6. How will we deal with changes from the original plan?
   - *Only need to explain change if it affects parts of the lesson that the other person will teach.*
   - *Give students a question to think about and then share ideas with their partner; discuss change as students share their ideas with each other.*

FIGURE 6.3. Completed Co-Teaching Decision Form.

Lesson Co-Taught by: <u>Leslie Simmons and Jeremy Wilton (5th grade)</u>

Date of Co-Taught Lesson: <u>March 4</u>

Purpose/Objective of the Co-Taught Lesson:

To help students define a simile, explain similes that come from their reading, and find similes in texts they have read.

Common Core Standards Addressed: *RL.5.4; L.5.5*

	Reflections	Aspects I Want to Discuss
What went well with the lesson? How did our teaching help the students meet the lesson's objectives?	*Explicit explanation and modeling went well. Students used the term "simile" in oral discussions and explained similes using the same sentence structures that had been used during the think-aloud.* *Oral rehearsal of simile explanations went well. Teacher guided students to clarify comparisons.*	*Were there aspects of the think-aloud that Jeremy might want to incorporate into his teaching?* *Two similes were discussed orally by the whole class. Should students have had more oral practice guided by Jeremy before the group work?*
What changes did we make and why? Were they helpful?	*I added another example to my think-aloud. It gave them a second opportunity to hear the language used to explain a simile.*	
What parts seemed most difficult for the students? How could our teaching have addressed those difficult areas better?	*Students had trouble locating similes on a given page of their novel. Giving them specific directions about how to locate information on a page would have been helpful.*	*How will students be provided with additional practice in locating similes within the texts that they read?*
By the end of the lesson, did the students demonstrate that they had met the objective? (Are there specific students who need additional instruction?)	*Most can, when working with a partner, write explanations of similes that are given to them. Most cannot find similes within text. Two students defined "simile" at the end of the lesson.* *Hannah, Nathan, and Simone would benefit from more practice explaining similes.*	*Small-group lesson with Hannah, Nathan, and Simone—start with oral explanations and move on to written ones.*
What is the next instructional step? How can the coach support the teacher as he or she moves on to the next step?	*More practice finding similes in text; lesson on metaphors.*	*What support does Jeremy think he needs as he moves forward?*

FIGURE 16.4. Completed Co-Teaching Reflection Form.

review those procedures, conducting a think-aloud to show students how they could use those same procedures when looking for similes. Then, after reading and discussing a short text that included at least two similes, students could work in pairs to locate and explain the similes. Next, he thought that he would introduce metaphor. When Leslie asked him how she could continue to support his work with Common Core Standard RL.5.4, Jeremy replied, "Well, our co-planning and co-teaching about similes really helped me see how I could actually explain these types of figurative language to my students. So I would like to plan the metaphor lesson myself and then share it with you to get your input. If I planned the lesson tonight, would you have time tomorrow to look it over so I could teach the lesson the day after tomorrow?" Leslie assured him that she would have time to review the lesson and was pleased that Jeremy was more confident about his ability to take the lead in planning what he saw as more challenging tasks.

Co-Teaching Decision Form

Teacher: _____   Coach: _____

1. What adjustments to the classroom arrangement will need to be made to accommodate the co-teaching lesson?

2. How do we plan to explain the co-teaching process to the students?

3. What language will we use when transferring the teaching responsibility from one person to the other?

4. Where will the person who is not teaching be standing (or sitting)? What will he or she be doing?

5. How will the nonteaching person indicate that he or she wants to share an example or ask a question during the lesson?

6. How will we deal with changes from the original plan?

Co-Teaching Reflection Form

Lesson Co-Taught by: _____

Date of Co-Taught Lesson: _____

Purpose/Objective of the Co-Taught Lesson:

Common Core Standards Addressed:

	Reflections	Aspects I Want to Discuss
What went well with the lesson? How did our teaching help the students meet the lesson's objectives?		
What changes did we make and why? Were they helpful?		
What parts seemed most difficult for the students? How could our teaching have addressed those difficult areas better?		
By the end of the lesson, did the students demonstrate that they had met the objective? (Are there specific students who need additional instruction?)		
What is the next instructional step? How can the coach support the teacher as he or she moves on to the next step?		

······················· **Strategy 17** ·······················

Observing

What Is It?

Observing classroom instruction allows the coach to provide targeted professional support to address specific questions or concerns raised by the teacher (Jay & Strong, 2008). At times, teachers may find that even with the best of intentions and efforts, their instruction is not as effective as they would like. Or, they may be concerned that specific students do not respond well to instructional approaches or strategies that work for most students. In these situations, teachers may ask the coach to observe their instruction to gather data and offer feedback related to a specific question or concern about their teaching and/or their students' learning (Knight, 2007). Observing allows the coach to see teachers and students in action in their own classrooms, which helps the coach to gain important insights about specific aspects of instruction. Because observation allows a coach to see instruction in action, Jay and Strong (2008) refer to it as "the heart of literacy coaching" (p. 43).

This type of collegial observation is very different from observation that administrators do as part of the evaluation process. Observation of instruction by the coach is considered a formative process because the findings from the observation can be used to revise and refine instructional practices (Jay & Strong, 2008). While other aspects of literacy coaching, such as setting goals and co-planning, address important aspects of instruction, they do not focus directly on the actual act of teaching. While a teacher may explain something he or she is doing in instruction, it is not the same as seeing it in action! When a coach is able to observe a teacher's instruction in action in the classroom, he or she is able to see exactly what is and is not happening. This information provides credible and useful data for the coach and teacher to discuss during a postobservation conference.

Observing a teacher requires that the coach has established a respectful, collegial relationship with him or her. The teacher must be comfortable enough to invite the coach in to watch his or her teaching (Jay & Strong, 2008). When a teacher is comfortable enough to invite you in to observe, you can be assured that he or she will be ready to discuss your observations honestly and openly. While observing is presented as a stand-alone coaching strategy here, it is often combined with other literacy coaching strategies such as a follow-up to co-teaching or in conjunction with goal setting and co-planning.

How Do I Do It?

Observing is a three-step process that begins with a pre-observation conference. Next, the observation takes place, followed by a post-observation conference.

Pre-Observation Conference

1 After a teacher has suggested that you observe his or her instruction, schedule a preobservation conference. Generally, this conference will be short, lasting between 10 and 15 minutes.

2 Explain to the teacher that your observation will be collegial, not evaluative. For example, you might say something like, "When I come in to observe, I'll be focusing on the specific issues or questions you have identified as the purpose for my observation. I'll be trying to gather information and insights so that we can discuss the observed lesson and determine ideas for enhancing instruction and learning. I will not be sharing this information with the principal or with anyone else."

3 Ask the teacher what purpose he or she has for the observation. The following prompts may be useful to help the teacher articulate and clarify the purpose for the observation.

- "What is going well with your instruction? With your students' learning?"
- "What concerns you? Why?"
- "When I observe in your classroom, what do you want me to look for? Why?"
- "What questions do you hope we can answer as a result of my observation?"

4 Confirm the teacher's purpose for the observation. You may want to say something such as "Let's make sure we are both clear on your purpose for the observation. Let's write it on the Observation Template so we keep that in mind throughout the entire observation process" (see Form 17.1).

5 Work with the teacher to fill in the top portion of the Observation Template.

6 Discuss where you will sit for the observation so you can see the teacher and students during the lesson but you do not distract them. Also determine whether you will take notes by hand or on your laptop.

7 Finally, discuss how to explain to the students what is happening during the observation. Generally, the teacher provides this information to the students so they do not wonder why the literacy coach is in the classroom during a lesson.

8 Set a date and time for you to do the observation.

9 You will also need to schedule the postobservation conference. It is recommended that you hold the conference on the same day as the observation or, if necessary, on the next day.

10 Remind the teacher of the observation the day before to ensure that the time still works.

During the Observation

1 Arrive several minutes early for the observation. Be sure to have the Observation Template (see Form 17.1) to remind you to focus specifically on the teacher's purpose for the observation. If you are taking notes by hand, bring a clipboard and pen or pencil. If you are taking notes on your laptop, be sure it is charged or that you bring your power cord and sit near an electrical outlet.

2 Sit in the area you and the teacher selected during your preobservation conference.

3 The teacher will briefly inform the children about the observation by saying something such as "Class, Mrs. Zappia will be observing our lesson to learn more about what I am teaching and what you are learning in our class. She will be watching and taking notes, but she will not be participating in our lesson."

4 During the observation, take notes on the Observation Template.

5 When the lesson is over, thank the teacher and class for allowing you to watch the lesson. Then excuse yourself from the classroom.

6 Read through your notes as soon after the observation as possible. Clarify your notes as necessary, being sure to avoid language that sounds evaluative. Consider ideas for the "Possible Actions" section of the Observation Template. Write them on the form, but remember that you will be gathering input from the teacher at the postobservation conference before he or she determines what the next steps will be. Make a copy of the template to share with the teacher at the postobservation conference.

7 If possible, send a short e-mail or handwritten thank-you note to the teacher for allowing you to do the observation. A sample note from literacy coach Sherrie Zappia is provided in Figure 17.1.

Dear Pam,

Thanks for inviting me to observe your classroom today. I enjoyed seeing the lesson, and I learned a great deal. I look forward to meeting with you in your classroom this afternoon at 2:15.

See you soon!

Sherrie

FIGURE 17.1. Sample thank-you note.

After the Observation Conference

1 Begin the conference by thanking the teacher for inviting you to observe the lesson.

2 Restate the purpose of the observation as noted on the Observation Template (see Form 17.1).

3 Begin the discussion by asking the teacher: "What aspects of the lesson were effective in helping you accomplish your purpose?"

4 Add your observations about aspects of the lesson that were particularly effective.

5 Ask the teacher: "What aspects did not seem as helpful in accomplishing your purpose?"

6 To share your observations, give the teacher a copy of your observation form. Focus on specific observations and try to avoid generalizations. Make sure your language is objective and not evaluative (see Figure 17.2).

7 Discuss the lesson and your observations, focusing on the "Possible Actions" column. Take notes about the possible actions that you and the teacher identify.

Avoid evaluative language.	Use objective language.
"You did a great job introducing the strategy."	"I saw that you introduced the strategy by telling the students the name and purpose for it."
"The students did not seem interested in the activity."	"I noticed that three of the students at the back of the reading rug did not look at the chart or follow along as you read it aloud."
"You should give more time for guided practice."	"I noticed that almost half of the students did not complete the guided practice activity."

FIGURE 17.2. Coaching language for postobservation conferences.

8 Ask the teacher which of the possible actions he or she would like to address in future lessons.

9 Record that information on the observation form.

10 Ask the teacher if he or she would like any follow-up support.

The Strategy in Action

Sherrie Zappia is a literacy coach who spends all of her time coaching teachers at Dover Heights Elementary School. Pam Hughes is a second-grade teacher who has 5 years of teaching experience. Sherrie meets with the second-grade team weekly to engage in a variety of coaching strategies such as developing implementation guides (see Strategy 8), reviewing assessment data to plan instruction (see Strategy 9), and examining student work (see Strategy 10). Sherrie also modeled a lesson in Pam's classroom on key ideas and details in literature to address standard RL.2.1. They then co-planned and co-taught a follow-up lesson to address this same standard. At the postconference for the co-planned lesson, Pam explained, "I learn so much from working with you. Now that we've co-planned and co-taught this lesson, I feel like I'm ready to do it on my own."

Later that quarter, the second-grade team discussed how second-grade students are now expected to integrate knowledge and ideas when reading literature. Sherrie and the team members discussed ways they address standard RL.2.9 in their teaching: "Compare and contrast two or more versions of the same story (e.g., Cinderella stories) by different authors or from different cultures." One of the teachers, Terri, talked about using fairytales to address this standard, and the other teachers agreed that the approach seemed to be a good one.

Several weeks after that meeting, Pam shared:

"The comparing and contrasting different versions of the same story is hard for me to teach because I'm used to teaching students to read and comprehend one book at a time. I took the ideas from our team meeting, and I just started a fairytale unit. I have already taught the first few lessons that focus on two versions of *Cinderella*, and I'm concerned that my students just seem to be focused on the little details that are similar or different rather than looking at the story elements or how the setting or culture are similar or different. They are focusing on things like both girls have blond hair or both boys are brave. I'm just not getting them to think about the stories deeply enough to compare and contrast. I'd like for you to come in and see what we are doing and give me some feedback."

Sherrie responded, "I'd love to visit your classroom to see how this unit is working. When I observe, I want to be sure to focus on *your* purpose for the observation. In order to do that, let's schedule a short meeting to talk about what you'd like me to observe and offer feedback on related to the lesson." Sherrie and Pam scheduled a preobservation conference to determine the purpose for the observation. Pam explained that her purpose for the observation was for Sherrie to "look at what I do in the lesson that helps students be able to compare and contrast the two versions of the fairytale and figure out what is missing that would help them be able to compare and contrast more effectively."

Sherrie observed Pam teaching the lesson, and they then met for a postobservation conference. Sherrie shared the Observation Template (Form 17.1) that she had filled in, and she took additional notes based on Pam's contributions to the discussion (see Figure 17.3 for the completed Observation Template). During the conference, Sherrie shared her observation that Pam provided a clear, explicit explanation of how to compare and contrast, but that the students seemed to need more instruction and support to actually begin comparing and contrasting two versions of the fairytale. Through their discussion, they agreed that adding a focused think-aloud would be an effective way to make the process clearer to the students. They also discussed how adding a structured graphic organizer to guide the students through the compare and contrast process would be helpful. At the end of the postobservation conference, Pam told Sherrie:

> "It was so helpful to have another pair of eyes and ears in the classroom. What you observed really helped me understand how I can revise my teaching for this standard to be more explicit by adding focused think-alouds and using a graphic organizer so the students could really understand how to compare and contrast the important elements of different versions of stories. If you hadn't observed, I may never have figured out that what changes to make to help my students understand this new and challenging skill."

Teacher: *Pam Hughes*   Date: *November 2*

Purpose of Observation: *To look at what the teacher does in the lesson that helps students be able to compare and contrast the two versions of the fairytale and to figure out what is missing that would help them be able to compare and contrast more effectively.*

Common Core Standard(s) Addressed: *RL.2.9: Compare and contrast two or more versions of the same story (e.g., Cinderella stories) by different authors or from different cultures.*

Observations	Comments	Possible Actions (developed by coach and teacher collaboratively)
Teacher provides explicit explanation of comparing and contrasting.	Students appear to be listening and engaged.	Keep doing explicit explanations for new skills and strategies!
Teacher reminds students of the two versions of Cinderella they have read.	Students say they remember both books, but are not asked to demonstrate their recall.	Since one book was read yesterday and one was read today, students may benefit from a quick review of the plot of each story. This could be teacher led or done with a partner and monitored by the teacher.
Teacher asks students to compare the two books and tell her how they are "the same or alike."		
Students raise their hands and teacher calls on them to share their responses. She writes them on the white board under the heading "Compare How Stories Are Alike."	Students do not refer back to the books to develop their responses.	Instruct students to refer back to the books so their responses are more text dependent. That process may need to be modeled if it is new to students.
Students share literal information such as both stories are about a beautiful girl and both stories end "happily ever after."	Student responses are offered and recorded as students think of them. Not organized around story elements or plot.	Before asking students to compare or contrast, do a focused think-aloud so they understand how to compare. Focus on story elements as a way to organize the comparison process.
Teacher asks students to contrast the books and tell how they are "different."	Student responses are the same as noted above.	
Students raise their hands and teacher calls on them to share their responses. She writes them on the white board under the heading "Contrast How the Stories Are Different."	Student responses are literal—one story is set in China—but the student does not share why or how that made the stories different in terms of plot.	Providing a graphic organizer to record (and prompt) student responses can give students a clear structure to guide their comparing and contrasting.
Teacher concludes lesson, "You have found lots of ways the books are alike and different."		

Next Steps
- ◆ Teacher: *I plan to develop and use a focused think-aloud for comparing and another for contrasting so students can understand the process more deeply. I want to use a graphic organizer that lists story elements to help students structure their responses, but I don't know what that will look like.*
- ◆ Coach: *I will locate or develop two good graphic organizers for compare-contrast and share them with Pam so she can choose or adapt one for her next lesson.*

FIGURE 17.3. Completed Observation Template.

FORM 17.1

Observation Template

Teacher: _____ Date: _____

Purpose of Observation: _____

_____

_____

Common Core Standard(s) Addressed: _____

_____

Observations	Comments	Possible Actions (developed by coach and teacher collaboratively)

Next Steps
Teacher:

Coach:

······················· **Strategy 18** ·······················

Implementing the Coaching Cycle

What Is It?

In a coaching cycle, the coach and teacher work together over a period of time to plan, implement, and reflect on instruction with the goal of enhancing teacher practice and increasing student literacy learning (Bean, 2009; Casey, 2006; Instructional coaching for teachers, n.d.). A coaching cycle incorporates all of the coaching activities that have been described previously in this chapter. These coaching activities may be linked in the following way. Before any instruction begins, the coach and the teacher meet to establish the goal(s)/purpose(s) for the cycle. The coach often models the first lesson, allowing the teacher to see a strategy or instructional approach in action with his or her own students. Then the coach and teacher co-plan and co-teach one or more lessons. If they engage in multiple co-taught lessons, the coach generally takes on the more challenging parts in the first lesson and then releases those challenging parts to the teacher in subsequent lessons. Following the co-taught lesson(s), the teacher takes over the teaching while the coach observes the lesson(s), providing focused feedback on the effectiveness of instructional practices to help students meet the learning objectives. This coaching cycle sequence reflects the gradual release of responsibility model (Pearson & Gallagher, 1983), where coaches provide just the right amount of support at each stage of the process to help teachers become independent in the planning, implementation, and evaluation of their instruction (Kruse & Zimmerman, 2012). The support provided through coaching cycles enable teachers to "refine specific procedures, but more important, [to] expand teachers' conceptual knowledge in a way that helps them learn from their own teaching over time" (Lyons & Pinnell, 2001, p. 139).

While coaching cycles contribute to building teacher capacity, they require a relatively large time commitment on the part of the teacher and the coach. Most coaching cycles involve the planning and teaching of four or five lessons on consecutive days. Not only does the coach need to be available at the same time on consecutive days, but the coach and the teacher need time to meet on each of those days as well, to conference about the lesson that was taught and to plan for the next lesson. Because of the time commitment and the fact that working with individual teachers is just one of many coaching responsibilities, coaches can generally engage in only a small number of coaching cycles at any one time.

How Do I Do It?

Implementing a coaching cycle is a bit like choreographing a dance. You are trying to design the perfect balance between you and your partner, incorporating each of your strengths in order to perform the piece for the audience. However, it is even more challenging because your audience (the students) must not only enjoy the piece (the instruction) but learn from it. In addition, you are trying to improve the dancing techniques (instructional practice) of your partner by providing just the right amount of support at just the right moment.

Figure 18.1 shows the typical sequence of the five phases of the coaching cycle and lists key details about each phase. While it may appear that the coaching cycle involves only three or four lessons, there is no set number of lessons for a coaching

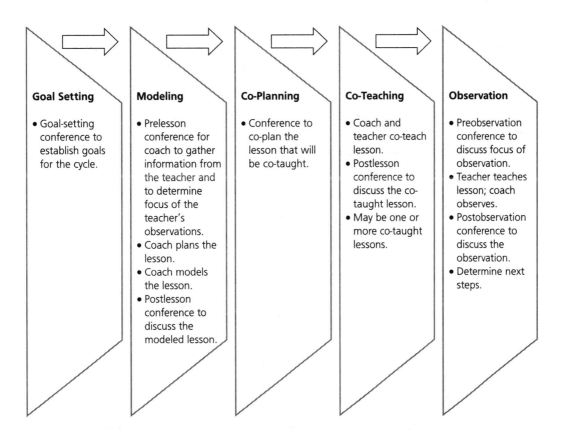

FIGURE 18.1. The coaching cycle.

cycle. The length of the cycle will depend upon several factors including the complexity of the instructional goal and the instructional needs of the teacher. Some cycles will necessitate just one modeled lesson, one co-taught lesson, and one observation lesson, while others may require multiple modeled, co-taught, and observation lessons.

Each phase of the coaching cycle shown in Figure 18.1 has been discussed in detail in Strategies 13 through 17. You may want to review one or more of these strategies as you prepare for a coaching cycle. You may also find it helpful to refer to Figure 18.2 to determine what forms from those strategies can be used as you implement a coaching cycle.

As mentioned earlier, coaching cycles require a commitment of time from both you and the teacher. The following considerations will ensure that your coaching cycles are productive.

1 Carefully determine which teachers might want to engage in a coaching cycle. You will find that many first- and second-year teachers welcome the close collaboration as they begin to incorporate instructional approaches, such as reading workshop or writing workshop, into their practice. In addition, teachers who are trying to implement new district initiatives, such as a new reading program or the Common Core standards, may want the type of ongoing support provided within the coaching cycle. Furthermore, teachers with whom you have developed a trusting relationship may see the coaching cycle as a way to work through an instructional challenge they are facing. As you can only engage in a small number of coaching cycles during the same time period, choose those teachers who are willing to commit the time and effort.

2 When you are planning your coaching activities for the week or month, try to schedule your coaching cycles first. This will ensure that you will be available at the same time on consecutive days to work with the teacher in his or her classroom. If your schedule doesn't allow for consecutive days (e.g., Monday through Friday), try to schedule the lessons as close together as possible (e.g., Monday, Tuesday, Thurs-

Phase of Coaching Cycle	Forms
Goal Setting	Form 13.1: SMART Goal-Setting Template
Modeling	Form 14.1: Modeling Planning Template Form 14.2: Observation Form for Template for Modeling
Co-Planning	Form 15.1: Co-Planning Template
Co-Teaching	Form 16.1: Co-Teaching Decision Form Form 16.2: Co-Teaching Reflection Form
Observation	Form 17.1: Observation Template

FIGURE 18.2. Forms for each phase of the coaching cycle.

day, Monday, Tuesday). Remember to schedule planning and conferencing time as well. Coaches and teachers often find it efficient to conference about the lesson they just taught and to plan for the next lesson during the same meeting.

3 Observe in the classroom before you begin a coaching cycle. Unless you have recently been in the classroom of the teacher with whom you will be working, schedule a time for an informal observation. To provide the appropriate support to the teacher, you need firsthand knowledge about the students' literacy skills and the teacher's instructional practices. Don't forget this step because "literacy coaches who do not observe find themselves making incorrect assumptions about instruction" (Walpole & McKenna, 2013, p. 206), and those incorrect assumptions could lead to the planning and implementation of instruction that does not achieve the teacher's goals.

4 Realize that the coaching cycle does not always follow the sequence shown in Figure 18.1. Suppose, for example, that, toward the end of a cycle, the teacher teaches a lesson that you observe. During the postobservation conference, you and the teacher agree that one aspect of the lesson was particularly difficult for all of the students. You have thought about a strategy that could support the students' learning. You and the teacher decide to co-plan and co-teach the next lesson where you will model the new strategy and the teacher will help the students apply that strategy.

5 Respect the teacher's time by adhering to the time frame established at your initial planning session. Extending the coaching cycle may frustrate the teacher. It may interfere with the teacher's curricular pacing, it may require additional planning and reflection conferences for which the teacher does not have time, or it may send a signal to the teacher that he or she is not making good progress with his or her instruction. Even when you would think it would be beneficial to extend a coaching cycle, it is better to work within the established time frame and document plans for future coaching activities during the final conference of the cycle.

The Strategy in Action

Oliver Dumont recently began his fourth year of coaching at Hawthorne Elementary School. He spends about two-thirds of his time coaching and the other third providing small-group interventions to intermediate students. He has adopted the layered approach to coaching. For example, he has provided several large-group professional development sessions, facilitated at least five small-group article studies, and worked with grade-level teams to develop implementation guides for the CCSS and to revise units of study so they better address those standards. He has also worked with individual teachers to model, co-plan, and co-teach lessons. Last year, he began to implement coaching cycles and has seen how teachers who engage in this close collaboration with him over a period of time form the habits of careful planning, targeted instruction, and data-based reflection needed to improve student learning.

Maureen Lennon, a fourth-grade teacher, is in her third year of teaching at Hawthorne. She loves teaching her students about all of the different literary genres and feels her students will have no trouble meeting the grade-specific Common Core standards for reading literature. However, she knows that, as she teaches toward the Common Core, she needs to focus more on informational texts. Realizing that this is not her area of strength, she approaches Oliver for support. She has participated in a number of small-group activities facilitated by Oliver, including an article study and a lesson study with her fourth-grade team. She sees him as a person who is knowledgeable about literacy, values others' ideas, and understands the complexity of teaching. He might, she thinks, be just the person to help her!

At their first meeting, Maureen shares her concerns with Oliver. She says:

> "I know that I need to do a better job of teaching students about informational texts, but it seems so much harder than teaching about literature. In science, for instance, there are so many different topics that I am not familiar with and each topic has a ton of vocabulary that the students are supposed to learn. And then there's all those graphics. I mean, in literature, there are illustrations that help students understand the text, but in science there are illustrations, diagrams, charts, and maps. I know my students often just read the science text and don't even look at the graphics. So, I'm just not sure where to start with helping them meet some of the Common Core standards for reading informational texts."

Oliver agrees that informational texts come with their own set of challenges. As they continue their discussion, it becomes clear that Maureen is mostly asking for support to help her students understand how graphics contribute to their understanding of informational texts. Oliver comments:

> "You know, Maureen, your goal fits right into the Common Core standard of RIT.4.7: 'Interpret information presented visually, orally, or quantitatively and explain how the information contributes to an understanding of the text in which it appears.' I think you can address this standard as you teach your next science unit. I see that your science period is during my coaching time, so maybe we could work together to develop a series of lessons that focus on the graphics within chapter 3 of the science textbook. Perhaps I could teach the first lesson, and we could then co-plan and co-teach some lessons. You said that you are starting the new chapter next Monday. Should I just reserve from 1:30 to 2:15 every day next week to work with you and your students?"

Maureen was excited about Oliver's plan and added "If you are available after school, we could do our co-planning and reflection then. I don't have any after-school meetings next week."

Whenever Oliver engages in a cycle of coaching, he uses the Coaching Cycle Summary (Form 18.1) to document important information about the ongoing collaboration. He completes the appropriate section at the end of each day, so he can see at a glance what has already been taught and what the next steps are. The summary of his coaching cycle with Maureen is shown in Figure 18.3. Of course, as Maureen and Oliver met to co-plan the lessons, they used many of the tools that have been described in this part. For example, when planning for the model lesson, Oliver used the Modeling Planning Template (Form 14.1) and Maureen prepared the Observation Form Template for Modeling (Form 14.2). As they co-planned the other lessons, they used the Co-Planning Template (Form 15.1). In addition, Oliver used the Observation Template (Form 17.1) when he observed Maureen teach. They modified the Co-Teaching Reflection Form (Form 16.2) to use for all of their postlesson conferences.

When they met after each lesson, Oliver and Maureen discussed their observations and examined student work to plan the next day's instruction (see Figure 18.3). For example, on October 8, they discussed the first co-taught lesson and noted that students had no difficulty finding examples of cycle diagrams when browsing the informational texts that Maureen and Oliver had provided for them. However, when students labeled the elements of the cycle diagrams they had found, many did not label the expositions (i.e., the explanatory paragraphs attached to the graphic). Maureen suggested that she could highlight that term during the next lesson and have the students reexamine their cycle diagrams to find any expositions.

Oliver's summary sheet (see Figure 18.3) also shows how he employed the use of the gradual release of responsibility model during the cycle. Oliver generally took on what Maureen saw as the most challenging parts of the lesson, but then made sure that Maureen had an opportunity to teach that part during a future lesson. For example, in the first co-taught lesson on October 8, Oliver used a think-aloud to model how to explain a cycle diagram. When they decided that the students would benefit from hearing the explanation using a different cycle diagram, Maureen presented the think-aloud during the second co-taught lesson. Oliver also took the lead, during the co-taught lesson on October 9, in explaining how to compare information from the text with information from the cycle diagram, with Maureen expanding on that explanation the next day.

At the end of the week, Maureen and Oliver met to discuss the last lesson in the cycle and what, if any, follow-up was needed. Maureen was very pleased with the progress both she and her students had made. She shared her thoughts with Oliver:

"I can't believe how much I learned about teaching graphical information to my students. I really see how explicit explanation, modeling, and guided practice helps the students understand challenging material! What excites me even more is that I have an approach to use when I introduce other types of graphics from our science and social studies texts. The only thing that still seems difficult is helping them compare the information they read in the text with the information they learned from graphics. I want them to realize that authors often provide a great deal of additional information through the graphics."

Coaching Cycle with *Maureen Lennon*

Goal-Setting Conference	Modeling	Co-Teaching 1	Observation 1	Final Notes
Date: *10-2*	**Date:** *10-7*	**Date:** *10-8*	**Date:** *10-10*	◆ *Maureen plans to follow a similar instructional sequence with other graphics as the semester continues. Would like to co-plan and maybe co-teach the lesson where students compare information from the text with information from the graphic.* ◆ *Maureen will have students incorporate appropriate graphics into informational writing projects.*
SMART Goal: *To develop expertise with instruction about graphic features in science and social studies texts to help students meet CCSS RIT.4.7 and L.4.2.*	**Focus of Modeled Lesson:** *Provide explicit explanation (overview) of graphics in science textbook.*	**Focus of Co-Taught Lesson:** ◆ *Teacher: Cycle-related vocabulary.* ◆ *Coach: Model how to explain cycle diagram.*	**Focus of Observed Lesson:** ◆ *Review—compare information from text and cycle diagram.* ◆ *Students explain cycles to peers.*	
	Notes: ◆ *Students able to correctly apply sticky-note labels to graphics in chapter 3 of science text.* ◆ *Maureen will attend more to graphics during informational read-alouds.*	**Notes:** ◆ *Need to review the term exposition.* ◆ *Needed larger cycle diagram for think-aloud.* ◆ *Need to review how to explain a cycle diagram.* ◆ *Student pairs able to label elements of cycle diagrams they had found.*	**Notes:** ◆ *Graphic organizer was helpful. Maureen explained it well.* ◆ *Student pairs had trouble completing graphic organizer about their own cycle. Need more practice with this.* ◆ *Didn't have time for peer sharing.*	
Next Step: *On 10-4, complete Modeling Planning Template (Form 14.1).*	**Next Step:** *Co-plan and co-teach lesson about the cycle diagram in chapter 3 of science text.*	**Next Step:** *Co-plan and co-teach lesson where Maureen models think-aloud.*	**Next Step:** *Students will explain cycles to peers and share what information was in cycle diagram that was not in text.*	

Co-Teaching 2	Observation 2
Date: *10-9*	**Date:**
Focus of Co-Taught Lesson: ◆ *Teacher: Review how to explain a cycle. Review exposition.* ◆ *Coach: Model—compare information in text about the cycle with information gained from cycle diagram.*	**Focus of Observed Lesson:**
Notes: ◆ *Maureen's think-aloud was so clear!* ◆ *Need a graphic organizer to show differences between information in text and in cycle diagram.*	**Notes:**
Next Step: *Co-plan observation lesson.*	**Next Step:**

FIGURE 18.3. Completed Coaching Cycle summary.

Oliver responded:

> "I'm so glad that you felt the time we invested in the coaching cycle was worth-while. Perhaps, when you are ready to teach the comparison part again, we could co-plan that lesson—building on the lesson we used this week. And I'd be happy to support you in other ways as well as you continue to work on addressing the Common Core standards for reading informational text."

Coaching Cycle Summary

Coaching Cycle with _____

Goal-Setting Conference	Modeling	Co-Teaching 1	Observation 1	Final Notes
Date:	Date:	Date:	Date:	
SMART Goal:	Focus of Modeled Lesson:	Focus of Co-Taught Lesson:	Focus of Observed Lesson:	
	Notes:	Notes:	Notes:	
Next Step:	Next Step:	Next Step:	Next Step:	
		Co-Teaching 2	**Observation 2**	
		Date:	Date:	
		Focus of Co-Taught Lesson:	Focus of Observed Lesson:	
		Notes:	Notes:	
		Next Step:	Next Step:	

Putting It All Together

*Profiles of Highly Effective
Literacy Coaches*

In Parts One through Four, we have presented key ideas and strategies related to coaching toward the Common Core. We've shared essential information related to adult learning theory, the change process, and layers of coaching (i.e., large group, small group, and individual). We've also provided examples of specific coaching strategies in action to address various CCSS at different grade levels. In Part Five, we share portraits of six highly effective coaches to illustrate additional key aspects of literacy coaching such as working with your principal, getting into classrooms, and staying organized. Each profile was selected to highlight a common challenge experienced by literacy coaches. For each profile, we present practical tips and tools to help you address the challenges associated with literacy coaching.

In Profile 1, we share how a literacy coach can establish and maintain principal support for literacy coaching at the school level. Having principal support is essential for setting literacy coaching as a school priority (Kral, 2007) and for promoting teacher engagement in coaching (Matsumura, Sartoris, Bickel, & Garnier, 2009). In Profile 2, the focus is on getting into classrooms through building positive, productive relationships with teachers and establishing the value of small-group and individual coaching activities. Profile 3 shows how a coach can reach out to and work with teachers who are hesitant or even resistant to engage in coaching support. Profile 4 discusses how a coach can "stay the course" when challenges and frustrations arise. In Profile 5, ideas for embedding literacy coaching into other assigned duties are discussed. This approach is particularly relevant for coaches who spend a great deal of their time engaged in activities such as teaching intervention groups or leading response-to-intervention (RTI) programs. Profile 6 provides useful ideas for getting and staying organized as a literacy coach.

Establishing and Maintaining Administrator Support

Kim Newton is an experienced reading specialist at Deer Park Elementary School. Her school district updated the roles and responsibilities of the reading specialist last year to include literacy coaching. Kim was excited about her new role, but she was also worried about how to announce it to the teachers and how to get started with literacy coaching. To address her concerns, Kim scheduled a meeting with her principal, Miss Sarah Moore, to discuss literacy coaching at their school. Kim knew that Miss Moore was very busy so she created a template to structure their meeting and to record notes (see Form 1).

Kim knew that she was expected to spend half of her time coaching, but she wanted to discuss the specific schedule with Miss Moore. For example, Kim thought that coaching in the morning, when teachers were teaching literacy and when the primary grades had their shared planning times, would enable her to work with those teachers on small-group and individual coaching strategies. That would mean that Kim's reading intervention groups would need to be scheduled in the afternoon. She knew this would be a change for many of the teachers so she wanted to make sure it was a topic of discussion at her meeting with Miss Moore.

Kim also knew that the teachers would be curious about what services and support she would be offering through the new coaching program. In addition, she wanted to discuss how to show that literacy coaching was a priority in the school, and how to explain changes in the number of students she could serve in reading interventions due to half of her time being shifted to literacy coaching. Therefore, Kim added these items to the meeting template. She then shared her template with Miss Moore several days before the meeting so they both had a chance to prepare for the meeting. Kim and Miss Moore agreed that having the template to guide their discussion during the meeting helped them address the critical issues in a timely manner.

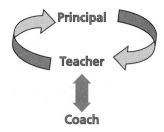

FIGURE 1. The principal–teacher–coach relationship model. From Elish-Piper, L'Allier, and Zwart (2009). Copyright 2009 by the Illinois Reading Council. Reprinted by permission.

A major issue that Kim and Miss Moore addressed early in the year was how to separate literacy coaching from supervision and evaluation (Toll, 2004). Some teachers expressed concern that information from coaching activities might be reported back to the principal and used in evaluations. Kim and Miss Moore understood that this concern needed to be addressed directly so the teachers knew that Kim's coaching support was not part of supervision or evaluation at the school. They decided to share a model that clearly illustrated how the literacy coach is neither a supervisor nor an evaluator (Elish-Piper et al., 2009). In this model (see Figure 1), the princi-

---

Meet with the Principal Regularly
- Discuss roles and responsibilities.
- Discuss necessary adjustments to current responsibilities to free up time for coaching.
- Determine coaching priorities that are . . .
  - Based on data, including needs assessment completed by teachers.
  - Aligned with district and school goals.
  - Focused on key aspects of the Common Core.

Develop a Plan to Share Literacy Coaching Program with Teachers
- The principal shares the principal–teacher–coach relationship model.
- The principal clarifies the following ideas:
  - The literacy coach is not part of the evaluation process; the coach is a support for teachers.
  - When the literacy coach is working in a classroom, the teacher is expected to stay to observe and/ or participate.
- The literacy coach explains how he or she is available to support teachers.

Ways the Principal Can Foster and Support Literacy Coaching in the School
- The principal and literacy coach need to establish and maintain a meeting schedule that fosters ongoing, frequent communication.
- Follow the principal–teacher–coach relationship model.
- To show support, the principal should be visible at staff development sessions facilitated by the literacy coach. Also, the principal should refer to and publicly support literacy coaching at faculty meetings, grade-level team meetings, and other settings.
- Celebrate progress, understand that change takes time, and foster a collegial and collaborative climate so that the school staff can work as a team to support and encourage one another.

FIGURE 2. Working with the principal to promote literacy coaching success.

pal does not discuss teacher observations with the literacy coach, and the literacy coach does not report back to the principal after observations or conferences with a teacher, because the literacy coach is a supportive colleague for teachers to think and problem solve with—not a supervisor or evaluator.

Throughout the year, Kim took notes about how she and Miss Moore worked collaboratively to get the literacy coaching program started on the right foot. A summary of Kim's notes is provided in Figure 2.

When we talked to Kim and Miss Moore at the end of the first year of literacy coaching at their school, they discussed how they learned a great deal and were excited by the outcomes of literacy coaching. They credited their collaborative relationship as one of the reasons for the early successes of the literacy coaching program at Deer Park Elementary School. Kim even commented: "Having my principal's support, understanding, and endorsement made all the difference to getting my coaching up and running!"

FORM 1

Principal Meeting Template

Coaching Consideration	Notes
Time and Schedule for Coaching ◆ Amount of time ◆ When coaching will be scheduled ◆ Adjustments to other aspects of schedule	

Beginning Coaching Priorities
◆ Consider:
  • Data, including needs assessment
  • District and school goals
  • Key aspects of CCSS	

Rolling Out Coaching to Faculty	When? Who? How?
Other Important Issues to Be Addressed	
Issues Still to Be Resolved	

Getting into Classrooms

Megan Schoenfeld was hired last year as a literacy coach, and she is expected to spend all of her time engaged in literacy coaching. During her first few months at South Ridge Elementary School, she struggled to get into classrooms to work with teachers. She explained, "The teachers are very engaged in large-group coaching activities, and I've been able to attend grade-level team meetings too, but none of the teachers were interested in working with me in more in-depth types of coaching activities such as co-planning, co-teaching, or lesson study." Megan worried that the effectiveness of her literacy coaching would be greatly limited if she was unable to implement small-group and individual coaching strategies.

To address her concern about getting into classrooms, Megan talked with other literacy coaches in her school district as well as her principal. She also consulted a variety of resources that offered suggestions for getting into classrooms to work with teachers (Bean & DeFord, 2012; Elish-Piper et al., 2009; Frost, n.d.). Because she was new to the school, Megan realized that the teachers had never seen her teach, so she needed to establish her credibility with her colleagues. To begin establishing her credibility as a teacher, she volunteered to go to every classroom in her school to meet all of the students by doing read-alouds using new children's literature from her extensive collection of children's books. Many of the teachers took her up on her offer, so she scheduled classroom visits with those teachers. As she prepared, she made sure to select new, engaging books that aligned with some aspect of the curriculum. She also used an interactive read-aloud approach (Fisher, Flood, Lapp, & Frey, 2004) that included a clearly stated purpose, modeled fluent reading, and incorporated text-based discussions as required by the Common Core. After the interactive read-alouds, she debriefed with the teachers to see how they thought the process went and whether they wanted to schedule a follow-up modeled lesson, to co-teach lessons using new books from her collection, or to co-plan a series of interactive read-alouds. The interactive read-alouds helped many of the teachers see Megan as an experienced and effective teacher; however, this did not mean that all classroom teachers opened up to working with her in a coaching capacity. Throughout her first year at South Ridge Elementary School, Megan tried many approaches to gain access to classrooms, and those that she found most effective are summarized in Figure 1. At first, some of these ideas for getting into classrooms may seem counterintuitive. For example, how does talking about TV shows with a teacher or offering to reorganize a classroom library lead to meaningful, intensive coaching? Because effective literacy coaching is built on respectful, trusting relationships, it is essential for teachers to feel comfortable working with you (L'Allier et al., 2010). Many of these suggestions focus on building such relationships, demonstrating your commitment to supporting teachers, and positioning yourself as a colleague and peer (Elish-Piper et al., 2009). While there is no magic formula for gaining access to classrooms, Megan suggests: "Don't give up. Just keep being friendly, offer to help, show that you are a team player, and keep on trying. Your efforts will eventually pay off!"

Strategy	Description and Considerations
Literacy Resource Open House	Literacy coaches tend to have access to excellent instructional and professional development resources. Invite teachers to visit your office to explore the materials. Discuss the resources with the teachers and encourage them to borrow relevant resources for use in their own teaching. Offer to model or co-plan a lesson using the instructional resources.
"How Can I Help?" Survey	Develop a survey to see what types of coaching support teachers are interested in accessing. The survey can also include topics related to the instructional shifts associated with the Common Core. See Form 1 for a sample survey.
Be Visible	Walk the halls. Eat in the teacher lunchroom, at different times, if possible. Visit the office and teacher workroom frequently. By making yourself visible, you can start conversations with teachers and begin to lay the groundwork for collaborative working relationships that include coaching in classrooms.
Classroom Library, Classroom, or Literacy Station Makeover	Offer to help teachers organize their classroom libraries, classroom, or literacy stations. Teachers will appreciate an extra pair of hands to complete these important, yet labor-intensive tasks. While working side by side, you will have the opportunity to discuss instruction and specific students, which may lead to additional coaching opportunities.
Focus on a Student	Offer to assess, observe, or provide instruction to a student about whom the teacher has concerns. Meet with the teacher to share your insights and suggestions for supporting this student. Offer to model, co-plan, or co-teach a lesson that addresses this specific student's needs.
Bond over Life Outside the Classroom	Let the teachers get to know you. Have casual conversations about your families, hobbies, or other topics of interest. Even talking about a TV show, sports team, or current event can begin to lay the groundwork for positive working relationships with teachers.
Provide "Crunch-Time" Support	There are predictable crunch times such as the first day of school, open houses, report cards, and parent–teacher conferences. Offer to help teachers prepare their classrooms, organize materials, or even grade assignments! Doing so will show that you are willing to "roll up your sleeves" and work. Teachers will appreciate your support and will be likely to invite you back to their classrooms for coaching activities.
Establish Yourself as a Helpful Resource by Getting Creative!	You can offer to cover a teacher's classroom so he or she can take a bathroom break or call a parent. If you have chocolate or coffee in your office, invite teachers to stop in any time they need a fix! Offer to track down books for classroom activities related to specific topics or themes. These types of helpful activities will lead to conversations, positive relationships, and opportunities to visit classrooms.
Start with Willing Teachers	If you start with willing teachers and ensure that they are pleased with the coaching support you provide, they will share the good work you are doing with their colleagues. Eventually the word about the value of working with the literacy coach will start to spread.

FIGURE 1. Useful strategies for getting into classrooms.

"How Can I Help?" Survey

Dear Teachers:

As the literacy coach at our school, there are many ways I can support your professional development and teaching as we move toward incorporating the Common Core standards into our instruction. Please review this list and identify those coaching activities that you believe will be most helpful to you this year. Please put a checkmark (✓) next to any coaching activities that you are definitely interested in and a question mark (?) next to any activities about which you'd like more information.

_____ Setting goals	_____ Modeling lessons in your classroom
_____ Co-planning	_____ Co-teaching
_____ Observing	_____ Coaching cycle
_____ Lesson study	_____ Reviewing units of study
_____ Examining student work	_____ Reviewing assessment data to plan instruction
_____ Developing a pacing guide	_____ Other (please specify)

I would like coaching support:

_____ Immediately   _____ Within a month   _____ Let's set a meeting to plan a time.

The best time for me to meet with the literacy coach is:

_____ Before school   _____ My plan period   _____ After school   _____ Other (specify)

I am most interested in coaching related to these Common Core standards:

_____ Reading (Literature)   _____ Reading (Informational)   _____ Reading (Foundational Skills)

_____ Writing   _____ Speaking and Listening   _____ Language

I want to learn more about these instructional shifts:

_____ Balancing literary and informational texts   _____ Increasing text complexity

_____ Developing evidence-based responses   _____ Writing from sources

_____ Building academic vocabulary

Please return this survey to my mailbox in the office as soon as you have completed it. Thanks!

Working with Hesitant Teachers

Reema Singh recently moved from being a fourth-grade teacher to serving as her school's literacy coach. She has been pleased with her transition to coaching the teachers in grades 3–5. She is concerned, however, with a small number of teachers who seem hesitant, or even resistant, to working with her. She has tried many of the suggestions that her colleague, Megan Schoenfeld, used (see Figure 1), but they have not been successful with these specific teachers.

Reema investigated a number of professional articles, books, and workshops to try and identify useful strategies for building positive working relationships with these teachers. After consulting these resources, she realized that there are several common reasons why teachers may be hesitant to engage with coaching toward new practices, and at times these teachers can even appear to be resistant (Knight, 2009b; Toll, 2005). Four reasons in particular helped her understand these teachers in her school. With the hesitant or resistant teachers who fell into each category, she tried some of the approaches that had been recommended in the professional books and articles. After several months, she documented the approaches that had worked well (see Figure 2).

As we discussed in Chapter 1, the change process can be difficult for both teachers and coaches, but there are fairly predictable stages that teachers progress through as they encounter a new initiative such as the Common Core. At times, you may believe that a teacher is hesitant or even resistant to change when in reality, he or she may just be trying to make sense of how to understand, implement, or evaluate the initiative. If coaching support is not answering the specific questions teachers have, they may become "stuck" and unable to move forward, which can look like resistance. By listening carefully to what teachers say and the types of questions they ask, you can identify the stage of the change process where the teacher is so you can adjust your coaching approach and stance accordingly to meet teachers where they are and help them move ahead toward implementation. If you refer back to Table 1 in Chapter 1, we offer several specific coaching suggestions related to each stage of the change process.

Causes of Hesitation or Resistance	Suggestions for Moving Beyond Them
Teacher questions the value of the initiative.	• Promote proven and powerful teaching strategies. • Explain the expectations and ramifications of the initiative on teaching and testing. • Provide or collect outcome data when possible. • Enlist other teachers who embrace the value of the initiative so they can share their perspectives.
Teacher doesn't have the time or energy to implement the initiative.	• Acknowledge that the teacher feels his or her "plate is full." • Be respectful of the teacher's time. • Focus on a small number of key instructional practices. • Streamline the work involved with implementing the initiative. • Promote collaboration so that no teacher feels he or she needs to work alone. • Share resources and offer to complete organizational tasks such as preparing materials that can free up the teacher to work on the instructional aspects of the initiative.
Teacher believes his or her expertise and experience are not valued.	• Invite and value teacher voices and input. • Provide teacher choice regarding how to address the initiative in his or her practice. • Provide meaningful opportunities for teachers to share, network, and engage in professional conversations related to the initiative.
Teacher is at a stage of the change process that is different from where coaching support is offered and provided.	• Listen carefully to what teachers say to determine the stage of the change process where the teacher is currently operating. • Adjust coaching to address that stage of the change process (see Figure 2).

FIGURE 1. Addressing causes of teacher hesitance or resistance.

Reema was particularly concerned when hesitant teachers would engage with her as a resource for information or materials, but they would not work with her on the more intense, intentional, and meaningful aspects of coaching. She found that listening carefully to what the teachers said and considering possible reasons for the teachers' comments helped her develop a response that was directly aligned to the situation. She generally used a variation of Toll's (2005) "The Question" to initiate these conversations with hesitant teachers (see Figure 2).

Teacher's Statement	Possible Reasons for the Teacher's Statement	Coach's Response
"Thanks for testing my student and offering to meet with me to discuss teaching ideas. I don't really think we need to meet."	The teacher wants to use the results to place the student in a group. The teacher sees assessment as the end product.	"When I tested him, I was only able to see him perform in a one-on-one setting. Now that you've placed him in a group, I'd like to come in and see how he works within a group setting. It may help us come up with answers to THE QUESTION: 'When we think about the reading and writing we want him to do in the small-group setting, what gets in the way?' We could then talk about ideas for supporting him in that setting."
"I just don't have time for this."	The teacher doesn't have time. The teacher is feeling overwhelmed.	"I understand. When would be a good time for me to come back?" "I understand how busy everyone is. That's why literacy coaching is great because I can help you manage the many things on your 'to-do' list."
"There's nothing I need help with."	The teacher does not have any specific goals. The teacher is hesitant to open up his or her practice to others. The teacher does not want to disclose that he or she does not understand or implement a specific instructional approach or strategy.	Use THE QUESTION . . . "When you think about the reading and writing you want your students to do, the kinds of teaching you want to do, the kind of classroom you want to have . . . what gets in the way?" "I'd like to learn about your work for my own sake. Because I work with everyone in the school, it's helpful for me to know what instruction and learning look like in every classroom in our school. Can we talk about your classroom so I can learn more about what you and your students are doing?" Then, ask THE QUESTION.
"I've been around for a long time. There's nothing new you can teach me."	The teacher has had previous negative experiences with literacy coaches and/or other "professional developers."	"I hear you. That's why my role is not to teach you *new* things. It's to support you as you work toward your goals." Then, ask THE QUESTION. "You probably have some things you could teach some of the newer teachers in our school. Could I learn more about your classroom so I can share what you're doing with others?"

FIGURE 2. How can I respond to hesitant teachers? Adapted from Toll (2005). Copyright 2005 by the International Reading Association. Adapted by permission.

Staying the Course

Rachel Norris is a literacy specialist who spends almost half of her time coaching teachers. The remainder of her schedule is filled with a combination of push-in and pull-out reading instruction for struggling readers in grades K–5. Rachel has been coaching for 5 years, and she finds that literacy coaching can be a demanding and lonely position at times. While she loves the contributions she is able to make to enhancing teacher practice and student learning through coaching, she worries about burnout in the literacy coaching role. She has seen literacy coaches in other schools in her district return to the classroom after several years because of the challenges of the position. As she explained, "I am the only one in my building with this job, so I don't have someone next door or across the hall to discuss my challenges, frustrations, and successes with. I need support, but I've found I have to either give myself that support or network with others inside and beyond my school district."

When asked what she does to provide support to herself as a literacy coach, Rachel responded:

> "I have three strategies that work for me. First, I have to remember that I do not own the change process or teacher practice or even student learning in our school. When teachers complain or are hesitant to try new practices, I have to remember that it's not about me as a person or even as a literacy coach; it's because change can be hard, teaching can be hard, and learning can be hard, too! Dr. Maryanne Morgan, an administrator in our central office, shared a phrase with me that has made a great deal of difference. She said, 'Quit taking it personally!' Those words make the acronym QTIP, so I have that written inside my planning folder, on my classroom visit clipboard, and on my desk [see Figure 1]. It helps to remember that teachers are not pushing back because they don't like me or don't think I'm a good literacy coach. They are pushing back because change can be hard!"

Another thing that Rachel has done to support herself is to remember that coaching is a process that takes time (L'Allier et al., 2010). She tries to document

FIGURE 1. "Quit Taking It Personally!"

successes, progress, and positive feedback from teachers about her coaching work so that she can refer to these when she is having a particularly challenging day, week, or month. She also sets SMART coaching goals so that she can focus her work and document her progress toward reaching these goals. She generally sets one SMART goal focused on her own professional development as a coach so she continues to hone her practice with coaching. She also sets at least one goal focused on teacher outcomes to ensure that her coaching work is impacting teacher knowledge and/or practice. A sample of Rachel's goals from October is provided in Figure 2.

Additionally, Rachel supports herself by reflecting on other major initiatives that were hard to implement but that were accomplished at her school. She recalls that RTI took 3 years until it was enacted fully. Knowing that she and the teachers at her school were able to implement other initiatives in the past is reassuring and reminds her that moving toward the Common Core will take time but can be done, 1 day at a time!

Since Rachel is the only literacy coach at her school, she has worked hard to build a support system that goes beyond her school. She and the literacy coaches at the other elementary schools in her district meet informally at a local restaurant for appetizers and drinks once per month, generally on a Friday afternoon after school. They also approached the district literacy coordinator, Dr. Morgan, about having regular meetings that focus on professional development in coaching and allow the coaches to share ideas and problem solve the challenges they are facing. Dr. Morgan has arranged for the coaches to meet once per month at the central office. During these meetings the coaches read and discuss professional articles, chapters, and books related to literacy coaching, and at times they have a guest speaker who presents on a topic related to literacy coaching. Dr. Morgan often takes an active role in these meetings by sharing copies of articles and books from ASCD and Learning Forward, professional organizations focused on teacher professional development and leadership. Rachel's favorite part of these meetings is the last 30 minutes where the coaches present "Coaching Conundrums," and the group members discuss possible solutions to these challenges. At times, Dr. Morgan also asks the coaches to share their successes so the group can celebrate these coaching accomplishments.

Rachel has also joined the International Reading Association and the National Council of Teachers of English. Through these memberships she receives and reads their journals, attends conferences, participates in webinars, and accesses online professional development resources. Rachel explains, "I even go beyond traditional types of professional development by gathering coaching resources on sites such as Pinterest and Facebook, and I follow coaching on several Twitter feeds. By combin-

Coaching Goals	Successes, Challenges, and Next Steps
For my professional development as a coach: *Before the end of the month, I will read at least two professional articles on literacy coaching. I will identify at least one idea from each article that I will incorporate into my practice.*	*Mission accomplished! Read two great articles and learned a lot! I am now using the ideas I got from each article in my coaching work. I am using a repertoire of coaching strategies suggested by Blachowicz, Obrochta, and Fogelberg (2005), as well as using differentiated coaching to promote teacher reflection as Stover, Kissel, Haag, and Shoniker (2011) suggested. So far these approaches are working well. I need to remember that the time I spend reading professional articles and books helps me to become a better coach! I plan to keep reading at least two articles or book chapters about coaching each and every month.*
For my practice as a coach: *I will work through at least one lesson study cycle with the fifth-grade team related to opinion (argument) writing (CCSS W.5.1) to get this process started at that grade level.*	*Slow start because of lots going on for these teachers professionally as well as personally. I was getting so frustrated, but once Pioneer Day was over near the middle of the month, they came to me and said, "We're ready." I learned an important lesson—I need to consider everything that teachers are juggling when I try to push a coaching strategy! It took us more time than I anticipated to revise the sample lesson so that it could serve as our research lesson, but the teachers really wanted to know and understand opinion writing and standard W.5.1, so that took time. The teaching of the research lesson went smoothly thanks to Karen and Wally, who agreed to teach the lesson for the team even though they were nervous. The discussions after each lesson observation were productive, supportive, and insightful. I am so impressed with this team's plans after the lesson study. They asked if we could work together to co-plan a unit of study on opinion writing, and we've already started that process.*

FIGURE 2. Rachel's SMART coaching goals for October.

ing all of these strategies, I get great ideas, connect with others who are coaching, and stay energized!"

Rachel also advises, "Don't make your coaching work harder than it already is." She explains that she has collected a set of protocols and templates for some coaching activities so that she is not always "reinventing the wheel." For example, she uses the same template for co-planning and the same protocol for lesson study, regardless of topic or grade level. She finds that this consistency not only saves her time but it has two additional benefits:

1 Teachers know what to expect and can focus more on the content and process they are learning about than on the actual steps of the activity.

2 Once teachers become comfortable with the protocols and templates, it is easier for teacher leaders to use them to facilitate the same processes with their colleagues.

Rachel explains, "I use an existing protocol or tool, modifying it if it doesn't fit the purpose exactly. By using these resources from books, articles, and workshops, I am not spending countless hours researching, developing, and refining tools." We hope you'll find the collection of protocols, templates, and tools in this book will enable you to use the same approach to efficiency that Rachel recommends.

Embedding Coaching into Other Assigned Duties

Joo-Hee Park is a reading interventionist who has only 2 hours per week designated for literacy coaching in her large elementary school. Her days are filled with reading intervention groups as well as serving on her school's RTI committee and data team. Her school district has asked that the reading interventionists take on coaching by infusing it into their other daily duties. At first, Joo-Hee and the other reading interventionists in her district were overwhelmed by this change to their responsibilities. Joo-Hee thought, "What can I do in 2 hours a week? I feel like I'm being asked to do the impossible!"

After examining their various responsibilities, the reading interventionists and the district's director of literacy developed a plan for infusing coaching into those duties. By using what they came to call a "coaching eye and ear," they now watch and listen carefully to identify places in conversations, meetings, and other activities where they can infuse coaching. Throughout the year they developed a manageable approach to infusing coaching into their other duties. That list is provided in Figure 1.

After using these ideas for several months and feeling like they were working well, Joo-Hee began to think more carefully about how she used the 2 hours per week she did have for coaching. When talking with Becca, Tim, and Marisol, reading interventionists in other elementary schools in the district, Joo-Hee learned that they each actually had different amounts of coaching time in their schedules. For example, Joo-Hee had the least time (i.e., 2 hours per week) and Becca had the most (i.e., almost 2 hours per day). They shared their coaching experiences and created a chart to show how some common coaching activities can be simplified or shortened for those coaches who have very little time and how they can be expanded if a coach has more time available. Those ideas are presented in Figure 2.

Existing/Assigned Responsibilities	Ideas for Infusing Coaching: Using a "Coaching Eye and Ear"
Data Teams	◆ Serve as a resource, helping to explain assessment results and recommend instructional approaches to address findings. ◆ Volunteer to facilitate data team meetings so you can guide the process and become aware of how teachers' students perform. Doing this can lead to opportunities for modeling, co-teaching, co-planning, and other coaching activities.
RTI Committee	◆ Serve as a resource to interpret assessment findings and progress monitoring outcomes. ◆ Model the selection of intervention strategies using data-based decision making.
Pull-Out Reading Services	◆ Talk with teachers about how their students are performing in the reading intervention program. Share and offer to model or co-plan instruction that incorporates instructional strategies that have been successful when working with these students. ◆ Observe students from the intervention program in the classroom setting to learn more about how you and the teacher can coordinate instruction to support these students.
Grade-Level Meetings	◆ Provide mini-workshops for the first 10 minutes of grade-level meetings to address relevant professional development topics, to model instructional strategies, and to share new resources.
Faculty Meetings	◆ Facilitate short-article discussions using frameworks such as text coding or 3–2–1 (as previously described in Table 3.1 in Strategy 3). Either ask teachers to read articles prior to the meeting or select short segments of a longer article for teachers to read and then discuss at the meeting. You can also encourage the teachers to read the rest of the article after the meeting.

FIGURE 1. Infusing coaching into existing/assigned responsibilities.

Activity	Limited Amount of Time	Greater Amount of Time
Study Groups	Article study or a section of an article.	Book study
Setting Goals	Work with a grade-level team to develop SMART goals for their professional development and instruction. Incorporate this coaching activity into an already-scheduled grade-level meeting.	Work with individual teachers to set SMART goals.
Modeling Lessons	Model for several teachers at once with a short postmodeling meeting so teachers can make comments, ask questions, and plan their own similar lessons.	Model for specific teacher(s) as part of coaching cycle.
Co-Teaching	Co-teach a single lesson and discuss it briefly immediately afterward.	Co-teach multiple lessons and conduct pre- and postconferences to plan and reflect on the co-taught lesson(s).
Postobservation Conference	Confer with teacher for a few minutes immediately after observing a lesson or a video of a lesson.	Observe and hold the postobservation conference as part of a coaching cycle.

FIGURE 2. Modifying coaching strategies depending on the amount of coaching time available.

Joo-Hee now jokes that she looks at and listens to everything with a "coaching eye and ear" so she can serve as a resource for the teachers in her school. Because she believes that coaching is an effective approach to providing professional development for teachers, she is now collecting data on her coaching activities and outcomes. She plans to share this data with her principal to determine whether her schedule can be revised for the next year to allow more time for coaching.

Organizing for Success

Ian Marshall is a reading specialist who spends about a third of his time on literacy coaching. The rest of his time is devoted to providing small-group reading instruction for students in his K–2 school. Because he does not have a great deal of time to devote to coaching, Ian has developed several effective strategies for organizing his time, materials, and activities so that he can use his time as wisely and efficiently as possible.

Ian keeps a daily coaching log so he can record his coaching activities, follow-up plans, and coaching outcomes. He has his coaching log on his iPad so he can save and modify it as well as compare logs over time. He finds this log useful to make sure that he is engaging in meaningful coaching activities rather than in "random acts of coaching" or spending his time on tasks that others could do such as organizing the book room or inputting assessment data. Ian uses this log to make sure he is serving all of the teachers and grade levels in his K–2 school. A blank coaching log template is provided in Form 1.

Ian has a coaching backpack that contains all of his basic coaching supplies. It holds his copy of the Common Core standards, classroom schedules, a copy of the school's literacy inventory (i.e., bookroom titles, instructional resources, and professional development resources) as well as a clipboard, paper, pens, pencils, file folders, sticky notes, highlighters, white board markers, stapler, and tape. When he is going to a meeting or to visit a classroom, he simply adds the items he'll need for that specific coaching activity. By having these basic supplies packed and ready to go, he is able to save time and also ensure that he has the supplies he'll need for any type of coaching activity.

Ian uses his iPad extensively to support his coaching. It contains his coaching log, the district's literacy framework, and grade-level pacing guides, as well as his calendar. Using his iPad, he takes photos of lesson plans, assessment results, and classroom white boards. He then organizes the photos in folders so he can easily access them for follow-up or to use with teachers for coaching purposes. He also saves articles and even professional books on his iPad so they are all located in one place for easy access. For each grade level he has a folder, and within that folder he has a subfolder for each teacher so he can keep files, notes, and relevant resources organized and at his fingertips for when they are needed. Ian knows other coaches who use a large binder, laptop computer, or wheeled crate to organize and store coaching resources, but he likes the compact design of the iPad and the electronic features it offers. As Ian recently told us, "It doesn't matter how a coach chooses to organize files, resources, and materials, but a coach MUST be organized!" Some of Ian's other favorite coaching organizational tips are summarized in Figure 1.

Ian has worked with Sheila, Wendy, and Madelyn, other coaches in his district, to create several tools that save time and help them be organized for their coaching work. The first tool focuses on having coaching prompts ready to go to jump-start any coaching conversation that may arise. While Ian and the other coaches in his district try to be prepared, on-the-fly coaching opportunities (L'Allier et al., 2010) may arise in the hallway, before a meeting begins, in the parking lot, and even in the bathroom! The coaches designed these prompts (see Figure 2) to help them shift gears quickly to respond to and support teachers at a moment's notice.

Ian and his coaching colleagues also created a set of easy-to-implement activities for professional development sessions (see Figure 3). They generally know far in advance when they'll be delivering a professional development workshop, but they are occasionally asked to prepare something at a moment's notice when the school schedule changes, when a workshop presenter cancels, or when an urgent

---

- ◆ Color coding saves time and ensures you can find what you need when you need it. Color code files and resources by grade level, month, or instructional shift.

- ◆ Take 10 minutes at the end of each day to put things back where they belong. That time will save you much more when you are looking for materials during a busy day of coaching.

- ◆ Label everything! Labeling files, shelves, and bins with descriptive titles will help you store and access them easily.

- ◆ Review your calendar at the end of each day so you can plan for the next day's coaching activities (or to ensure you are prepared for the next day's coaching activities). Review your calendar at the beginning of each day so you know where you need to be, when you need to be there, and what you need to bring with you.

- ◆ Wear a watch or use the clock on your phone or iPad so you can keep track of time. If you get off schedule with one coaching activity, the rest of the day can tumble like dominoes!

- ◆ Make a check-out system for your books and instructional materials so you can keep track of which items teachers have borrowed.

- ◆ Organize electronic files that contain graphic organizers, sample lesson and unit plans, bookroom inventory, and other relevant resources on the school's shared computer drive so teachers and teacher leaders can access them when they need them.

- ◆ Organize your office so it is comfortable and inviting so teachers want to stop by to visit and browse. Learn a lesson from stores—put the materials that relate to school or grade-level goals in a visible place, organized in an appealing manner so teachers are drawn to them! Change the displays often so teaches will want to visit regularly.

FIGURE 1. Organizational tips for literacy coaches.

- ◆ "I wonder . . ."
- ◆ "Tell me more . . ."
- ◆ "What are you considering?"
- ◆ "What have you already tried?"
- ◆ "What do you plan to do next?"
- ◆ "What would like to see the students do better?"
- ◆ "What do you want to work on?"
- ◆ "What concerns you?"
- ◆ "What's going well?"
- ◆ "What can I do to help?"

FIGURE 2. Useful coaching prompts for any situation.

need arises. The activities described in Figure 3 all promote interaction and discussion so that teachers will be actively engaged.

As Ian points out, being an organized literacy coach is a work in progress. He picks up tips from other coaches, from the Internet, and from the organized teachers with whom he works. He explains, "Being organized is not really my goal, but it does help me meet my other coaching goals." He went on to say, "As I try new strategies to be more organized, some work perfectly, others need to be modified, and some just don't work for me. As long as I'm finding, developing, and using organizational strategies that help me be more effective and efficient, that's all that matters!"

Format	Description	Considerations
Where I draw the line (based on Choice Literacy, 2006)	The coach presents an issue or question, and teachers line up according to whether they agree or disagree. They then break into small groups, according to their degree of agreement, to discuss their responses. Next, each group presents its most compelling argument for why they think as they do. Teachers can move from one group to another if their minds are changed. Finally, the whole group discusses the issue.	This activity works best with a controversial or provocative prompt such as "Close reading should not begin until students are in the upper grades and can decode automatically" or "The Common Core standards are the same things we've always been doing. They just have a new name now."
What would you do?	The coach presents one or more scenarios that describe a teaching problem or decision that needs to be made. Teachers work in small groups to discuss how to address the situation, and if time permits, they present their ideas to the whole group.	Preparing the scenarios is essential to ensure teachers will have to think deeply to come up with viable responses. Focus scenarios on school or grade-level goals to make them directly relevant to the teachers' work.
Strategy demonstrations	Demonstrate an instructional strategy with the teachers participating as students. "Push *pause*" periodically to explain what you are doing and why, so that teachers understand the instructional decisions involved with the strategy.	Align the demonstration with a school or grade-level goal or an instructional shift associated with the Common Core.
Video-based discussions	Select a video that shows an instructional practice that aligns with a district or school goal or a Common Core instructional shift. Ask teachers to view closely and be prepared to discuss the open-ended prompts you have provided.	Use meaningful discussion prompts such as: ◆ "How does this connect to instructional practice at our school? In my classroom?" ◆ "If I were to use this practice in my teaching, what changes would I make and why? What would I be sure to include and why?"
Four A's protocol (based on Gray, 2005)	After reading a text, viewing a video, or listening to a presentation, ask teachers to respond to four prompts: ◆ "What **A**ssumptions does the author or presenter hold?" ◆ "What do you **A**gree with?" ◆ "What do you **A**rgue with?" ◆ "What parts do you want to **A**spire to?"	These prompts help teachers examine their own beliefs and practices in relation to a text, video, or presentation.

FIGURE 3. Easy-to-implement activities for professional development sessions.

Coaching Log Template

Day and Time	Coaching Activity	Teachers and Grade Levels	Topics, Common Core Standards, or Instructional Shifts	Outcomes	Coach Follow-Up
Monday					
Tuesday					
Wednesday					
Thursday					
Friday					

Weekly Coaching Summary and Reflection: What went well, what was challenging, what did I learn, and what do I need to do next?

Final Thoughts

As you take on the challenge of coaching teachers toward the Common Core, we hope the strategies, tools, and tips we've included in this book will be helpful. In closing, we want to share several ideas that we hope will be the biggest "take-aways" you have from this book. First, coaching adults requires that you understand how adults learn. By keeping those adult learning principles in mind, you will be able to support the teachers' professional learning and growth. Second, adoption of the Common Core presents a major change for teachers, and it will take time for them to update their teaching to address these new standards. Understanding the change process and using CBAM to plan and implement your coaching strategies will help you ensure that you are providing the types of support that teachers need so they can continue to move their teaching toward the Common Core. Third, by implementing the three layers of coaching—large group, small group, and individual—you can use your time wisely and ensure that teachers understand "the big picture," as well as how new instructional standards and strategies operate at their grade level and in their own classrooms. Fourth, the targeted coaching model provides guidance about the characteristics of effective literacy coaching programs, and it can serve as a reminder to spend the bulk of your coaching time working directly with teachers, devoting most of that time to the research-based coaching activities of conferencing with teachers, working with assessments, modeling, observing, and co-planning. This model also argues that your remaining coaching time should be devoted to large- and small-group coaching activities such as providing professional development workshops and facilitating grade-level meetings, study groups, PLCs, and lesson-study groups.

As you work with the teachers at your school to move their instructional practices toward the Common Core, we offer words of wisdom from one of the most skilled coaches we know, Carly Barnett. She recently told us:

"Over the past few years, I've learned that coaching takes four different types of skills and knowledge. I have to understand how to work with adults, even when they are struggling or frustrated with expectations for change. I have to know the curriculum and standards inside and out. I have to know how to build productive, respectful, collaborative relationships with teachers. And, I have to be reflective, resilient, organized, efficient, and willing to take a risk. My work as a coach is the hardest but most rewarding thing I've done as an educator. As a teacher, I used to impact the learning of the 25 children in my classroom. As a reading specialist, I had a direct impact on the 40 children in my reading intervention programs. Now, as a coach, I impact the learning of every teacher and child in my school. That is why I keep working hard to continue to grow to become the best coach I can be."

As you embark on your work of coaching teachers toward the Common Core, we offer these parting words: Be patient; embrace the change process; remember that building and maintaining relationships takes time, effort, and compromise; and be the kind of literacy coach that you would have wanted as a teacher. By implementing the large-group, small-group, and individual coaching strategies outlined in this book, you can provide the type of support necessary to enhance teaching practice and learning outcomes at your school.

References

Agamba, J., & Jenkins, S. (2012). Idaho total instructional alignment: The Common Core state standards and teacher professional development. In P. Resta (Ed.), *Proceedings of Society for Information Technology and Teacher Education International Conference 2012* (pp. 4800–4807). Chesapeake, VA: AACE.

Allen, J. (2006). *Becoming a literacy leader: Supporting learning and change.* Portland, ME: Stenhouse.

Allen, J. (2007). *Layered coaching* [DVD]. Portland, ME: Stenhouse.

Allison, E., Besser, L., Campsen, L., Cordova, J., Doubek, B., Gregg, L., et al. (2010). *Data teams: The big picture.* Englewood, CO: Lead+Learn Press.

Au, W. (2007). High-stakes testing and curricular control: A qualitative metasynthesis. *Educational Researcher, 36*(5), 258–267.

Bandura, A. (2001). Social cognitive theory: An agentic perspective. *Annual Review of Psychology, 52,* 1–26.

Barton, K. C., & Smith, L. A. (2000). Themes or motifs? Aiming for coherence through interdisciplinary outlines. *The Reading Teacher, 54*(1), 54–63.

Bean, R., Cassidy, J., Calo, K., Elish-Piper, L., Frost, S., Goatley, V., Kern, D., et al. (2013, April). *Roles and responsibilities of reading specialists/literacy coaches: An update.* Paper presented to the Specialized Literacy Professionals Special Interest Group at the annual conference of the International Reading Association, San Antonio, TX.

Bean, R., & DeFord, D. (2012). *Do's and don'ts for literacy coaches: Advice from the field* [Literacy Coaching Clearinghouse Brief]. Retrieved from *www.literacycoachingonline.org/briefs/DosandDontsFinal.pdf.*

Bean, R. M. (2009). *The reading specialist: Leadership for the classroom, school, and community* (2nd ed.). New York: Guilford Press.

Bean, R. M., Draper, J. A., Hall, V., Vandermolen, J., & Zigmond, N. (2010). Coaches and coaching in Reading First schools: A reality check. *Elementary School Journal, 111*(1), 87–114.

Beck, I. L., McKeown, M. G., & Kucan, L. (2013). *Bringing words to life: Robust vocabulary instruction* (2nd ed.). New York: Guilford Press.

Benedict, A. E., Park, Y., Brownell, M. T., Lauterbach, A. A., & Kiely, M. T. (2013). Using lesson study to align elementary literacy instruction within the RTI framework. *Teaching Exceptional Children, 45*(5), 22–30.

Biancarosa, G., Bryk, A. S., & Dexter, E. R. (2010). Assessing the value-added effects of Literacy Collaborative professional development on student learning. *Elementary School Journal, 111*(1), 7–34.

Blachowicz, C. L. Z., Obrochta, C., & Fogelberg, E. (2005). Literacy coaching for change. *Educational Leadership, 62*(6), 55–58.

Block, C. C., & Israel, S. (2004). The ABCs of performing highly effective think-alouds. *The Reading Teacher, 58*(2), 154–167.

Blythe, T., Allen, D., & Powell B. S. (2007*). Looking together at student work* (2nd ed.). New York: Teachers College Press.

Bryk, A. S., Sebring, P. B., Allensworth, E., Luppescu, S., & Easton, J. Q. (2010). *Organizing schools for improvement.* Chicago: University of Chicago Press.

Buhle, R., & Blachowicz, C. L. Z. (2008). The assessment double play. *Educational Leadership, 66*(4), 42–46.

Burbank, M. D., Kauchak, D., & Bates, A. J. (2010). Book clubs as professional development opportunities for preservice teacher candidates and practicing teachers: An exploratory study. *The New Educator, 6*(1), 56–73.

Burkins, J. M. (2009). *Practical literacy coaching: A collection of tools to support your work.* Newark, DE: International Reading Association.

Calkins, L., Ehrenworth, M., & Lehman, C. (2012). *Pathways to the Common Core: Accelerating achievement.* Portsmouth, NH: Heinemann.

Casey, K. (2006). *Literacy coaching: The essentials.* Portsmouth, NH: Heinemann.

Casey, K. (2011). Modeling lessons. *Educational Leadership, 69*(2), 24–29.

Choice Literacy. (2006). *The dog ate my study group plans: Four instant (and fun and reflective) no-prep teacher workshops* [Choice Literacy e-guide]. Retrieved from *https:// pennleadershipfacilitators.wikispaces.com/file/view/Dog+Ate+MY+Study+Group. pdf.*

Commeyras, M., Bisplinghoff, B. S., & Olson, J. (Eds.). (2003). *Teachers as readers: Perspectives on the importance of reading in teachers' classrooms and lives.* Newark, DE: International Reading Association.

Darling-Hammond, L., & Richardson, N. (2009). Teacher learning: What matters? *Educational Leadership, 65*(5), 46–53.

David, J. L. (2008). What research says about . . . /pacing guides. *Educational Leadership, 66*(2), 87–88.

De Alba-Johnson, N., Rodriguez, M., Arias, L., Johnson, C. Z., McConnell, S., McEvoy, M., et al. (2004, April). *Is professional training enough? The effect of coaching in the practice of early literacy instruction.* Paper presented at the annual meeting of the American Educational Research Association, San Diego, CA.

Desimone, L. (2002). How can comprehensive school reform models be successfully implemented? *Review of Educational Research, 72,* 433–479.

DuFour, R., DuFour, R., & Eaker, R. (2008). *Revisiting professional learning communities at work: New insights for improving schools.* Bloomington, IN: Solution Tree.

DuFour, R., DuFour, R., Eaker, R., & Many, T. (2010). *Learning by doing: A handbook for professional learning communities at work.* Bloomington, IN: Solution Tree.

DuFour, R., & Marzano, R. J. (2011). *Leaders of learning: How district, school, and classroom leaders improve student achievement.* Bloomington, IN: Solution Tree.

Elish-Piper, L., Hinrichs, S., Morley, S., & Williams, M. (2012). The assessment to instructional planning (ATIP) framework: A multidimensional, contextualized approach to using assessment to plan instruction. In E. Ortlieb & E. H. Cheek, Jr. (Eds.), *Using informative assessment towards effective literacy instruction* (Vol. 1, pp. 251–292). Bingley, UK: Emerald.

Elish-Piper, L. A., & L'Allier, S. K. (2010). Exploring the relationship between literacy coaching and student reading achievement in grades K–1. *Literacy Research and Instruction, 49*(2), 162–174.

Elish-Piper, L. A., & L'Allier, S. K. (2011). Examining the relationship between literacy coaching and reading gains in grades K–3. *Elementary School Journal, 112*(1), 83–106.

Elish-Piper, L. A., L'Allier, S. K., & Zwart, M. (2009). Literacy coaching: Challenges and promising practices for success. *Illinois Reading Council Journal, 37*(1), 10–21.

EngageNY. (2012). *Common Core instructional shifts.* Retrieved from *http://engageny. org/resource/common-core-shifts.*

Examining student work to inform instruction. (n.d.). Retrieved July 29, 2013, from *http:// mdk12.org/data/examining.*

Fisher, D., Flood, J., Lapp, D., & Frey, N. (2004). Interactive read-alouds: Is there a common set of implementation practices? *The Reading Teacher, 58*(1), 8–17.

Fisher, D., & Frey, N. (2008). *Better learning through structured teaching: A framework for the gradual release of responsibility.* Alexandria, VA: ASCD.

Fisher, D., Frey, N., & Uline, C. L. (2013). *Common Core English language arts in a PLC at work: Leader's guide.* Bloomington, IN: Solution Tree.

Frost, S. (n.d.). Eight tips for building relationships: A tale of two literacy coaches [Choice Literacy]. Retrieved from *www.choiceliteracy.com/articles-detail-view.php?id=456.*

Frost, S., & Bean, R. M. (2006, September 27). *Qualifications for literacy coaches: Achieving the gold standard.* Denver, CO: Literacy Coaching Clearinghouse.

Fullan, M., & Knight, J. (2011). Coaches as system leaders. *Educational Leadership, 69*(2), 50–53.

Gray, J. (2005). National School Reform Faculty. Retrieved from *www.nsrfharmony.org/ protocol/doc/4_a_text.pdf.*

Hall, G. E., & Hord, S. M. (1987). *Change in schools: Facilitating the process.* Albany: State University of New York Press.

Hall, G. E., & Hord, S. M. (2006). *Implementing change: Patterns, principles, and potholes* (2nd ed.). Boston: Allyn & Bacon.

Harrison, C., & Killion, J. (2007). Ten roles for teacher leaders. *Educational Leadership, 65*(1), 74–77.

Hord, S. M., & Tobia, E. F. (2012). *Reclaiming our teaching profession: The power of educators learning in community.* New York: Teachers College Press.

Hoy, W., & Tschannen-Moran, M. (1999). Five faces of trust: An empirical confirmation in urban elementary schools. *Journal of School Leadership, 9,* 184–208.

Hurd, J., & Licciardo-Musso, L. (2005). Lesson study: Teacher-led professional development in literacy instruction. *Language Arts, 82*(5), 388–395.

Instructional coaching for teachers. (n.d.). Retrieved August 15, 2012, from *http:// teachers21.org/wp-content/uploads/2010/09/Instructional-Coaching-for-Teachers. pdf.*

International Reading Association. (2004). *The role and qualifications of the reading coach in the United States. A position statement of the International Reading Association.* Newark, DE: Author.

Jay, A. B., & Strong, M. W. (2008). *A guide to literacy coaching.* Thousand Oaks, CA: Corwin.

Jones, J. P. (2000). Interdisciplinary units: An introduction to integrated curriculum in the intermediate and middle school. In K. D. Wood & T. S. Dickinson (Eds.), *Promoting literacy in grades 4–9: A handbook for teachers and administrators* (pp. 207–219). Boston: Allyn & Bacon.

Knight, J. (2007). *Instructional coaching: A partnership approach to improving instruction.* Thousand Oaks, CA: Corwin Press.

Knight, J. (2009a). Instructional coaching. In J. Knight (Ed.), *Coaching approaches and perspectives* (pp. 29–55). Thousand Oaks, CA: Corwin Press.

Knight, J. (2009b). What can we do about teacher resistance? *Phi Delta Kappan, 90*(7), 508–513.

Knowles, M. S. (1970). *The modern practice of adult education: Andragogy versus pedagogy.* New York: Association Press.

Knowles, M. S., Holton, E. F., & Swanson, R. A. (2005). *The adult learner* (6th ed.). Burlington, MA: Elsevier.

Kral, C. (2007). *Principal support for literacy coaches* [Literacy Coaching Clearinghouse Brief]. Retrieved from *www.literacycoachingonline.org/briefs/PrincipalSupportFinal3–22–07.pdf.*

Kruse, S. D., & Zimmerman, B. (2012). Does literacy coaching provide a model for school-wide professional learning? *Educational Research Journal, 2*(9), 279–291.

L'Allier, S. K., & Elish-Piper, L. (2006–2007). Ten best practices for professional development in reading. *Illinois Reading Council Journal, 35*(1), 22–27.

L'Allier, S. K., & Elish-Piper, L. (2011). *The literacy coaching series* [DVD]. Elburn, IL: LearnSure.

L'Allier, S. K., & Elish-Piper. L. (2012). Literacy coaches in elementary schools. In R. M. Bean & A. S. Dagen (Eds.), *Best practices of literacy leaders: Keys for school improvement* (pp. 43–62). New York: Guilford Press.

L'Allier, S. K., Elish-Piper, L., & Bean, R. M. (2010). What matters for elementary literacy coaching? Guiding principles for instructional improvement and student achievement. *The Reading Teacher, 63*(7), 544–554.

Larrivee, B. (2008). Meeting the challenge of preparing reflective practitioners. *New Educator, 4*(2), 87–106.

Learning Forward. (2010, December). Key points in Learning Forward's definition of professional development. *Journal of Staff Development, 31*(6), 16–17.

Leithwood, K., Seashore-Louis, K. S., Anderson, S., & Wahlstrom, K. (2004). *How leadership influences student learning.* Minneapolis: University of Minnesota, Center for Applied Research and Educational Improvement.

Lewis, C. (2004). Lesson study. In L. B. Easton (Ed.), *Powerful designs for professional learning.* Oxford, OH: National Staff Development Council.

Lewis, C., Perry, R., & Hurd, J. (2004). A deeper look: Lesson study. *Educational Leadership, 61*(5), 18–22.

Lewis, C., Perry, R., Hurd, J., & O'Connell, M. P. (2006). Teacher collaboration: Lesson study comes of age in North America. *Phi Delta Kappan, 88,* 273–281.

Lipton, L., & Wellman, B. (2007). How to talk so teachers listen. *Educational Leadership, 65*(1), 30–34.

Lyons, C. A., & Pinnell G. S. (2001). *Systems for change in literacy education: A guide to professional development.* Portsmouth, NH: Heinemann.

Matsumura, L. C. (2009). Leadership for literacy coaching: The principal's role in launching a new coaching program. *Educational Administration Quarterly, 45,* 655–693.

Matsumura, L. C., Sartoris, M., Bickel, D. D., & Garnier, H. E. (2009). Leadership for literacy coaching: The principal's role in launching a new coaching program. *Educational Administration Quarterly, 45*(5), 655–693.

May, P. J. (2010). *Literacy coaching: The role of reflective thought in teacher decision making.* (Order No. 3430333, University of Rhode Island). *ProQuest Dissertations and Theses,* 153. Retrieved from *http://search.proquest.com/docview/763603640?accoun tid=12846.*

McLaughlin, M., & Overturf, B. J. (2012). The Common Core: Insights into the K–5 standards. *The Reading Teacher, 66*(2), 153–164.

McLaughlin, M., & Overturf, B. J. (2013). *The Common Core: Teaching K–5 students to meet the reading standards.* Newark, DE: International Reading Association.

McNulty, B. A., & Besser, L. (2011). *Leaders make it happen: An administrator's guide to data teams.* Englewood, CO: Leadership Learning Center.

McTigue, E. M., & Flowers, A. C. (2011). Science visual literacy: Learners' perceptions and knowledge of diagrams. *The Reading Teacher, 64*(8), 578–589.

Moran, M. C. (2007). *Differentiated literacy coaching: Scaffolding for student and teacher success.* Alexandria, VA: ASCD.

Murawski, W. W. (2012). 10 tips for using co-planning time more efficiently. *Teaching Exceptional Children, 44*(4), 8–15.

National Governors Association Center for Best Practices & Council of the Chief State School Officers. (2010). *Common Core State Standards for English language arts and literacy in history/social studies, science, and technical subjects.* Washington, DC: Author. Retrieved from *www.corestandards.org/assets/CCSSI_ELA%20Standards. pdf.*

Paris, S. G. (2001). Linking reading assessment and instruction in elementary grades. In C. M. Roller (Ed.), *Comprehensive reading instruction across the grade levels* (pp. 55–69), Newark, DE: International Reading Association.

Pearson, P. D., & Gallagher, M. (1983). The instruction of reading comprehension. *Contemporary Educational Psychology, 8,* 317–344.

Reeves, D. (2008/2009). The learning leader: Looking deeper into the data. *Educational Leadership, 66*(4), 89–90.

Reeves, D. B. (2009). *Leading change in your school.* Alexandria, VA: ASCD.

Roberts, K. L., Norman, R. R., Duke, N. K., Morsink, P., Martin, N. M., & Knight, J. A. (2013). Diagrams, timelines, and tables—oh, my!: Fostering graphical literacy. *The Reading Teacher, 67*(1), 12–23.

Rosemary, C., & Feldman, N. (2009). *Professional development setting checklist: A literacy coach's tool for planning and assessing professional learning.* Retrieved from *www.literacycoachingonline.org/briefs/tools/Rosemary_%26_Feldman_PD_setting_ tool_4.5.09.pdf.*

Saunders, W. M., Goldenberg, C. N., & Gallimore, R. (2009). Increasing achievement by focusing grade-level teams on improving classroom learning: A prospective, quasi-experimental study of Title I schools. *American Educational Research Journal, 46*(4), 1006–1033.

Shanahan, T. (2012/2013). The Common Core ate my baby and other urban legends. *Educational Leadership, 70*(4), 10–16.

Short, K. G., Lynch-Brown, C. G., & Tomlinson, C. M. (2013). *Essentials of children's literature* (8th ed.). Boston: Pearson.

Sivers, D. (2010, April). *How to start a movement.* Retrieved from *www.ted.com/talks/ derek_sivers_how_to_start_a_movement.html.*

Spandel, V. (2013). *Creating writers: 6 traits, process, workshop, and literature* (6th ed.). Boston: Pearson.

Stiegler, J. W., & Hiebert, J. (1999). *The teaching gap: Best ideas from the world's teachers for improving education in the classroom.* New York: Free Press.

Stover, K., Kissel, B., Haag, K., & Shoniker, R. (2011). Differentiated coaching: Fostering reflection with teachers. *The Reading Teacher, 64*(7), 498–509.

Stronge, J. H. (2007). *Qualities of effective teachers* (2nd ed.). Alexandria, VA: ASCD.

Sweeney, D. (2003). *Learning along the way.* Portland, ME: Stenhouse.

Sweeny, B. (2002). *The CBAM: A model of the people development process* [Teacher Mentors]. Available at *www.teachermentors.com/CBAM.php.*

Symonds, K. W. (2003). *Literacy coaching: How school districts can support a long-term strategy in a short-term world.* San Francisco: Bay Area School Reform Collaborative (ERIC Document Reproduction Service No. ED477297).

Taylor, B. M., Pearson, P. D., Peterson, D. S., & Rodriguez, M. C. (2003). Reading growth in high-poverty classrooms: The influence of teacher practices that encourage cognitive engagement in literacy learning. *Elementary School Journal, 104,* 3–28.

Teachers learn from looking together at student work. (n.d.). Retrieved from *www.educationword.com/a_curr/curr246.shtml.*

Terehoff, I. I. (2002). Elements of adult learning in teacher professional development. *NASSP Bulletin, 86*(232), 65–77.

Toll, C. A. (2004). Separating coaching from supervising. *English Leadership Quarterly, 27*(2), 5–7.

Toll, C. A. (2005). *The literacy coach's survival guide: Essential questions and practical answers.* Newark, DE: International Reading Association.

Toll, C. A. (2006). *The literacy coach's desk reference: Processes and perspectives for effective coaching.* Urbana, IL: National Council of Teachers of English.

Trotter, Y. D. (2006). Adult learning theories: Impacting professional development programs. *Delta Kappa Gama Bulletin, 72*(2), 8–13.

Vescio, V., Ross, D., & Adams, A. (2008). A review of research on the impact of professional learning communities on teaching practice and student learning. *Teaching and Teacher Education, 24*(1), 80–91.

Vogt, M. E., & Shearer, B. A. (2011). *Reading specialists and literacy coaches in the real world* (3rd. ed.). Boston: Pearson Allyn & Bacon.

Wagner, T. (2003). Beyond testing: The seven disciplines for strengthening instruction. *Education Week, 23*(11), 28–30.

Walpole, S., & McKenna, M. C. (2013). *The literacy coach's handbook: A guide to research-based practice* (2nd ed.). New York: Guilford Press.

Wills, J. S., & Sandholtz, J. H. (2009). Constrained professionalism: Dilemmas of teaching in the face of test-based accountability. *Teachers College Record, 111*(4), 1065–1114.

Children's Literature Cited

Averill, E. (1960). *The fire cat.* New York: Harper-Collins.

Buchanan Smith, D. (1973). *A taste of blackberries.* New York: Crowell.

Cannell, J. (2008). *Stellaluna.* New York: Scholastic.

Cleary, B. P. (2011). *Skin like milk, hair of silk: What are similes and metaphors?* Minneapolis: Millbrook Press.

Deedy, C. A. (2000). *The yellow star: The legend of King Christian X of Denmark*. Atlanta: Peachtree.

Farley, W. (1982). *The black stallion*. New York: Random House.

Jansson, T. (1990). *Finn family moomintroll*. New York: Farrar, Straus and Giroux.

Kalman, B. (Ed.). (2002). *The life cycle of a bird*. New York: Crabtree.

Kalman, B. (Ed.). (2006). *The life cycle of a bat*. New York: Crabtree Publishing.

LaMarche, J. (2000). *The raft*. New York: HarperCollins.

McCloskey, R. (1943). *Homer Price*. New York: Viking Press.

Minarik, E. H. (1957). *Little bear*. New York: Harper-Collins.

Osborne, W., & Osborne, M. P. (2001). *Rain forests*. New York: Random House.

Smith, K. B. (2001). *Rain forest animals*. Lutherville, MD: Flying Frog.

Soltis, S. (2011). *Nothing like a puffin*. Sommerville, MA: Candlewick.

White, E. B. (1952). *Charlotte's web*. New York: Harper-Collins.

Index

Page numbers followed by *f* or *t* indicate a figure or a table.